The Dawning of Democracy:
Ireland 1800–1870

DONAL McCARTNEY

HELICON LIMITED

First published 1987

Helicon Limited
Ballymount Road,
Walkinstown,
Dublin 12.

Distributed by
The Educational Company of Ireland
Ballymount Road, Walkinstown, Dublin 12

© 1987 Donal McCartney

Cover: O'Connell's monster meeting at Clifden, Co. Galway, Sept. 20, 1843
Maps: Bob Rogan

Printed in the Republic of Ireland by
Criterion Press Limited, Dublin

Contents

Foreword	v
Preface	vi
1 The Union	1
2 The Question of Religion	26
3 Secret Societies and Agrarianism	63
4 Emancipation and Reform, 1823–40	110
5 Repeal, Famine and Fenians, 1840–70	149
6 Epilogue: Society and Democracy	192
Notes	215
Bibliographical note	220
Index	224

For my mother, Sarah

Foreword

The growing interest in the history of Ireland in recent decades has led to a substantial increase in the number of scholars engaged in research and study. Old and cherished interpretations have been questioned, as historians discover new sources or ask new questions of the old. Much of this new thinking is, however, hidden from the public in learned journals, which are not easily accessible. The aim of this series is to make available to a wider readership the fruits of the most recent researches. Each volume is self-contained, and each author, a specialist in the field, has been free to put forward his own analysis of the period with which he deals. Taken together they form a lucid and stimulating account of Ireland's history from the earliest times.

Art Cosgrove
Elma Collins
General Editors

Preface

In 1800 a solution to the Irish question was sought by integrating the two islands into one constitutional unit — the United Kingdom of Great Britain and Ireland. The solution then imposed was tested over the first forty years of the nineteenth century, found wanting by Irish nationalist leaders and ultimately rejected by them. Social and agrarian problems, as well as grievances related to civil rights for catholics, were among the major factors contributing to growing dissatisfaction with the union. Dissatisfaction, as it spread, gradually expanded into a nationalist ideology which was fed from many sources. Because nationalism became such a powerful force in the late nineteenth and early twentieth centuries, it was only natural that the view of early nineteenth century Ireland should have been obscured or coloured by a concentration on nationalism in its formative period. Nationalism, however, was by no means the only force at work in Ireland in the first half of the nineteenth century, and it is possible to argue that it may not have been the primary influence. There is indeed little evidence to suggest that the ordinary people were at that time at all concerned with nationalist politics. In this concentration on nationalism, however, what has been so easily overlooked is the progress and power of democracy — arguably the greater, more widespread and basic influence for at least half of the century. The continuing acceptance of the union settlement depended on how the gathering strength of democracy would react towards it. The fact that Irish democracy was channelled increasingly into nationalist politics sealed the fate of the union.

The protestant aristocracy was very much in the ascendant in 1800 and for several decades afterwards, and dominated the political and social life of the country. This dominance was based on ownership of the land, membership of the established church and political allegiance to the union. Its semi-feudal privileges were regarded as a right; and the Williamite revolution which established those privileges was looked upon not only as 'glorious' but also as immutable. By 1870, however, the protestant ascendancy had been severely undermined, and Gladstone's first Land Act of that year merely began the process of the legal dismantling of the landlords' absolute right to private property. Between 1800 and 1870 much had occurred to advance catholic democracy at the expense of protestant aristocracy. In the 1820s there had been launched, under the genius of O'Connell's leadership, a civil rights campaign for catholic emancipation. The parliamentary, municipal, social and administrative reforms of the 1830s amounted to a limited experiment in what may be called powersharing between O'Connell and the whig government of the day. In the country-wide repeal agitation of the 1840s the Irish masses were organised for an onslaught on the union. The Young Irelanders created the intellectual climate in which separatist republican ideas could grow. But it was the Fenians who by the late 1850s and throughout the 1860s actually enrolled and produced working-class republicans.

The period 1800–1870 was an age of the emerging people: the secret society was organised among the people; education was provided by church and state for the people; the churches incorporated the religion of the people; political pressure was maintained by the people whose leader, O'Connell, was labelled the 'man of the people'; significantly the Fenian newspaper was called the *Irish People*; the drift towards catholic democracy was opposed by the 'protestant people'; and the land of Ireland was demanded for the people of Ireland.

This book attempts to trace the development and examine the character of Irish democracy in its formative period between the passing of the Act of Union in 1800 and the passing of Gladstone's first Land Act in 1870.

However inadequately expressed, I wish to acknowledge assistance I have received from the editors of the series, from Louise Richardson, Maeve Bradley and my wife, Peig.

The dedication is to a grand old lady who has always represented for me all that is best in the Irish people.

University College
Dublin

Donal McCartney

Ireland: 1800

1 The Union

Any proper understanding of Irish history must begin with Ireland's geographical position. Of tremendous significance in the story of Ireland is the fact that the larger island of Britain stands between Ireland and continental Europe. Over the centuries Ireland has lived in the shadow cast by its powerful neighbour.

> I am the tall kingdom over your shoulder
> That you would neither cajole nor ignore.[1]

Other small nations in Europe have had connections with more than one imperial power. Holland and Belgium, for example, have been involved deeply with Spain, France, England and Germany at different phases of their history. It has been possible in the case of small continental states to play off one great neighbour against a rival, and to cancel or modify the impact of one great power by utilising the influence of another. Ireland, indeed, has had military and diplomatic dealings with Spain in the sixteenth century and with France in the seventeenth and eighteenth centuries. These contacts, however, were more in the nature of a response to than a replacement of British dominance. Because of the circumstances of its geographical location Ireland has been influenced or restricted or suffocated throughout its history by a single powerful neighbour.

Proximity to Britain has had profound psychological effects on the Irish. Although geographically a north European people, the Irish developed characteristics and outlooks which differentiated them from their northern neighbours. They remained, generally speaking, the only catholic people in northern Europe. And in contrast with the British, the Dutch, the Danes, the Germans or the Swedes, the Irish during the nineteenth century had the reputation of being more carefree and less industrious; more emotional and less serious-minded; more rebellious in politics and less successful economically than the other north European peoples. Whatever the causes of national distinctiveness, and they are undoubtedly complex, there seemed to be some grounds for the observation of the Spanish philosopher, Menendez Pidal, that the Irish were a Latin or mediterranean people who had gone astray in the cold north Atlantic and never found their way home. National characteristics which in the nineteenth century were often wrongly attributed solely to race or solely to climate are now more widely understood to have been responses to the historical and sociological environment. So tangled were the relations between the two islands, and so largely did Britain loom in Ireland's history, that the Irish got into the habit of always measuring themselves against England, and of looking over their shoulders, as it were, to see what England was doing, and then perhaps going the opposite way. It was the psychological reaction of the weaker unit trying to assert its independence. It was akin to the natural reaction of the teenager to the domineering parent. If the English, for example, had remained Roman catholic at the time of the reformation, it is at least open to discussion whether the Irish chieftains might have embraced protestantism.

And if most Irish were not only catholic in religion but also had the reputation of being easily attracted to political activity, both at home and in America, the reason must again be attributed, in part, to England's direct and indirect stimulation of the Irishman's nationalism. To maintain his separate identity throughout modern history, the Irishman — with of course some notable exceptions — had to remain intensely catholic and effectively political. The northern protestants in contrast asserted their Britishness.

Geographical position has determined that the constitutional and political history of Ireland has been dominated by the question of Anglo-Irish relations. Interference by England in Ireland's affairs stretches back over 800 years, beginning with the Anglo-Norman invasion of Ireland in 1169. During the following few centuries the Anglo-Normans were always sufficiently strong to disrupt native Irish political development, but they were never powerful enough to effect a complete conquest of the whole island. Until the sixteenth century Ireland was a lordship over which the kings of England claimed sovereignty. Actual allegiance, however, was not always forthcoming from the Irish lords and chieftains. In the reign of Henry VIII Ireland was raised to the more dignified status of a kingdom. She had now, in theory at least, become a sister kingdom to England with the same king but separate parliaments. In practice, however, the Irish parliament remained inferior to the English, a position which was modified, although hardly eliminated entirely, by the period of so-called Irish legislative independence 1782–1800. The Act of Union which came into force on 1 January 1801 abolished the separate Irish parliament, instituted instead direct rule from Westminster, and declared the constitutional integration of the two islands under the official title of 'The

United Kingdom of Great Britain and Ireland'. A new phase in the history of Anglo-Irish relations had begun.

For centuries a parliament in Dublin had been the main instrument of English rule in Ireland. From its earliest foundations in the thirteenth century it had acknowledged the kings of England as lords of Ireland also. In the fourteenth century parliament had passed the infamous statute of Kilkenny to protect the colonists against Gaelic culture and marriage to the mere Irish. In 1541 the Dublin parliament had declared Henry VIII king of Ireland. In the seventeenth century it deposed King James II and put William of Orange in his place and excluded catholics from parliament as well as from other civil rights. In the eighteenth century it passed a whole series of savage penal laws against the Irish catholic majority who formed more than three quarters of the population. In the later eighteenth century, however, under the influence of the European enlightenment the Irish protestant ascendancy became more liberal, and the penal laws against the catholics were relaxed. Inspired by the example of the American colonists, Irish protestants became more patriotic and demanded more freedom from England for their parliament in Dublin. During the 1790s, under the influence of the French revolution, liberalism showed signs of turning into radicalism; and colonial patriotism showed signs of developing into Irish nationalism. At the same time the protestant ascendancy was beginning to feel threatened by catholic democracy. In these circumstances the British government decided to put an end to the Irish parliament. The instrument which had served English dominion in Ireland so well was not to be allowed to become the instrument of catholic democracy. The proposal was made that the Irish parliament should abolish itself, and that Ireland should henceforth be integrated into the United Kingdom and ruled directly from Westminster. This is what the Act of Union of 1800 meant and it was passed in the English parliament as well as in the Irish parliament. It has determined the whole course of the unhappy relationship between Ireland and Britain ever since.

Act of Union
The details of this very important act may be outlined under five general categories — constitutional, religious, commercial, financial and legal. The four constitutional articles declared that the two kingdoms of Great Britain and Ireland be forever united under the name of the United Kingdom of Great Britain and Ireland, and that the United Kingdom be represented in one and the same parliament,

namely Westminster. Out of a total of 658 members in the house of commons at Westminster, Ireland was to be represented by 100 MPs. Two MPs were to be elected for each county in Ireland, two for the city of Dublin, two for the city of Cork, one for Dublin University (Trinity College), and one for each of thirty-one other boroughs. Thirty-two Irish lords were to sit in the house of lords — twenth-eight of these were lords temporal elected for life by the peers of Ireland, and four were anglican bishops who represented the lords spiritual by rotation.

The fifth article dealing with religion specified that the churches of England and Ireland be united into one protestant episcopal church, that the doctrine, worship, discipline and government of the united church remain in full force forever and that the established united church be deemed to be an essential and fundamental part of the union.

The commercial clauses of the sixth article established a free trade area between the two islands; treated the two countries as one; placed his majesty's subjects in Ireland on an equal footing with his majesty's subjects in Great Britain; and extended to them the same privileges in the export and import of agricultural produce and manufactured goods, in trading and navigation and in all commercial treaties with foreign powers.

The financial clauses of the seventh article specified the respective contributions which Britain and Ireland should make towards the imperial expenditure of the United Kingdom. The proportion fixed for the first twenty years of the union was that for every £15 contributed by Great Britain, Ireland was to contribute £2. National debts incurred by either kingdom before the union and the separate national exchequers were to be retained until the debts were paid off or until the ratio which Ireland's national debt bore to England's was the same as the ratio which the Irish imperial contribution bore to the English imperial contribution. (This contingency happened in 1816 and so from 1 January 1817 the two exchequers were amalgamated and the fiscal union completed.)

The eighth article of the union declared that in each of the kingdoms all laws and the civil and ecclesiastical courts in force at the time of the union should remain as established.

To be fair to the British and Irish politicians involved in the passing of the Act of Union, its terms were not intended to be unfavourable to Ireland. The financial clauses were based upon economic calculations, and had to do with the ratio between the resources, wealth and trade of Ireland and those of Great Britain. (Hence the ratio of two to fifteen in imperial charges.) The free trade clauses removed restrictions on Irish trade, and gave Ireland free access to England's world markets. They also provided protection for certain specified exports from Ireland until such time as they might be able to compete more favourably with English goods. It is true that Irish representation in the United Kingdom parliament was less than would have been merited if representation had been based on population. Because the ratio of England's population to Ireland's greatly increased during the nineteenth century, Ireland, on that score, came to be in fact over-represented in the United Kingdom parliament. At the time of the union Irish representation was based, as indeed it was in England itself in that period, on the estimated wealth of the country in comparison with that of Great Britain. The intention as stated in the Act of Union itself was to provide such measures as might best tend to strengthen and consolidate the connection between the two kingdoms; to promote and secure the essential interests of Great Britain and Ireland; and to consolidate the strength, power and resources of the British Empire.

Union attitudes
Why was it considered necessary to strengthen and consolidate the connection between the two kingdoms? From Britain's point of view the union was, in the first place, a pressing military need. The recent war with America had shown that Britain had no allies in Europe. France, the old enemy, was never so powerful or never so threatening as she was now, for this was the hour of France's revolutionary and democratic fervour, and her mission was to liberate the nations of Europe from aristocratic regimes. And the revolution was followed by the years of Napoleonic expansionism. Never, since the Spanish Armada in the sixteenth century, had Britain felt so threatened, and never again until Hitler's Germany in 1940 stood poised for attack, was invasion of Britain more likely. Ireland could be used for a back-door assault on the neighbouring island. Indeed, revolutionary France, aided and abetted by the republican United Irish Society, had recently attempted three invasions of Ireland, once in 1796 under General Hoche, and twice in 1798 under General Humbert and Admiral Bompart. A vulnerable Ireland increased the insecurity of Britain. A disturbed Ireland was the dagger held at the back of Britain by her continental enemies. If, throughout history, Britain had always been too close for Ireland's comfort, Ireland, in time of war, was always too near for Britain's security. As part of the geographic unit known as the British Isles, Ireland was at the heart of the empire. Ireland, therefore, would have to be held securely if the empire itself was to survive. It is

not really surprising that conservative prime ministers since William Pitt in the 1780s have always allowed the prime consideration of the defence and security of Britain to determine their policies towards Ireland. The defence and security of Britain were the crucial considerations in promoting the union with Ireland.

There was also from Britain's point of view a constitutional need for the union. In 1788 there had occurred what is known in English history as the regency crisis. This was brought about when the king had an illness that developed into insanity, and which looked to some as if it might become permanent. John Mitchel put it less charitably if more picturesquely, when he wrote that George III, who never had much of a mind anyway, completely lost the little bit he did have in 1788. Differences arose between the Irish parliament and the prime minister, Pitt, over the installation of the regent in office, and the limitation of his powers. The temporary recovery of the king resolved the immediate crisis, but the incident had convinced Pitt of the danger that Ireland might appoint a regent who would have full sovereign powers while in England he would be limited by an act of parliament. In these circumstances the Irish parliament might go its own independent way. To prevent the possibility of the emergence in the British Isles of a constitutional monster with two different kinds of head, Pitt determined that a full union was necessary. He bided his time until, following the 1798 rebellion, circumstances were more favourable. One can only admire the skill of the statesman who had then presented an imaginative solution to the Irish problem which combined attractions of a constitutional, commercial and defensive nature, all in this one piece of legislation — the Act of Union.

The protestant colonists who had been allowed to rule Ireland, with the backing of England, felt the need to be protected against the democratic revolutionary forces that had been unleashed. The nationalism, republicanism and jacobinism of the United Irishmen had sought to forge links with the awakening giant of catholic democracy. Discontent among the peasantry and a threat of invasion from revolutionary France added to the ascendancy's fears. Their regime, based upon earlier political, religious and land settlements, was in grave danger of being undermined and destroyed by revolution. Lord Clare, one of the leading Irish architects of the union, had reminded his colleagues in the Irish house of lords that, despite all rhetorical claims to the contrary, they were not the Irish nation. They were, instead, colonials who owed all they held in Ireland to successive English monarchs. These monarchs had conferred the power and property of the land upon three sets of adventurers who had poured into the country at the end of three Irish rebellions. Confiscation was their sole title, and they were 'hemmed in on every side by the old inhabitants of the island brooding over their discontent in sullen indignation'. The catholic natives were awaiting the opportunity to retake their lands, re-establish their persecuted religion and re-assert their political supremacy. Faced with the choice of a separate catholic Ireland or an Ireland united with Britain which would defend the protestant interest, Lord Clare and his colleagues chose the latter. To secure their ascendancy Irish protestants accepted the union. They surrendered the privilege of having their own parliament in order to provide themselves with a shield against catholic democracy. The price they extracted was a guarantee of security for their protestant religion, for the lands they had colonised, and for their continuing social domination. Fears of losing their supremacy had driven the protestant ascendancy into the union. But Lord Clare and his unionist colleagues could put a brave face on it, and convince themselves that what they had done in accepting the union was justified on the grounds that it was in the best interests of Ireland. Clare argued that Ireland, once a mercenary province under her own parliament, would become, under the union, an integrated part of the most progressive and powerful nation in the world. Irishmen, he felt, could be proud to play a role on the world stage of the imperial parliament at Westminster. England and Wales had been joined together in the sixteenth century. Scotland had been united with England and Wales at the beginning of the eighteenth century to form Great Britain. And now, at the end of the eighteenth century, Ireland was to be united with Great Britain in a United Kingdom of Great Britain and Ireland. It could all be made to sound like the onward march of historical inevitability.

The great mass of the catholics were apathetic to the union. In an age of aristocracy they were given no say in political matters and therefore had not to be consulted. Catholic emancipation, however, was still one of the major issues confronting the government and parliament. The leaders of catholic opinion — the bishops, the few catholic noblemen, the middle-class catholic merchants and barristers in the towns and the forty shilling catholic freeholders who had been given the vote in 1793 — were politically important. The catholics, as Cornwallis and Castlereagh feared, had it in their power to frustrate the intentions of the government by their opposition and to throw the country into confusion. If that opposition did not prove altogether fatal to the union it could at least have delayed its progress especially in the south and west.

Both sides in the union debate, needing all the support they could muster, courted the catholics, and the latter found themselves in one of the strongest bargaining positions they had been in during the eighteenth century.

But organised catholicism had to await the political genius of an O'Connell in the next generation. Meanwhile the bishops and the catholic noblemen like Kenmare and Fingall concluded that Pitt and the pro-unionists had more to offer the catholics, were more tolerantly disposed towards them and were in a better position to deliver even on half promises. Allurements in the event of a union and threats in the event of its failure were dangled before them. They were given to understand that emancipation was likely to be conceded by a United Kingdom parliament and that it would be firmly rejected by the government as long as the Dublin parliament existed; that sectarianism would not be countenanced in an Ireland incorporated into the United Kingdom; that peace and harmony would follow the union and that sedition and disturbances would have a less fertile soil in the expanded kingdom. State financial provisions for the catholic clergy, reform of the hated tithe system of support for the clergy of the established church, the house of commons open to Irish catholic representatives and the house of lords open to Irish catholic peers were other prospects which catholics were encouraged to see in the union. While no direct pledge was given, catholic leaders were assured of the government's intention that catholics would be fully integrated as citizens and given equal rights with the protestants. The support of the bishops and of the catholic lords was all the more readily forthcoming when they were reminded by Pitt's negotiators that they could never expect such generosity of spirit on the part of a frightened protestant minority.

The fiercely anti-papist atmosphere that followed the '98 rebellion convinced the catholic bishops and many of the clergy that justice and fair government were more likely to be obtained from a United Kingdom parliament than from an orange oligarchy entrenched in Dublin. So, despite the fact that some of the most bitter and bigoted opponents of emancipation were on the same side, leading catholics supported the union. Some of the bishops — Troy of Dublin, Bray of Cashel, Moylan of Cork, Caulfield of Ferns, Dillon of Tuam, O'Reilly of Armagh and Lanigan of Ossory — actively promoted the measure. No catholic bishop publicly opposed it. The attitude of Dr Daniel Delany of Kildare and Leighlin was fairly typical. It was reported to Castlereagh that Delany spoke highly in favour of the union, but he availed of the opportunity to say that the excesses still committed against many catholic clergy were offensive. Just how far the bishops were prepared to go in their efforts at this time to reach an accommodation with the government, is illustrated in the fact that they were also willing to consider the so-called two 'wings' of emancipation, namely state payment of the clergy and a royal veto on the appointment of catholic bishops. A mixture of self-interest, practical politics and concern for the welfare of their religion and their flock determined the policy pursued by the catholic bishops and lords. And as the bishops and the catholic peers did not wish to appear to be endangering the union by insisting that emancipation should be part of the union legislation, they were prepared to postpone emancipation until the United Kingdom parliament had been established.

In Dublin where opposition to the union was most pronounced, and where the influential legal profession and the banking and commercial interests had come out strongly against it, catholic merchants and catholic barristers like the young Daniel O'Connell could be found in alliance with their professional and business protestant colleagues in opposition to the measure. O'Connell, making his first appearance in politics, denied that catholics were ready to sell their country for a price or abandon it on account of the unfortunate animosities which the wretched temper of the times had produced. And probably in response to a threat made in the English parliament he replied that were the alternative offered him of the union or the re-enactment of the penal code, he would prefer the latter as a lesser evil. He would rather confide in the justice of the Irish protestants than lay his country at the feet of foreigners. (O'Connell's uncle and brother were active in Kerry on the side of the union.)

The two camps in the union argument attached importance at least to the appearance of popular support. In this campaign to win signatures both for and against the union the forty shilling catholic freeholders in the counties, therefore, were involved in the political excitement. Their importance in politics was recognised for the first time during the union debate by Dublin castle and by the local political magnates. In what then passed for public opinion the signatures of these new voters counted for something. Which petition they signed depended, of course, upon the political views of the local magnate. Support for the union from these catholic freeholders was in some places influenced by their clergy's stand. In this way, the catholic electorate and the catholic clergy with the encouragement of the government had joined forces on an issue that was national and not sectarian. Previously the traditional concern of the catholic community had been mainly with the sectarian issue of the penal laws, and the first tentative steps towards emancipation. The union debate had involved them with national politics, and having got a taste of the wider politics and a recognition of their role they were unlikely in the post-union situation to surrender their involvement and revert to their eighteenth-century political passivity. Ironically, therefore, it was the British government, and to a lesser extent the protestant landlords, that brought the catholic bishops and the forty shilling freeholders into politics long before O'Connell succeeded in involving them in his emancipation or repeal agitations of the early nineteenth century. Important also was the fact that the union took the government and administration of Ireland out of the hands of the protestant ascendancy, out of the hands of the men of property and the Irish upper classes generally. Into this political vacuum came the men of no property, the men of talent, the middle-class catholics and their clergy to lead Irish public opinion and political agitation. As Lecky said, the ascendancy politicians were compelled to register and proclaim their own incapacity in their own parliament. They were forced to declare themselves incapable or unworthy of running the country.[2]

Opposition to the union was articulate and extensive but eventually ineffective. In parliament the opposition was led by the brothers George and William Ponsonby whose family had been among the great magnates of eighteenth-century Ireland. At the time of the union they controlled almost two dozen parliamentary seats. Grattan and Plunket provided the patriotic anti-union oratory. The Ponsonbys, Grattan and Plunket were supporters of reform and catholic emancipation and belonged to the whig opposition. In uneasy alliance with this whig wing were the speaker of the house, John Foster, Sir John Parnell, chancellor of the exchequer, and J C Beresford, inspector-general of imports and exports. The members of this 'orange' wing (Beresford was general secretary of the united Orange lodges) were generally hostile to catholic claims, and apart from the union were mainly supporters of the government in which they held office. As men of commercial experience their opposition to the union was based largely on the conviction that the commercial and fiscal clauses of the union would be seriously damaging to the Irish economy. The inability of these two rival wings to agree on an alternative to the union was one of the main reasons for its success. Of the sixty-four MPs who represented the counties, more than half were in opposition to the union measure. Outside of parliament the city and county of Dublin, fearing the adverse social and economic effects which the removal of parliament might have on the capital, were the centre of anti-unionism. The counties nearest the capital — Louth, Meath, Kildare, Wicklow, Carlow and Wexford — tended to follow Dublin's lead. In the Ulster 'frontier' counties of Fermanagh, Tyrone, Armagh, Cavan and Monaghan where sectarian bitterness was strong and where orangeism feared that an English parliament would be 'soft' on catholics, resistance to the union was also strong.

In Munster and Connaught, where catholics were proportionately the most numerous, the union found considerable support. The catholic unionist, Lord Kenmare, carried his catholic tenantry with him in Kerry. Among linen manufacturers in Ulster there was some support for the union on the grounds that free access to English markets would lead to an expansion of the Ulster linen industry. Others, like the United Irishman Hamilton Rowan, shed no tears for the passing of what he regarded as one of the most corrupt and venal assemblies that had ever existed. The union, said Rowan, 'takes a feather out of the great man's cap; but it will, I think, put many a guinea in the poor man's pocket.'[3] The cities of Cork, Waterford and to a lesser extent Limerick and Galway hoped to benefit from the prospects of greater commerce in the United Kingdom free trade area. If the anti-union camp was made up of the most unlikely alliances, so too did the pro-union group produce equally strange bed-fellows. Troy, catholic archbishop of Dublin, found himself, albeit for different reasons, on the same side as the bigoted anti-catholic Lord Clare (leader of the unionists in the house of lords).

The union found its most able promoters in the lord lieutenant Cornwallis, the chief secretary Castlereagh and the chancellor Lord Clare. The house of lords, which contained the protestant bishops and many of the greatest Irish landowners, voted overwhelmingly in favour of the union (75 to 26 on the first vote). If most of the county representatives in the commons were on the anti-union side (38 against, 26 for), the government and the lords between them carried more influence with the boroughs. And if the anti-unionists could claim that more signatures were obtained against the union than for it, the unionists could claim that a preponderance of the owners of the landed wealth of the counties upon whom they had concentrated for signatures had signed in favour of the union. (From the counties were received 28 petitions against the union and 19 for.) The only counties in which no petition could be got up against the union, thanks to the exertions of the local landlords, were Antrim, Derry, Waterford and Kerry. Most of the bishops of the established church, because of their close connection with the government and because the union proposed to guarantee their position and their security, supported the measure. The presbyterians generally acquiesced.

The union carried
It would be old-fashioned, too nationalistic and much too simplistic to hold that the Act of Union was carried mainly because of the corrupt methods employed by the government. The measure passed through the Irish parliament because of a variety of interwoven reasons including the government's determination; the lack of co-operation and the failure to offer any constructive alternative to the union on the part of a divided opposition; disillusionment with 'Grattan's parliament'; the shock of the '98 rebellion; the threat from France; the fears of the protestant ascendancy; the expectations of the catholics; economic and regional considerations; apathy and acquiescence on the part of many, and the failure to whip up that kind of patriotic feeling which had inspired the volunteers and the country during the agitation for legislative independence in 1782. But it would be equally wrong, and a grave misunderstanding of the situation, to ignore the charge of corruption or to underestimate or underplay its significance.

Despite the fact that many liberal protestants opposed the union for patriotic reasons, and that others opposed it on grounds of self-interest, it was eventually carried by a majority in the Irish parliament. A parliament that had existed for more than five hundred years had extinguished itself. Pitt and his Irish agents, Lord Castlereagh and Lord Clare, had organised a majority by the use of various means — by having seats in parliament purchased from the borough owners for some supporters of the union; by giving out promotions in the peerage to others; by holding out the prospect of the employment of government influence to ensure that others would be returned as representative Irish peers in the house of lords; by compensating all those traffickers in politics, whether unionist or anti-unionist, who would lose by the abolition of Irish constituencies (the value of a borough was declared to be £15,000, so that over £1 million was paid out in compensation alone); and by the provision of ecclesiastical and legal jobs to the families of others who voted for the union. One of Pitt's biographers has argued that the sordid bargainings could not be said to have amounted to wholesale corruption, and did not much exceed those which normally were needed to carry any important bill through parliament.[4] It is also true that the opponents of the union were not themselves adverse to the use of 'bribery' for their own ends. (They established a fighting fund to purchase seats for anti-unionists.) The difference lay in the fact that the government possessed more money and more patronage and was able to dispense more favours. Modern historians have indeed pointed out that all these rewards which were bestowed on individuals for support of the union measure are no different from the practice today of doling out ambassadorships, honours and jobs to political adherents, and to all those who contribute finance to the party. These historians also prefer to use the word 'management' instead of 'corruption' when describing the manipulations of eighteenth-century politicians. However, the scale and significance of the whole sordid business, and the charges and counter-charges of corruption that were made, left a bad taste. And it does not matter much, politically, how your modern academic historian may palliate or explain away the deals that were done or the methods that were employed. What mattered was the view that came to be taken of these things by those who were never consulted at all, i.e. by the bulk of the Irish people, as democracy and nationalism spread among them. What was remembered was that the union was passed in a protestant assembly by a comparatively small group of protestant landlords whose vote was influenced by England and who regarded themselves, in any case, as British. How the majority of Irish people from the mid-nineteenth century onwards came to regard the methods by which the union was carried was well expressed in the ballad written by the Young Irelander, John O'Hagan:

> How did they pass the union?
> By perjury and fraud;
> By slaves who sold their land for gold
> As Judas sold his God.
> By all the savage acts that yet
> Have followed England's track,
> The pitchcap and the bayonet,
> The gibbet and the rack;
> And thus was passed the union
> By Pitt and Castlereagh;
> Could Satan find for such an end
> More worthy tools than they?[5]

The union had been effected by management or corruption, depending on one's point of view. One thing, however, is certain: it was not a love-match. It was not the culmination of a happy relationship between the two partners. It was not the result of any love that Britain had for Ireland or of any devotion that Ireland had for Britain. It was a marriage of convenience. The convenience was mainly Britain's. It also served the interests of some Anglo-Irish protestants. It was opposed, however, by some of the most patriotic and idealistic among the Anglo-Irish — by Grattan, Plunket, Sir John Parnell and the Ponsonbys. And one of its great weaknesses was that the marriage never had the full consent of the catholic majority. What followed the wedding was not even a pretence of a honeymoon. The charade would finally end in the divorce courts in 1922.

Lecky wrote that the union was not only a great crime, but was also, like most crimes, a great blunder.[6] Instead of binding the two islands closer together it only drove them further apart. And yet, one must not anticipate the marital breakdown too readily. It is arguable that it had as reasonable a chance of success as most political unions in history. The prospects seemed no worse than in the case of the union of England and Wales or of their union with Scotland. And unlike the unification of Germany or Italy or the USA later in the century, no bloodshed was necessary in the case of the Irish union. English ministers wanted the union to be a success. Yet, Ireland was never fully integrated constitutionally into the United Kingdom, but was administered from Dublin castle by a lord lieutenant and a chief secretary as if she were an Indian outpost of the empire.

To Irishmen, it seemed that Britain had not been able to make up its mind whether it wanted Ireland or not. The catholics, who had been promised that emancipation would follow the union, ultimately wrung emancipation from the government nearly thirty years later after a massive and prolonged civil rights campaign. The economic and fiscal union was not seen to work, as promised, in Ireland's favour either. Far from being treated as wife and partner, Ireland was the Cinderella of the household. The worst-ever social disaster in Ireland's history when one million people died in the great famine and another million emigrated from the starving land, would take place only forty years after the Irish economy allegedly became part of what was then the foremost economy in the world. Only the north-east of Ulster would share in Britain's industrial revolution, and this would have the effect of widening the gap still further between northern protestants and southern catholics. Despite all mounting evidence to the contrary Britain would cling, throughout the nineteenth century, to the view that the union was the final solution to the Irish problem. The word 'forever' had, in fact, been used three times in the Act of Union document.

A modern historian has written that the Act of Union was the most important single factor making Ireland a nation in the modern world.[7] Indeed, Irish history, at least down to 1922, has been a history of Ireland under the union. Every nationalist movement, whether constitutional and parliamentary or republican and physical force, has aimed at the abolition of that union. Every unionist movement has aimed at its maintenance. The first principle for every political leader in Irish history since 1800 has been his attitude to the union. Irish nationalist leaders, whether of the constitutional or physical force variety, never accepted the morality or legality or practicality of the act. Their followers, therefore, were instructed that they did not have to obey an illegitimate rule. Passive resistance, civil disobedience and active rebellion were offered in turn and sometimes simultaneously as long as the union survived.

Effects of the union
During the immediate aftermath of the union national politics on the surface, and local politics, in particular, remained unaltered. Nevertheless, the establishment of the United Kingdom of Great Britain and Ireland had the consequence of producing something akin to a political earthquake with delayed effects. It threw Ireland and Britain into a new relationship with each other. Britain now had direct responsibility for the good administration of Ireland. The United Kingdom parliament had the duty of ruling Ireland, and of attempting to impose remedies for the country's ills. This was not an easy task for there were great differences between the two countries — religious, social, economic and cultural. As the century progressed the differences often became more marked. The United Kingdom parliament would have to give Ireland a great deal of attention and time. Awkward and unresolved Irish problems would lurk like so many landmines threatening to blast individual careers and to destroy the unity of cabinets, parliamentary majorities and the solidarity of political parties. Every major parliamentary crisis during the nineteenth century, or so it seemed to John Russell during a debate on Maynooth in the 1840s, had been caused or complicated by Irish issues. Full integration, as envisaged in the act of 1800, was even more ambitious than simple government, for it imposed a legal, constitutional and political unity that made no allowance for any difference in the two traditions. A uniformity of such proportions would demand great skill and attention and the necessary force to sustain it. The hostility of Napoleonic France, the expansion of the empire overseas, the strides taken at home in industrialised Britain, and the great complexity of the problems associated with these de-

velopments meant that Ireland was just one more challenge facing British statesmanship in a very crowded hour. The imperial energy required might ensure that the Irish question would be tackled with success. On the other hand, the challenge might prove to be too much of a strain and of a distraction considering all else that demanded the attention of British statesmen.

As long as the Irish parliament existed, Irish protestantism had drawn Irish catholic fire. Now that it was abolished, the aggression was redirected at Britain and the angry drama would be played out on the stage of the imperial parliament, thereby raising the Irish question to a greater significance and ensuring for it a world audience. By removing the buffer of the Irish protestant parliament the union brought Irish nationalism and British imperialism face to face. In the end, the intransigence of imperial uniformity produced, by way of reaction, the intransigence of nationalist separatism, expressed in its ultimate form in Pearse's pronouncement that the Irishman who accepted 'anything less by one fraction of one iota than separation from England' would be guilty of an immense infidelity and of an immense crime against the Irish nation.[8] An Ireland, which during the nineteenth century was willing to compromise politically, found no satisfactory response from the British authorities who were grown quite imperial by the end of the nineteenth century. With every passing decade the constitutional road to independence became more difficult, and republican violence became more probable, as in the insurrections of 1803, 1848, 1867, 1916 and 1919–21. Britain resisted all concessions to constitutional nationalism whether repeal under O'Connell or later still, home rule under Butt, Parnell or Redmond. Ireland responded with a more extreme nationalism, and demanded a separatist republic with ever-growing support and increasing effectiveness. In the long term, the union, ironically, had only enhanced confrontation between the sister islands. The shock waves would be felt eventually in other parts of the empire.

Dublin, which up to 1800 had been the second city in the British Isles and an administrative and legislative capital, suffered geopolitical dislocation as a consequence of the Act of Union. The abolition of a parliament which had housed 300 MPs and nearly a hundred peers meant that Dublin as a political and social centre was gradually, but severely, diminished. The abolition of the Dublin parliament affected the city's housing and business, and altered the pattern of its architecture. The former MPs and peers of the Irish parliament now had less reason for maintaining residences in Dublin. And as the great political figures withdrew from Dublin it was felt that the luxury trades, and the other forms of business that had flourished due to their presence, must inevitably suffer. As a consequence of their withdrawal the more imposing residences of the Irish ascendancy lost their function as centres for political intrigue, and were in time transformed into commercial and other offices. The biggest of the Dublin houses reflected the political changes most obviously. The Parliament House in College Green, built between 1729 and 1739, and whose grandeur and architectural elegance dominated the city, was bought by the Bank of Ireland in 1802. Its interior was adapted and additions were made by the architect, Francis Johnston, to facilitate banking purposes. The transformation was symbolic of the fact that the middle-class world of business and commerce was making inroads on the world of the ascendancy. The largest of the great town houses was Leinster House, begun in 1745 by the architect Richard Cassels for the Fitzgerald family, the earls of Kildare. Fifteen years after the union the duke of Leinster sold the house to the Royal Dublin Society. (In 1921, Dáil Éireann moved into Leinster House and the RDS was moved to Ballsbridge.) Tyrone House in Marlborough Street was designed by Cassels about 1740 as a town house for Marcus Beresford, later earl of Tyrone. It was bought by the government in 1835 to become the headquarters of the board of national education.

This transformation could also be seen as a symbol of the victory of a democratic age over that of an aristocratic regime. Aldborough House was built in the 1790s. It became a school in 1813 and was later turned into the stores department of the general post office. Lord Annesley's town house in Marlborough Street was bought in 1803 as the site for the pro-cathedral — emerging catholicism was replacing protestant ascendancy. Belvedere House became a Jesuit school in 1841. Powerscourt House was bought by the commissioners of stamp duties in 1807, and was purchased in 1835 by a wholesale drapers. The age of the magnificent town houses of Dublin had ended with the abolition of the Irish parliament. The Customs House, the Four Courts, the Parliament House and the great town houses which were the show pieces of Dublin's architecture belonged to the age of the protestant ascendancy of the eighteenth century. Of course, some magnificent buildings were erected after the union. But like the GPO, built between 1814 and 1818, or the railway stations, or the big catholic churches, they belonged to an age that saw the democratisation of Irish society. The building of these city churches in prominent locations, replacing the back-lane chapels of the penal era, reflected more than anything else the ending of the age of the protestant ascendancy and the dawning of the new age of catholic democracy.

The economic consequences of the union for Dublin in particular, and for Ireland in general, are still a matter of debate among economic historians. The fact that Dublin appeared to prosper in the days of Grattan's parliament and that its industry declined during the post-union period led earlier commentators to assume a connection between a legislative act and economic circumstances. Modern economic historians have emphasised that the one was not necessarily the consequence of the other. They have pointed to the complexities of the problem and have shown how the operation of international economic laws have had more to do with the circumstances than any constitutional change. They have stressed that the decline was coincidental rather than consequential and has more to do with appearances. Appearance, of course, influenced the formation of political attitudes. In 1810, for example, Dublin corporation would condemn the union largely on economic grounds because of its alleged detrimental effects.

The material impact of the union on Dublin, although great, was perhaps less important than the psychological impact on its status. London, not Dublin, became the new centre of Irish political interest, since London was responsible for all Irish legislation. Belfast, which at the time of the union was no more than a small town, began to grow dramatically, largely as a result of the industrial revolution. And as it grew it became a rival to Dublin, no longer a metropolitan city, but merely another provincial capital. Belfast began to see itself as the unionist capital of Ireland. And it looked upon that union as the symbol and guarantee of its own prosperity and security. The union had brought Belfast, along with London and Dublin, on to the centre of the stage in the unfolding drama of Anglo-Irish relations.

The merging of Ireland with Britain into one political, constitutional entity was a great experiment, holding out prospects of many advantages for both islands. During the 1830s, for example, Ireland was to enjoy the benefits of liberal and progressive legislation in the areas of education, emancipation, protestant church reform, tithes, municipal reform, poor law, policing and fair administration. From any point of view, it was to Britain's advantage to pursue a policy of pacifying Ireland. If military security had been the main reason for the union, it followed that in time of war a friendly and contented Ireland would always be the best guarantee that Britain had of avoiding the stab in the back. A discontented and disloyal Ireland only increased the threat to British security. If the union failed it was not for any lack of attention to Ireland on Britain's part, though some of the attention may have turned out to be misplaced or insensitive. A great amount of parliamentary time was devoted to the Irish question. India, with a population a hundred times that of Ireland, received only a fraction of the attention which was given to Ireland. For long periods British statesmen were preoccupied with the embarrassment or the nuisance of Irish troubles. Parties and cabinets split over the Irish question; and governments were defeated or, alternatively, supported in office because of their Irish policies. Henry Grattan once said: 'You have swept away our constitution, you have destroyed our parliament, but we shall have our revenge. We will send into the ranks of your parliament and into the heart of your constitution a hundred of the greatest rascals in the kingdom.'[9] Grattan's prophecy was fulfilled in the days when Parnell and his Irish party of land leaguers and Fenians held the balance between the two major parties in England, and pursued a policy of obstruction aimed at destroying Westminster's control over Ireland. In retrospect, none of the aims of the union measure and none of its great promised benefits appeared to have been realised. The union had not worked.

The quest for political identity

It is the prerogative of the novelist to choose any one of several possible endings to his story. The historian is restricted by his knowledge of what has actually happened. One of the problems in studying the history of Ireland under the union is that we know the end of the story. The knowledge that the union ended in dissolution tends to intrude itself between the actual events and developments in early nineteenth-century Ireland and the way in which we understand and analyse them. That intrusion consequently colours our description. We need to keep on reminding ourselves, therefore, that the final outcome was by no means the inevitable or only ending. From the viewpoint of the people involved the story of Ireland within the United Kingdom could have had several different endings. The historian, if he is to understand properly the period about which he writes, must put himself from time to time in the position of the participants and with them look ahead along the avenues that open out before his vision and not be content with standing at the terminus and looking backwards. The latter practice blurs the vision by its habit of creating too many straight lines, and by not appreciating the twists and turns and false starts. Looking backwards only, one fails to take adequate notice of how the actions of the statesmen involved, the reactions of the people concerned, and the forces that were at work combined to produce the result we know, and not one of any number of other possibilities.

At the time of the union there were three contemporaries who charted the direction of Irish political thinking and who established traditions which echoed down through the nineteenth century. These three offered separate images of Irish political identity, and held out to the people of Ireland three distinct objectives. In the immediate post-union period it remained to be determined which of these might establish precedence over the others. The first of these was Henry Grattan, who may be described as the father of Irish constitutional nationalism. Grattan's objective was the establishment of an independent Irish parliament which would have control over domestic affairs. But his Ireland would be linked with Britain through the crown for all imperial purposes. Because of his insistence on the sisterhood relationship between the two countries, Grattan might truly be described as a father of the British commonwealth idea. He was hardly exaggerating his own role in the establishment of Irish legislative independence in 1782 — the first abortive experiment in dominion status — when he declared:

> I found Ireland on her knees, I watched over her with an eternal solicitude; I have traced her progress from injuries to arms, and from arms to liberty. Spirit of Swift, spirit of Molyneux, your genius has prevailed. Ireland is now a nation; in that new character I hail her, and bowing to her august presence, I say, *Esto perpetua*.[10]

Grattan had cast himself in a particular role as the father of Irish political liberty. His version of Irish history, which he had thus launched upon the world, would be as popular and influential in the nineteenth century as Pearse's version in the twentieth. In Grattan's view, the Act of Union, though it might abolish the parliament of Ireland and the Irish state, could never destroy the nation nor Irish aspirations for the restoration of a national parliament. In his celebrated speech against the union Grattan had said:

> Yet I do not give up the country; I see her in a swoon, but she is not dead; though in her tomb she lies helpless and motionless, still there is on her lips a spirit of life, and on her cheek a glow of beauty. 'Thou art not conquered; beauty's ensign yet is crimson in thy lips and in thy cheeks, and death's pale flag is not advanced there.'

And Grattan had concluded:

> I will remain anchored here with fidelity to the fortunes of my country, faithful to her freedom, faithful to her fall.[11]

Grattan the politician soon cooperated in the union settlement. But Grattan of the patriotic myth remained ever steadfast to the ideal of an Irish nation. The legislative independence which he had achieved for Ireland between 1782 and the Act of Union of 1800 would become the objective of every major constitutional nationalist movement throughout the nineteenth century.

To the right of Grattan stood his exact contemporary, John Fitzgibbon, afterwards Lord Clare. Although Fitzgibbon had originally supported the legislative independence ideal of Grattan, the increasing liberalism towards the catholic majority and the spreading influence of the radicalism of the French revolution frightened Fitzgibbon into an extreme conservative position and made him, in the process, the father of Irish unionism. Unlike Grattan, 'Black Jack' Fitzgibbon's reputation among the people always remained as low as it was on the day when some citizens of Dublin allegedly threw dead cats at his coffin. Insofar as he was remembered at all by the nationalist mind of Ireland, this Irish architect of the union with Britain occupied a position which was the very opposite to that held by the memory of Grattan. Yet, in his own way and on his own terms, Fitzgibbon was a patriot though not a nationalist. And where Grattan by his rhetoric injected something of the poetry of politics into nineteenth-century Ireland, Fitzgibbon introduced into the union debate a contrasting and stark political realism.

In a four-hour harangue to the Irish house of lords on 10 February 1800, Lord Clare contrasted the cold facts of history with the glowing myth of Anglo-Irish colonial nationalism. 'We have been for twenty years in a fever of intoxication and we must be stunned into sobriety', said Fitzgibbon, in what must have been the most clinical historical lecture ever delivered in the old Irish parliament. In his unionist image of Irish identity he marked out the political pathway which he felt the Irish people should follow.

> I hope I feel as becomes a true Irishman for the dignity and independence of my country. I would therefore elevate her to her proper station in the rank of civilised nations. I would advance her from the degraded post of a mercenary province to the proud station of an integral and governing member of the greatest empire in the world.[12]

The ballad, written by Thomas Davis some forty years later with the refrain 'Ireland long a province, be a nation once again', was merely the nationalist version of Lord Clare's unionist speech. Grattan and Lord Clare, while going divergent ways, could both claim to be true patriots concerned for the dignity and independence of their country.

To the left of Henry Grattan stood the third of the three contemporaries — Theobald Wolfe Tone. This third influential image-maker of the late eighteenth century was a younger contemporary of Grattan and Fitzgibbon, and also like them was a member of the Irish protestant ascendancy. He was too young to have shared with them any political responsibility for the achievement of legislative independence in 1782. But as an impressionable and ambitious boy in his teens, he imbibed all of the emotional atmosphere of the time. The realities of the post-independence decades left him disillusioned and prepared him for the enthusiastic adoption of French revolutionary ideals which he proceeded to adapt to Irish circumstances. Under the influence of the French revolution he came to despise Grattan's parliament. He wrote that: 'The revolution of 1782 was the most bungling imperfect business that ever threw ridicule on a lofty epithet by assuming it unworthily'.[13] And it is often overlooked that Tone's rebellion in 1798 was as much an attempt to overthrow Grattan's parliament as it was to break the connection with England. So, where Grattan had proposed a link with England and Fitzgibbon had proposed integration, Tone advocated total separation. He was the father of Irish republicanism. The image which he proffered to the Irish people was formulated in the passage:

> To subvert the tyranny of our execrable government, to break the connection with England, the never-failing source of all our political evils, and to assert the independence of my country — these were my objects. To unite the whole people of Ireland, to abolish the memory of all past dissensions, and to substitute the common name of Irishman in place of the denomination of Protestant, Catholic and Dissenter — these were my means.[14]

The interplay of these three distinct ideals — Lord Clare's unionism, Tone's republicanism and Grattan's moderate nationalism — would constitute Irish political history in the nineteenth century. As the new century opened, however, it was the union with Britain that constituted the reality. And it is remarkable how acceptable this union initially turned out to be. Those among the ascendancy who had opposed it most vehemently soon made it quite clear by their actions and their involvement in the settlement that they were anxious to cooperate fully with the constitutional arrangement of 1800.

Of the 100 Irish MPs returned to the United Kingdom parliament in 1801, 50 had opposed the union. They caused no disruption in the United Kingdom parliament, nor did they form anything like a separate party. Even for those like Foster, Parnell, Grattan and

Plunket who had bitterly and strenuously opposed the union, adjustment to its reality became a relatively easy and simple matter. MPs in the Irish parliament had always been tories or whigs, and appendages of the political factions in England. As their patriotism or colonial nationalism of the late eighteenth century subsided into history, their role as the Irish versions of English parties increased. For them the union had become a *fait accompli*: they no longer debated its justification nor questioned its legality. Established now as part of the majority in the United Kingdom they had no wish to revert to being a besieged minority in an independent Ireland. This was especially true of those who had supported the union. They had been handsomely compensated in money and in titles for any losses they had suffered by the abolition of the Dublin parliament. They were, therefore, in no position to complain about the union. Their lands, religion, prosperity and security were guaranteed by the union. These former members of the Irish parliament fitted into the United Kingdom institutions quite naturally. The more able among them, like Lord Castlereagh, had their talents recognised by being advanced to ministerial office. A former strong opponent of the union, Speaker Foster, was appointed to the board of trade, and then became chancellor of the Irish exchequer. Ponsonby became for a while leader of the opposition. The more impressive of the former 'patriots', like Grattan, when eventually he entered the United Kingdom parliament (1805), were always afforded a respectful hearing in its debates. In the first thirty years of the nineteenth century, Irishmen in the London parliament did not form a distinct group. They continued with their allegiances to the tories or the whigs. The vast majority of them joined the former. Their policies were indistinguishable from those of the English MPs with whom they were allied.

The war with Napoleonic France, the threat which it posed and the general opposition which French imperialism evoked among the Anglo-Irish, helped to cement together the new structure. The war had the further effect of keeping prices high, and while the Irish economy was thus inflated by the war prices, the union was not seen to have any immediate detrimental effects on the country. Despite the initial setback to their hopes with the resignation of Pitt, the expectations of the catholics remained high, and friends of emancipation were seen to occupy places of responsibility in several of the cabinets in the early nineteenth century. In these circumstances the catholics felt no need for any organised opposition to the union.

In the years immediately following the union, then, the dream of reestablishing Grattan's parliament was in abeyance. Tone's separatist dream had made no great impact, but it flickered into life briefly with Robert Emmet's insurrection on a July evening in the streets of Dublin, in 1803. The abortive rebellion was a pathetic affair. In one sense, it was no more than the embers of the '98 rebellion, but unlike '98 it lacked any real threat of foreign intervention, despite Emmet's contacts with France. The youthfulness of the executed leader (he was only 21), the sincere glowing patriotism of his speech from the dock, and the utter hopelessness of the venture ensured that Emmet would live on in the memory of the people. And when a later generation romanticised the episode, Emmet's rising became more effective in nationalist myth than it ever had been in reality. The rebellion was roundly condemned by those politicians who had led the opposition to the union. O'Connell said about it 'that no madder scheme was ever devised', and that it was 'as wild as anything in romance'.[15] Among his prized possessions at Derrynane was a blunderbuss which was said to have been taken by him in a raid on a house in Dublin, while serving in the lawyers' corps against the rebels.

In the opening decades of the nineteenth century Lord Clare's option of the union was seen to have been firmly established. Grattan's tomb in Westminster Abbey is over-shadowed by the monument raised to Lord Castlereagh. This was symbolic of the abolition of the Dublin parliament and its replacement by Westminster.

How long the stability might last, or how long the union settlement might persist without being seriously challenged, depended on the forces at work. Some of these forces were operating to preserve the established order; others were working to effect change. One of the chief agents of conservatism was Dublin castle — the administrative nerve-centre of British rule in Ireland. The castle and its officers — the lord lieutenant, chief secretary, under-secretary and civil servants — had responsibility for operating the constitutional *status quo*. And emanating from the castle were the whole paraphernalia of law and order — the police, the magistrates, the courts and the local government system, all charged with the upholding of British rule. Outside of the castle administration unionism was also strongly entrenched among the Irish parliamentary representatives, even though no unionist party as such emerged until the end of the century. These MPs regarded the union not only as something that was eminently desirable, but also as a given condition which was not to be questioned. Another of the pillars of the union was landlordism. The landlords were not only politically conservative, they were socially and economically conservative as well. They wished, naturally, to preserve the political and land settlements which had established their power and status. The established church, too, firmly supported the union, since the union and the established church were regarded as inseparably linked. Any attack on the one was looked upon as also endangering the other. Insofar as Trinity College Dublin was associated with the protestant clergy and the landlord and ruling classes it, too, was a conservative institution. The catholic church, also, and especially the hierarchy often acted in the interests of conservatism.

Each of these agents of conservatism was countered to some extent by an antidote working to effect change. Dublin castle, for example, although concerned with maintaining the constitutional *status quo* was also committed to the implementation of reforms and of good administration leading to some progress and change. The emerging political and economic philosophy of the day — liberalism — fostered the concern for improvement. In an age of reform, even the Irish administration was unable to avoid the influence of the spirit of the time in areas like education, local government, police, church and land reforms.

The conservative force of unionism had its antidote in the threat of nationalism which would grow in confidence and strength throughout the nineteenth century. Nationalists of all kinds aimed at undoing the union settlement. Secret agrarian societies and land reformers challenged and sought to destroy the landlord system that had been inherited from the previous centuries. And the revival of the catholic church led to the expansion of its influence over a number of different fronts in nineteenth-century Ireland. Thus the government itself, together with liberalism, nationalism, agrarianism and catholicism constituted some of the most powerful agencies in post-union Ireland. But perhaps the most powerful force of all was expanding democracy. Linked with the massive ground swell of social and economic change caused by the population explosion, the rise and organisation of democracy was to pose the biggest threat to the settlement which had united Ireland with Britain.

2 The Question of Religion

In few centuries did organised religion play so large a part in the life of the nation as it did in the nineteenth century. Catholics, episcopalians and the dissenting churches all experienced a period of revitalisation — within the protestant churches the revival was known as the second reformation. Orangeism, it might even be said, was a distorted or political expression or extension of protestantism: and catholic and nationalist came to be almost interchangeable terms. The fact that the three major branches of the christian church in Ireland permeated all levels of society meant that developments inside the churches were a microcosm of changes in society in general. It also meant, however, that not only were the churches responsive to the external forces of change, but were powerful and pervasive enough to be themselves a major cause of those changes that were taking place in society.

Episcopalian protestants
The church of Ireland which claimed to have been instituted by St Patrick had close doctrinal and disciplinary ties with the church of England since the Anglo-Norman invasion, and these ties had been strengthened by the reformation. Ever since the sixteenth century it had constituted an integral part of the protestant ascendancy. In accordance with the terms of the Act of Union the church of Ireland was united with the church of England, and this united church was declared to be the established church of the United Kingdom of Great Britain and Ireland. This union of the two branches of the anglican church was, however, more abstract than practical: for the church of Ireland remained administratively separate in much the same way that Ireland had remained administratively separate from the rest of the United Kingdom. It was a union of the churches in name only. One of the most immediate results of the Act of Union was the pressure for the appointment of bishops as part of the political debt incurred in wooing support for the measure. These 'union engagements' to aristocratic Irish families and to bishops in the Irish house of lords had the side-effect of making the church of Ireland more Irish in its leadership than it had been in the eighteenth century.

The big difference between the church of Ireland and that of

England was that while the latter broadly embraced a majority of Englishmen, the former always represented only a minority of Irishmen, no more indeed than about 12 per cent in the census returns of 1861 — the first reliable statistics to deal with Irish religious affiliation. That percentage was very unevenly and disproportionately spread both geographically and from the point of view of social status. In Ulster in 1861, 21.5 per cent of the total population were church of Ireland; in Leinster 12.3 per cent; in Munster 5.3 per cent and in Connaught 4.2 per cent. The concentration was clearly in the north (about half of the church of Ireland membership was in Ulster) and in the east (Dublin and Wicklow especially). The vast majority of landowners — ranging from peers with tens of thousands of acres to gentlemen farmers with a few hundred — belonged to the church of Ireland. In these hands lay the bulk of the political and social patronage of the counties. Apart from the landed proprietors church of Ireland members outside of Ulster were largely urban dwelling and belonged to the high professional classes. Fifty per cent or more of all barristers, solicitors, civil engineers, medical men, architects, bankers and persons described in the census as of independent means were members of the church of Ireland. And, as befitted a ruling elite, 80 per cent of the serving army officers belonged to the established church. One third of all clergymen were church of Ireland ministers, and in the years before disestablishment in 1869 up to one third of Trinity College Dublin graduates took orders. At the other end of the social ladder only 8 per cent of shopkeepers, less than 4 per cent of greengrocers and 1 per cent of vagrants were church of Ireland.

In the early nineteenth century the church of the establishment reflected many of the failings and abuses of a ruling oligarchy. Because it was a state church, appointments to bishoprics and other ecclesiastical offices in the church of Ireland were made by the prime minister, often as a result of political solicitation and patronage, on the advice of the lord lieutenant. Although much rarer than in the eighteenth century the practice of placing Englishmen in the top ecclesiastical jobs in the Irish church through the influence of political friends in government had not quite died out. When Beresford was appointed to Armagh in 1822 he was the first Irishman in over a century to become primate. Archbishop Laurence, appointed to Cashel in the 1820s, was an Englishman, as was Whately, archbishop of Dublin (1831–63), and his successor, Archbishop Trench. More often, however, the bishops of the church of Ireland belonged to leading Anglo-Irish families. Tuam, for example, was held throughout the nineteenth century by members of the Irish aristocracy including Beresford, Le Poer Trench, and Baron Plunket. At one stage in the early nineteenth century three members of the Beresford family were bishops of Tuam, Cork and Kilmore respectively. Since no clear line of demarcation existed in the anglican church between the temporal and the spiritual the men appointed to Irish bishoprics were not always noted for their spirituality. In vain did Archbishop Stuart of Armagh complain that if the intended transfer of a bishop from Clonfert to Kilmore took place then he would have among the six bishops under him in Ulster three of 'the most profligate men in Europe'.[1] Non-residency and pluralities, also rife in the church of England, were among the other abuses that had persisted into the nineteenth century.

The big incomes attached to the richest of the Irish sees made the office of bishop in the church of Ireland a sought-after and lucrative post. In 1831 the archbishop of Armagh held over 100,000 acres in episcopal land and a gross episcopal revenue of over £17,000; the bishop of Derry held 77,000 acres and £14,000; and the archbishop of Dublin held 34,000 acres and over £9,000. Irish bishops' revenues were nearly equal to those of their English colleagues and they had far fewer parishioners. The incomes also compared favourably with those of many lay offices: the under-secretary, who was in effect the head of the Irish civil service, was paid £2,000 per annum.

The part of the revenues of the church which caused the most bitter controversy was the tithe system. This was so because the tithe was a tax on agriculture, and in Ireland this meant that the burden fell heaviest on the catholic peasantry who were expected to support a church which they believed to be heretical. The clergyman did not usually collect the tithes himself, but hired a proctor or tithe farmer who managed the business for him by paying over an agreed amount and keeping whatever surplus there was as profit. In theory tithes were exacted at the rate of 10 per cent on all agricultural produce. In practice, however, most payments were in cash at a set rate per acre of produce. The tithe proctor assessed the yield and calculated the rate which led to much wrangling and even crime. The system satisfied no one — not even the clergymen who received all of the odium attached to an unpopular tax and not much by way of adequate monetary compensation.

Numerous critics from among the catholics and the dissenters had little difficulty in finding fault with the established church. They pointed to its weaknesses as the church of the oppressive landlord oligarchy, and as the adjunct of the 'big house' and the 'handmaid of the ascendancy'; they described it as the tool of the state; they condemned its privileges and its intolerance of other denominations, and its proselytising missions to the vulnerable poor; they remarked upon clerical laxity and the unconcern of some of its clergy with the spiritual welfare of their parishioners; they pointed to the underemployment of its ministers and its overenjoyment of the wealth of the country; above all they complained about the financial oppression of the tithe system which was enforced for its support; and catholics were disturbed by the close association which many of its members had with the Orange Order.

What was perhaps of even greater significance for the church of Ireland than the criticism levelled at it by catholics and dissenters was the fact that the union of Great Britain and Ireland had opened the way to criticism by radicals and liberals in the United Kingdom parliament, and even to that of friendly tories like Peel, who were embarrassed by the evils under which it continued to labour and which cried out for reform. It was as a consequence of this kind of pressure that far-reaching reforms of the church of Ireland took place. Sustained attempts to amend the tithe system culminated in the Tithe Rent-charge Act of 1838. The Church Temporalities Act of 1833 reformed the administrative structure by reducing the number of dioceses from twenty-two to twelve, by increasing centralisation and by improving the administrative machinery; episcopal lands and revenues were gradually reduced; ecclesiastical commissioners established by the act abolished pluralities and enforced standards of residence and religious observance throughout the church.

The church of Ireland had its own critics within, but what was more important, it had its share of internal reformers. Following the union the reduction in the numbers of Irish bishops sitting in the house of lords diminished the political role of the hierarchy, and this had the effect of lessening preoccupation with political affairs and of allowing more time for the ecclesiastical. Internal revival owed much to the evangelicals in the church. Evangelicalism spreading from England emphasised personal salvation and reliance on the bible. By the 1840s the spirit of evangelicalism had spread to some of the bishops. The evangelicals concerned themselves in humanitarian and charitable causes, but it was the extremely missionary-conscious among them who aroused most hostility from the catholics.

The story is told of how one of the rebels sentenced to death by hanging in 1798 was accompanied to the scaffold by a catholic priest praying in Latin, and by a protestant clergyman who whispered prayers in Irish into the poor man's ear. Over the next seventy years that little drama was to go on repeating itself in a variety of different stage settings as the protestant and catholic churches battled it out for the possession of the Irishman's soul. Left to their own devices in the early decades of the nineteenth century the protestants and the catholics accepted the situation of having to accommodate themselves to a pluralist society. On the catholic side a bishop like the celebrated James Doyle of Kildare and Leighlin advocated mixed education, saying that he did not know 'any measures which would prepare the way for a better feeling in Ireland than uniting children at an early age, and bringing them up in the same school ...'.[2] Bishop Doyle also suggested a union of protestant and catholic churches in Ireland for patriotic as well as charitable motives. On the protestant side the state of the established church was such that it was difficult to convince anyone that it was the true church of the Irish people.

What changed the situation from one of accommodation between 'the two nations' to one of deadly religious warfare between two sects was interference — outside interference in particular. The evangelical movement in England with its headquarters at Exeter Hall chose Ireland and its Roman catholic people for a great missionary crusade. Agencies for this protestant crusade — called proselytising societies by those on the other side of the religious divide — spread rapidly throughout the land: the Hibernian Bible Society; the British Society for Promoting the Religious Principles of the Reformation; the Association for Discountenancing Vice and Promoting Christian Knowledge; the Irish Evangelical Society; the Society for Irish Church Missions to the Roman Catholics; the Connaught Home Mission Society; the Sunday School Society for Ireland; the Ladies Hibernian Female School Society; the Religious Tract Society for Ireland; the Scripture Readers of Lady Huntingdon's Connection; the Baptist Society; the Irish Society for Promoting the Education of the Native Irish through the Medium of their own Language. One of the principal tactics employed in this mid-nineteenth century religious war involved the showering of hundreds of thousands of tracts through the post on the heads of the Roman catholics of Connemara and elsewhere at a time when the people were suffering the worst famine in Irish history.

Interference by English evangelicals encouraged counter-interference from Rome. And the general dispatched by Rome to organise resistance and launch the catholic counter-offensive was none other than Archbishop Paul Cullen. It was Cullen's considerable administrative skills; his pastoral concern for the provision of churches, schools, hospitals and orphanages; his role in inspiring the devotional revolution among Irish catholics; and his political pressure for the disestablishment and disendowment of the protestant church in Ireland which ensured ultimate victory in Ireland to Rome over evangelical England.

Presbyterianism
No drastic variations in the relative demographic strength of catholics, anglicans and presbyterians occurred during the first three quarters of the nineteenth century. In the 1861 census out of a total population of over 5.75 millions, 4.5 millions were classified as Roman catholics, over 693,000 were members of the church of Ireland, and 523,000 were presbyterians, or 77.7 per cent, 12 per cent and 9 per cent respectively. While this was the statistical picture over the whole of Ireland, Ulster, or more accurately the north-east, had its own distinctive religious as well as social and economic structures. In what is now the six counties nearly 41 per cent were catholic, 33 per cent were presbyterians and 23 per cent were church of Ireland. Ever since the colonisation of the early seventeenth century Scottish settlers and their descendants, who were mainly presbyterians, were concentrated in this region, more specifically in Antrim and Down. English colonists, mainly anglican, inhabited mid and south Ulster, more specifically Co. Armagh and Co. Fermanagh. As in the rest of the island the landlord minority in Ulster was mainly anglican. These colonists, whether English or Scottish, saw themselves as the inheritors and defenders of the civil and religious liberties established in the 'glorious revolution' of 1688.

Although the presbyterians numbered less than one in ten of the total population of Ireland, they were one in three of the population of what is now the six-county area. Another way of stressing this concentration would be to note that 87 per cent of all Irish presbyterians resided in the six-county area of Ulster. By contrast less than half (46 per cent) of the members of the church of Ireland resided in the area. This concentration of presbyterians assured them of a powerful and distinctive influence in the region. The very structure of their church encouraged democratic sentiment and social and political independence, and even inclined them towards political radicalism. The minister's function was not so much to instruct as to assist on the road to salvation. All through the eighteenth century the presbyterians had kept up their connections with the parent kirk of Scotland, and until the establishment of the Belfast Academical Institution in the early nineteenth century many of the ministers received their academic training in the Scottish universities. Until the nineteenth century presbyterians were for the most part small farmers who also engaged in weaving in their homes. They had their own independent culture and sense of separate identity; they placed great store on the role of education, and had their own parish reading societies; their bards were in the tradition of the Scottish vernacular poets; their educated were influenced by the British radicals; and their strong ties with the rebellious American colonists, many of whom had emigrated from the province during the eighteenth century, stimulated democratic and liberal ideas among them.

The presbyterian church with its emphasis on the bible and on the liberty of the individual conscience was quite distinct from the church of the landlords and of the political establishment. Presbyterians took the lead in the tradition of religious dissent in eighteenth-century Ireland; and penal laws had effectively excluded them also, like the catholics, from civil or military office under the crown, from the government of Ireland and from the ascendancy. In these circumstances the Ulster presbyterians in the late eighteenth century opposed protestant ascendancy, supported reform of parliament and greater independence of Westminster, advocated catholic emancipation and the more radical amongst them were leading participants in the republican United Irishmen. The republicanism of the presbyterians went back to the anti-monarchical tradition of the English civil war, and therefore ante-dated that of the French revolution with which for a while in the 1790s it coalesced originating its own brand and tradition of Irish republicanism. However, the involvement of a radical minority of presbyterians in the United Irish movement and in the '98 rebellion must not be exaggerated. The vast majority of presbyterian clergy remained critical of their own radicals and suspicious of catholic objectives. Such political radicalism as did exist among them in the 1790s was transformed rather briskly after the union into conservatism and the defence of the *status quo*. This transformation was due to a variety of complex causes: the sectarianism of the '98 rebellion, particularly in Wexford, awakened memories of the 1641 massacres, especially since sectarian clashes had remained endemic in Ulster despite the best efforts and principles of the United Irishmen; the attraction of orangeism was that it seemed to afford security against sectarian attack; a time of growing prosperity helped the shift away from radicalism; haunted by the growing fear of catholic ascendancy based on sheer numbers replacing protestant ascendancy, the presbyterians were driven into closer alliance with the anglicans in defence of the protestant religion and in support of the union; the increase in the royal grant (*regium donum*) for the support of the presbyterian clergy underlined the developments in close co-operation between the state and the presbyterian church.

Although the liberal tradition was never totally extinguished among the presbyterians, and although they were to remain as sturdily independent in some respects as ever (notably in education), they ceased to interest themselves in Irish parliamentary independence or nationalism or republicanism, or the union of Irishmen of all creeds. Instead, in an age of expanding democracy, they committed themselves to the defence of the union with Britain and the maintenance of a new protestant ascendancy of which they had become more and more a part. In these circumstances the Orange Order which initially was in very large measure an alliance between episcopalian small farmers and gentry against the catholics held out attractions for the presbyterians. Even where they were slow to join the Orange Lodges they composed their differences with the episcopalians and joined forces in defence of the union and the protestant religion.

The emphasis on individual conscience, at all times characteristic of the presbyterians, gave rise to many schisms within their church, and to the emergence from time to time of strong personalities who provided the colourful leadership for these theological divisions. The controversy between 'old light' and 'new light' theology raged throughout the eighteenth and into the early nineteenth century. The 'old light' were the orthodox, conservative, evangelical presbyterians who claimed to be more interested in salvation than in doctrine. They had broad, popular support. The 'new light' were latidudinarian, liberal, intellectual and preached enlightenment theology. In the early nineteenth century the 'new light' was led by Rev. Henry Montgomery and the 'old light' by Dr Henry Cooke — two outstanding disputants. To Cooke the pope was antichrist; Montgomery, on the other hand, supported catholic emancipation. In 1830 Montgomery and his 'new light' and unitarian followers withdrew from the synod. A few years later at a huge loyalist demonstration at Hillsborough in 1834, Cooke proclaimed 'the banns of a sacred marriage' between the presbyterian church and the church of Ireland. Although not all presbyterians would have agreed with this political marriage it was a measure of the general move to the right taken by the presbyterians.

In the theological struggle between presbyterians one tendency — 'intellectualism' — stressed personal discipline, the denial of extreme impulses, the rational pursuit of duty, and acceptance of the role of the ministry in the systematic instruction of the scripture. The other tendency — 'fundamentalism' — held the bible to be the only guide to salvation, saw it as representing the literal truth, and saw 'conversion' as the test of admission to the fellowship of Christ and personal salvation. Fundamentalist enthusiasm triumphed. One flowering of this was the revival of 1859 with its prayer meetings and hysteria and female possession, which were the presbyterian counterparts of the reported miracles and millenarianism in the catholic church, or the fanatical evangelicalism of the episcopalians. This revival of enthusiasm provided the weavers with a cultural solidarity in their new environment as they migrated to the linen-mills being established in the towns, and created a popular following upon which orangeism was to build.

The religious and cultural *imperium* which arose in Ulster owed much to the forms adopted by presbyterianism. The presbyterians were much less anxious than the episcopalians to conduct missions for the conversion of the Roman catholics of the south. The comparatively weak efforts which they made in this direction failed to win converts from Roman catholicism, and when these efforts failed it was taken as verification that the catholics could not be counted among the elect. This was the presbyterian equivalent of catholics saying that outside the one true church there was no salvation. Orthodox presbyterianism and official catholicism were mutually exclusive, and this had far-reaching political or partitionist implications for Irish society. The presbyterians concentrated less on proselytising and more upon revival within themselves. The self-sufficiency of this inner light of the elect produced a kind of religious insularity and, geographically, they seemed satisfied to restrict themselves to what, ominously, they called 'their own province'.

The Orange Order
These strongly conservative tendencies in Ulster politics owed much to the strength of the Orange Order in the province. Recent scholarship has shown that the disturbances in Armagh preceding the establishment of the Orange Order had much to do with the labour market for weavers. The competition for land between catholics and protestants, which was once thought to be the sole and immediate cause of the origin of orangeism, increased the bitterness of sectarian rivalry and helped the spread of sectarian organisations. Like the catholic Defenders and Ribbonmen, the Orange Order was a secret society with all of the ceremonial associated with masonic organisation, and an oath of loyalty to the king conditional on his upholding of the

protestant ascendancy. It provided a bond of security between protestants at all levels of society who felt themselves under threat from the catholics, and it represented the revival of a militant protestant spirit. The yeomanry (local military defence corps in the 1790s under the command of the gentry) soon became the preserve of the Orangemen. Orangeism spread to Dublin where respectable but ultra-conservative protestants found it a useful counterpart to catholic emancipation moves. As orangeism spread throughout the north a Grand Lodge of Ulster was founded and supported by many of the province's gentry. In time the order got a foothold among the militia, the regular troops and the police — a development which made it difficult for catholics to distinguish between the government, the governing classes and the Orangemen. The Grand Lodge of Ireland was established in Dublin, 1798. To suppress the rebellion of 1798 the castle entered into an informal alliance with the Orangemen. Their position with the administration was weakened because of the division among the lodges on the question of the union. In Ulster, however, it had become a popular movement. Peel as chief secretary (1812–18) approved of their principles although sometimes cautious about their methods, and he defended them against the attempts of liberals to have them investigated by parliamentary commission. He agreed with the Orange attorney-general Saurin's observation:

> We ought not to deceive ourselves. Ireland must be either a Catholic or a Protestant state — let us choose.[3]

Catholicism

Irish catholicism shared in the general revival that took place in the church following the disruption caused by the enlightenment and the French revolution. The removal of the penal laws, which had obstructed its growth in the eighteenth century, also allowed it to flourish in the decades after the union. The catholic church in Ireland was administered by four archbishops and twenty-three bishops. By the mid-nineteenth century most of the bishops and a big number of the parish clergy had been educated in the national seminary founded at Maynooth in 1795. Doctrinally the Irish clergy were conservative in the tradition of the Council of Trent, and as the century progressed they became closely identified with the defensive policies of Rome. The Irish catholic clergy were totally dependent on voluntary subscriptions from the people. The fact that they received no salaries from the state helped to make them the most independent clergy in Europe. Politically they tended to be much more democratic than their continental colleagues who had closer ties with the European secular establishments. A close and loyal relationship, which was both spiritual and social, existed generally between the parish clergy and the people. During the nineteenth century priests and people moved forward together confidently, determined to solve the social and political problems that faced them.

The most tangible evidence of the revival of Irish catholicism was to be seen in the great expansion that took place in the building of churches, schools, diocesan colleges, seminaries, hospitals, convents, monasteries, orphanages and other institutions. During Dr Murray's term as archbishop of Dublin (1823–52), 97 new churches were built in the archdiocese alone. This activity was continued under his successor, Dr Cullen (1852–78), so that by the time of Cullen's death the archdiocese could boast of major new churches like St Andrew's in Westland Row and the Three Patrons in Rathgar; religious houses like the Passionist monastery at Mount Argus, and the Jesuits in Milltown Park; hospitals like St Vincent's and the Mater; Magdalen asylums like that at Drumcondra, or female blind asylums like that at Portobello Bridge, or a hospice for the dying like Our Lady's, Harold's Cross; educational colleges like St Patrick's Training College, Drumcondra, for men, or Baggot Street, which was later moved to Carysfort, for women; seminaries like Clonliffe and All Hallows; orphanages like St Vincent's, North William Street, or St Vincent's, Glasnevin; a catholic university in Stephen's Green, and a catholic medical school in Cecilia Street. The other dioceses reflected a similar growth, and cathedrals were built in several of these. The *Catholic Directory* claimed in 1844 that within the previous thirty years 900 catholic churches had been built or restored throughout the country. With this expansion in buildings the number of nuns and clergy increased.

Table 1

Date	Total Diocesan Clergy	Catholic population	Ratio of diocesan clergy to catholic population	Regular clergy
1834	2,156	6,436,060	1:2,985	200
1861	2,527	4,505,265	1:1,783	528
1871	3,056	4,150,867	1:1,375	406

Table 2

Date	Churches	Convents of nuns	Monasteries or brothers' schools
1845	2,218	91	42
1871	2,342	213	85

The involvement of the catholic clergy in politics tended, if anything, to increase as the century progressed, and apart from personal involvement their influence was immense. Alongside this spate of catholic building the new railways were opening up travel and commerce between the towns which were growing in prosperity in the post-famine decades. Shops, in particular, expanded rapidly in these towns, and big department stores emerged in the cities. Post offices and banks, police barracks and town halls also became characteristic features of the Irish urban scene.

These material developments in the Irish landscape reflected a greater variety of opportunity for the emerging catholic middle class. The children of the farming classes were drawn into the building trades, transportation and the worlds of business, banking and the civil service. The increased demand for priests, teachers, journalists, doctors, clerks and officials also stimulated the growth of the middle classes which in turn provided an impetus to the spread of democracy.

According to Richard Lalor Sheil's evidence before an 1825 house of commons committee the proportion of catholics to protestants at the bar was about 1:5, but he recognised that the number of catholic barristers was rapidly increasing. He said that it was a feather in the cap of a Roman catholic who had made money in trade to have a barrister in the family. By the time of the 1861 census the catholic middle classes had attained a substantial foothold in the profession.

Table 3

	Catholic	(Percentage)
Barristers	216	28%
Attorneys	674	35%
Physicians & Surgeons	761	32%
Apothecaries	210	50%
Other Professions (Architects etc.)	358	33%

Twenty years before the union thirty-eight per cent of the merchants of Dublin were catholic. By 1825 O'Connell estimated that more than half the commerce of Dublin was in catholic hands, and by 1829 de Beaumont claimed that ninety per cent of the funds in the Bank of Ireland belonged to catholics.

As the world of Gaelic civilisation dissolved in the harsh economic light of the early nineteenth century and the social gloom of the great famine, the cultural vacuum was filled with the all-pervasive catholicism of what one historian has called the 'devotional revolution'.[4] Between two to three thousand churches throughout the country were filled every Sunday and holyday for mass, and at other times for the great variety of devotional occasions that were being introduced — first communions, confirmations, benediction, novenas, sodalities, confraternities, first Fridays, forty hours adoration. The annual missions or retreats launched by the Vincentians in 1842, and conducted also by the Passionists, Redemptorists, Jesuits, Dominicans, Franciscans and Carmelites, lasted a couple of weeks and became great spiritual experiences in the parishes. If it is not possible to prove that the catholics had become more religious it is at least easy enough to show that they had become more devotional because of this explosion in facilities for holiness. Those who have lamented the passing of the Gaelic culture have referred to the 'great silence' or the 'cultural desert' that replaced it. But the silence and the desert were present only to those who because of their fascination with what had vanished were deaf to the sounds of catholic Ireland. Taking into account the tolling of innumerable church bells for mass or the angelus, the sermons of the great preachers from pulpits all over the country, the instructions of the parish clergy, the pastorals of the bishops, the hymns from innumerable choirs, the new church organs, the outdoor processions, the litanies, the Latin responses of the altar-boys, the catechism being learned off by rote by the school-children, the public recitations of the rosary, the renewal of baptisimal vows, the proclamation of faith, the public prayers for all occasions — then silence there was none, and 'cultural desert' depends upon a point of view. Catholicism, indeed, had an influence on nineteenth-century Ireland analogous only to the powerful cultural influence of the church in the age of faith in medieval Europe. The culture of the emerging democracy in Ireland was supplied in large measure by expanding catholicism. Democracy itself received an injection from the constant insistence on the principle of the equality of catholics before the law and their rights as full citizens of the United Kingdom. The acceptance of the primacy of merit over birth for promotion within ecclesiastical structures enhanced democratic principles in a secular world.

The Catholic Question 1800-23
Immediately after the union had come into effect Pitt tried unsuccessfully to get his cabinet and the king to agree to emancipation. The idea of giving every catholic in his dominions the right to sit in parliament and to hold office in the state was too much for George III. Anyone supporting emancipation was regarded by the king as a 'personal enemy'. After the king had suffered another bout of insanity Pitt resigned, and gave a formal assurance that he would never again trouble the king with the question of emancipation.

In Ireland the opposition of certain protestants to emancipation was virulent and even more vociferous than that of George III. A great deal of this was caused by the sectarianism aroused by the rebellion of '98. For a few years after the rebellion a flood of frantic accounts and descriptions was published which kept alive the bitterness of the sectarian debate. Narratives by Musgrave, Duigenan, Jackson and Taylor stressed the part which popery allegedly played in the rebellion. It was claimed that religious fanaticism had been the chief cause of all the rebellions in Ireland since the reformation. Popish bigotry was said to have caused the massacre of protestants by catholics in 1641, and the same cause was alleged to be the origin of the rebellion of '98. Two separate solemn powers — civil and ecclesiastical, or the monarchy and Rome — could not, according to Sir Richard Musgrave, co-exist in the same state without perpetual collision, discord and rebellion. This aggressive protestantism was not approved of by the administration in Dublin which had negotiated the union and won the support of the catholics. Dublin castle had employed pamphleteers like Father Arthur O'Leary to prove that Roman catholic doctrines were not incompatible with a devoted loyalty to the protestant constitution. Musgrave had dedicated his book, *Memoirs of the different rebellions in Ireland*, to the lord lieutenant, Cornwallis. After its publication, Cornwallis requested that in any future edition the dedication to him be omitted. He was not prepared to lend the sanction of his name to a work which, he said, tended so strongly to revive

> the dreadful animosities which have so long distracted this country, and which it is the duty of every good subject to endeavour to compose.[5]

The Rev James Bentley Gordon made genuine efforts to be fair-minded. In his treatment of the '98 rebellion, he said he was 'in favour of the speedy annihilation of those disqualifying laws against the catholics'.[6] He repudiated Musgrave's idea of religious intolerance.

Catholic writers like Edward Hay, Denis Taaffe and Denys Scully, while resenting the bigotry and vindictiveness of the extreme protestant propagandists, showed that they were prepared to respond in a liberal spirit of conciliation to the overtures from the castle, and from the more liberal of the Irish protestants. Taaffe, who had advocated breaking the connection with England in 1796, took part in the Wexford rising in '98 and wrote in opposition to the union in 1800. Like many of his co-religionists by 1801, he was content to await the promised benefits of the union, while writing pamphlets in an effort to provide what he called 'antidotes to cure catholicophobia and Iernephobia'. Catholic protestations of an historical loyalty were, at this time, prevalent.

The man who replaced Pitt as prime minister, Henry Addington, led a government between 1801 and 1804 which deliberately steered clear of the catholic issue. The Addington administration, however, commissioned an English catholic, Francis Plowden, to write a history, reconciling the public mind in Ireland to the union, but as the *Edinburgh Review* put it, it was found that the undertaker had outwitted the doctor. Plowden wrote, indeed, as a champion of the union, but he insisted also — too indelicately for ministerial taste — that it should be a proper union without any discrimination against his majesty's catholic subjects. His interpretation of Irish rebellions was the opposite to that of Musgrave. In Plowden's view, it was the rulers of Ireland who had been responsible for Irish uprisings in the past.

When Pitt returned to office as prime minister in 1804 it was to lead the defence of England against Napoleon. The imminent threat of invasion, and the sanctity of the institution of monarchy were, for Pitt, far more important matters than the emancipation of the Irish catholics. With Pitt back in office and no sign of their expectations which had been aroused during the union negotiations being fulfilled, catholics realised they would have to become more active and strongly remind the government of their situation.

At a meeting of catholics in November 1804, a committee of twenty-five was established to prepare a petition to be presented to parliament for the total abolition of the penal laws. This was the first meeting of any importance held by the catholics since the union. Among the members of that committee were no less than four peers, three baronets (almost one third of the committee was aristocratic), the young barrister, Daniel O'Connell, and Denys Scully, barrister and landowner in Co. Tipperary, who at this time devoted a lot of detailed attention to the catholic cause. A catholic delegation which went to London in March 1805 to present the petition to Westminster consisted of Lords Fingall, Kenmare and Trimleston, Sir Edward Bellew, James Ryan and Denys Scully. Scully kept in touch with the committee in Dublin through O'Connell. Prime Minister Pitt was asked to present the petition in the house of commons but he refused. O'Connell wrote that this rejection by Pitt 'has created a sentiment of contempt for him that is finely contrasted by the readiness of Irish enthusiasm for the Prince [of Wales] and his friends [Grenville and Fox]'. Lord Grenville presented the petition to the lords, and Charles J. Fox presented it to the house of commons. Henry Grattan gave his maiden speech in Westminster in suport of it. In both houses, however, consideration of the petition was defeated by large majorities: 178–49 in the lords, 336–124 in the commons.

One of the delegates, the merchant, James Ryan, assumed leadership on his return to Dublin. That Ryan had formed a 'junta' or a 'knot of dependants' was resented by others, and in April 1806 it was announced that an *association* had been formed which was hoped would comprise 'the full respectability of the catholic body'.

When Pitt died in January 1806, Lord Grenville became prime minister and Charles James Fox took over as foreign secretary. The hopes of the catholics ran high, for these were the same two men who had presented their petition less than a year earlier, and there were other friends of emancipation in this new administration, known as the ministry of all the talents. Among them was Lord Moira who for years had been the chief intermediary between the prince of Wales and the whigs, and another emancipationist, George Ponsonby, became Irish lord chancellor. When Fox died within the administration's first year of office, the reformers lost a great driving force.

Meanwhile, in Dublin, important changes were taking place in the composition and style of the Catholic Committee. Until now, Anglo-Irish peers and wealthy merchants had shared the leadership. The approach of the leadership to catholic relief had been in the manner of the humble petition to parliament. And the committee placed a heavy reliance on the friends of emancipation among the more liberal politicians. A third group, however, was at this time making its presence felt in the Catholic Committee. Since 1792, catholics had been allowed to practise as lawyers. A first generation of catholic barristers now appeared in the debates of the committee — Denys Scully, Thomas Bodkin Hussey, Eneas MacDonnell, Clinch and O'Connell.

They added a new dimension and fresh, forceful emphasis to the emancipation struggle, and were eloquent and skilful in debate because of professional experience acquired at the bar. They made vivid appeals to the ordinary people whom they had been in the habit of defending in the courts, and lent a legal gravity and dignity to the proceedings of the committee. Confident in their knowledge of the law, and emboldened by the success and reputation attending their professional efforts, they stated the wrongs and grievances of their fellow catholics with a new daring; condemned petty tyranny with a scornful disregard of any censure from the Orange establishment; and signalised that a new epoch had begun in catholic affairs. For the moment, they needed the peers as a sort of social window-dressing for their cause. But the lawyers and the merchants, whom they succeeded in carrying with them, showed that they were wary of Fingall's close relationship with English politicians; they barely tolerated the extravagantly French manners of Lord Trimelston who seemed to them to be more interested in the patrician blood of the Barnwalls than in what was called, in the oratorial flourishes of the lawyers, the 'slavery' of the entire country; and they smiled condescendingly at the foibles of Lord Ffrench. To say, as did an admirer of O'Connell, that the first was a traitor, the second a a coxcomb, the third a brute, may reflect the ultimate attitude towards them by the middle-class leaders, but it failed to appreciate the contribution which the peers made in the initial stages of the struggle. The barristers dealt effectively with the pretensions of a merchant like Ryan, when he stepped out of line and tried to form his own clique within the committee. They also helped to keep in check the fanaticism of a doctor like Dromgoole whose armoury was said to have come 'almost exclusively from the Vatican', and who was described as 'the Duigenan of the catholic cause'. What the barristers contributed was not always regarded by the others as beneficial. It was alleged that they brought with them cunning and intrigue and a constant contention for the leadership of the committee in the years 1805–1808; and they left a suspicion with their non-legal colleagues that the barristers were using the catholic cause for promoting their own self-interest.

At a meeting of the catholics in February 1807 a group led by O'Connell displayed their growing impatience and their annoyance at the delay in granting emancipation. O'Connell appealed for a more aggressive attitude towards the Grenville ministry. He would place the catholic claim, he said, 'on the new score of justice — of that justice which would emancipate the protestant in Spain and Portugal, the Christian at Constantinople'.[7] At this meeting signs of a class division among the catholics reappeared. The catholic peers advised moderation. They were not prepared to embarrass their friends in Grenville's government. And Lord Ffrench argued that to put a petition forward at that time would injure the empire. He tried to delay consideration of the petition until feelings in the country could be more widely ascertained. O'Connell persisted, however, and asked was it injury to the empire to tender it the services of five million subjects, and he asserted that expediency, right, present policy and eternal justice demanded emancipation. When he went on to attack the union for delaying emancipation and for what he considered to be its other deplorable consequences, he was reminded by the chairman, Lord Fingall, that the union had no connection with the subject before the meeting. But O'Connell and the lawyers backing him were determined to push forward. 'Let us renew our petitions', argued O'Connell, 'away with delay — the man does not merit freedom who would hug his chains for a day'[8]. O'Connell was beginning to realise, however dimly, that if he was going to achieve a victory for democracy over the protestant ascendancy, he would first have to overcome the aristocracy among his co-religionists. At this meeting he had taken the first step and it was decided that Lord Fingall would transmit a petition to Henry Grattan. Grattan, however, advised withholding the petition, for his friends in government were already in deep trouble. Even so mild a measure as a bill to allow catholics to hold commissions in the army and navy created disagreements among the politicians and greatly annoyed the king. George III tried to get Grenville's ministry to give him a pledge not to bring in emancipation, and when they refused to do this they were replaced by a new government under the duke of Portland in March 1807. It was the second time in the nineteenth century that the king had broken up a ministry on the catholic question.

Parallel with these developments in the Catholic Committee, and not unrelated to them, were signs of the emergence of a more aggressive spirit in the country at large. A staunch protestant friend of emancipation, William Parnell, commenting on Plowden's argument that the Irish catholics had borne five centuries of indignity with perfect loyalty, wrote in 1804:

> This is singular praise but it sufficiently proves the degradation of their minds ... this great mass does not possess a degree of spirit, either collectively or individually that would support a rustic virgin of sixteen on her entrance into life.[9]

In 1807 Parnell published *An historical apology for the Irish catholics* in which, developing the thesis of Plowden, he argued that it was British administration in the past, not the catholic religion, that had been responsible for catholic disaffection. The injuries suffered by the catholics, he said, had goaded them into revolt. He warned that the lesson to be learned from Irish history was the grave danger involved in retaining the present restrictions on the catholics. 'Be angry and sin not', was the advice he gave to the disspirited catholics of 1807.

That Parnell's spiritless rustic virgin of 1804 had turned into something of a saucy young miss four years later, was becoming abundantly evident, not only in the emergence of the barristers' group in the Catholic Committee, but even more so in the writings of catholics outside of that group. Watty Cox had been silent since the days of his association with the United Irishmen. In November of 1807 the first number of his *Irish Magazine* was published, and it continued to appear as a monthly until Cox emigrated to America in 1815. (O'Connell, on circuit, used to remind his wife to send him copies of it.)[10] The *Irish Magazine*, militantly catholic, Irish and anti-establishment, was one of the most independent and spirited journals in the first half of the nineteenth century. The policy of conciliation and loyalty preached by catholic writers in the earlier years of the century, and practised by the leadership in the Catholic Committee, was unceremoniously brushed aside by Cox. The *Irish Magazine* reflected a more radical, popular and nationalist response to the situation in which the catholics found themselves. There was a constant emphasis on the historic oppression of the Irish which contrasted sharply with other contemporary publications. Cox was critical of the moderate leadership displayed by the Catholic Committee. His sympathy was with the mass of the people and not with the ambitions of the middle-class society, or the expectations of the catholic peers. His *Irish Magazine* carried in serial form 'accounts of the massacres of the Irish', in which only those atrocities attributed to protestants were included. The 'murders, slaughters and wretched sufferers' were all on one side, according to Cox's unbalanced narrative. In a review of writers who had concerned themselves with rebellions in the past, something of Cox's style can be caught in the passage in which he hits out at friend and foe alike:

> Plowden was hired by an English minister to write such a history as would make the Union palatable to the Irish; Hay did not tell half the facts for which he had documents in his possession; Gordon was a prejudiced clergyman of the established church, with sometimes the appearance of liberality; and Musgrave was an historical cur.[11]

As a catholic antithesis to the protestant Musgrave, Cox was anticipating a catholic nationalist offensive. When, in 1808, it appeared that English catholics were prepared to accept a royal veto on the appointment of their bishops, Cox's hostility to the English showed itself with his assertion that:

> An Englishman is the same invariable creature after seven centuries experience with the English nation; history informs us, and records written in blood, that we have no remission of pains or penalties from the English catholic no more than from an English protestant.[12]

Portland's administration was not only ready to shelve the emancipation issue, but fought the general election of 1807 successfully on a 'no popery' platform. It was in these unfavourable circumstances that Grattan presented in May of 1808 a petition from the Roman catholics of Ireland — 'As the brethren of Englishmen and co-heirs of the constitution ... seeking full enjoyment of those privileges which every Briton regards as his best inheritance'.[13] In the course of his speech, in which he tried to allay the 'no popery' fears, he addressed himself to the argument that the pope's right to nominate Roman catholic bishops was dangerous to the state. He then said that he had a proposition to make, a proposition which the catholics authorised him to make. He proposed that in the future nomination of bishops his majesty might interfere and exercise his royal privilege and that no catholic bishop should be appointed without the full approval of his majesty. Grattan pointed out that such approval was by no means incompatible with the catholic religion, or indeed with practice elsewhere. The veto which he proposed would eliminate any alleged danger that Bonaparte, by controlling the pope, could control the catholic bishops of the United Kingdom. George Ponsonby, supporting the petition, also outlined the veto scheme, apparently with the consent of Lord Fingall, and claimed that it had the approval of the bishops. Ponsonby had understood from an interview which he had had with Bishop Milner, the agent of the Irish bishops in England, that this was indeed the situation. He also reminded the government of the pledges which Cornwallis had given to the catholics at the time of the union. He claimed that nine-tenths of the protestants of Ireland would support emancipation, and explained the procedure that was followed on the death of a Roman catholic bishop when three names were submitted by the other bishops to Rome. Now, he said, the bishops have agreed to send the three names first to the lord lieutenant of Ireland, who would have the right to strike out any he found objectionable. Only then would they be sent to Rome for the pope's approbation. This, he argued, would give the real and effectual nomination to the crown. He used an unfortunate phrase to the effect that by conceding the veto the bishops had no objection to making the king 'virtually the head of their church'.

Apart from this general petition, separate petitions were also presented to the house from the catholics of Wexford, the city of Waterford, the county and city of Kilkenny, the counties of Kerry and Tipperary. Only one counter-petition, that from the lord mayor, aldermen, and common council of the city of Dublin, was received against the Roman catholic claims. Despite the offer of a veto, the petition was defeated by big majorities in both houses, and it marked the beginning of a controversy which would split the catholics over the next few years into vetoists and anti-vetoists.

So, at a time when both Austria and Prussia had fallen before Napoleon's might, and when it was considered necessary to unite all of the people of the United Kingdom, the friends of emancipation in parliament were willing to offer the security of the veto in order to allay the fears of the more extreme anti-catholics. The catholic peers in Ireland were prepared to go along with the idea. A majority of the catholics in England also showed a willingness to accept the veto. In Ireland, however, where the O'Connell camp came out strongly against it, it gave rise to an excited public debate. In the course of this debate it was revealed that in 1799 during the pre-union negotiations the ten bishops — including the four archbishops — who were the trustees of Maynooth, in response to a government official's enquiry had indicated their willingness to consider the acceptance of a royal veto. They did so in the belief that a UK government would grant emancipation and a scheme of state payment for the catholic clergy. The concession on the veto was also made in the immediate aftermath of the 1798 rebellion and the sectarian animosities which it had aroused and the continuing threat of a French invasion. The bishops were in no position to allow any hint of a possibility of disloyalty on their part. But by 1808 the circumstances had changed: emancipation had not followed the union, and its likelihood had further receded rather than advanced; opinion in England among leading statesmen had hardened, and was more hostile than among Irish protestant politicians; overwhelming majorities in parliament had rejected emancipation; 'no popery' had become a cry in the recent general election; catholic hopes had been dashed on a number of occasions since 1799; and the catholic laity under O'Connell were showing that they were in no mood for compromise or further concessions. By the time the Irish bishops met in September to consider the matter, a great deal of hostility to it had been aroused. From their meeting the bishops issued a statement that it was inexpedient to introduce any alteration into the mode hitherto observed in the nomination of the Irish Roman catholic bishops, which long experience proved to be wise. They also pledged themselves, however, to recommend to his holiness only such persons as were of unimpeachable loyalty and peaceful conduct. Bishop Milner retracted his earlier approval of the veto scheme and gave the Irish bishops his full support.

It was in these circumstances of the continued opposition of the government to emancipation and the raising of the veto issue, that a general committee of the catholics of Ireland was formally re-established at a meeting in May 1809. In that same year Perceval, who was one of the most outspoken opponents of emancipation, became prime minister on the death of Portland, and continued what was regarded by the opposition as a conspiracy of silence on the emancipation question.

Early in 1810, during the preparation of a new petition to parliament, it was being widely circulated in Dublin that the English catholics intended offering the crown a veto on the appointment of bishops. At the same time Grenville, in a letter to Fingall, suggested that Irish catholics should do likewise. This was rejected strongly in Dublin. A vague resolution of the English catholics then offered that arrangements which might tend to general conciliation could be made. The former catholic leader, John Keogh, advised O'Connell that Grenville and Grey 'were candidates for power', and would therefore be content with the substance of the veto under any other name. O'Connell made it clear to the English catholic board that the Irish catholics would not be bound by vague arrangements which might be made for them by others. When Grattan presented the petition on 27 February 1810 in the house of commons, he announced that, unlike the position two years earlier, the catholics would no longer agree to the veto, although he himself felt that some securities were necessary especially since the pope, due to Napoleon's military success, was likely to become a French subject. A few days later the Irish bishops passed sixteen resolutions expressing their hostility to the idea of granting the veto.

In the opinion of the parliamentary friends of emancipation the need for securities became all the more pressing when the pope lost his temporal dominions and became virtually a French subject, and later, even the prisoner of Napoleon. But these developments did nothing to diminish the opposition of the Irish catholics generally to the veto. If anything, the pope's predicament left opposition to the veto even more entrenched in Ireland. The firm stand on the veto reflected the growing toughness and aggressiveness of the Irish catholics. The veto issue stimulated their independent-mindedness, increased their alienation and emphasised their distinctiveness. The veto stood as a wedge which drove the catholic middle classes and the aristocracy ideologically further apart, with the clergy on the side of the middle classes. It also helped to distance the protestant parliamentary friends of emancipation from the aggrieved catholics in Ireland. It placed the Irish catholics in the apparent position of declaring themselves unable, for conscientious reasons, to give that degree of loyalty to the crown which came more easily to the English catholics. Insofar as the controversy emphasised the distinctiveness of Irish catholicism, it tended to separate the two islands of the United Kingdom. It was not so much that the controversy marked and underlined national differences already in existence but, after a decade during which there seemed to be a genuine willingness on the part of the Irish catholics to grow into the United Kingdom, the veto issue created divisions, and around the controversy there crystallised a distinctively Irish catholic attitude which marked the first stage in the turning away from the union on the part of the Irish bishops who, only eight years earlier, had accepted it. Lay activists like O'Connell and Scully had spoken from time to time about their dissatisfaction with the union, and now they were being joined, if only tentatively and indirectly, by the bishops. This was the real significance of the veto controversy.

The bitterness of the debate showed up in the writings of the vetoist, Rev. Charles O'Conor, and in the replies to O'Conor by the antivetoists, Plowden and Bishop Milner. O'Conor was the grandson of the celebrated antiquarian, Charles O'Conor of Belanagare, who had been one of the leading organisers of the original Catholic Committee in the 1760s. The grandson had become chaplain to the marchioness of Buckingham and librarian to Lord Grenville's brother at Stowe, where the library housed an important collection of Irish manuscripts. He had also been an unsuccessful candidate for the bishopric of Elphin. The violence of his advocacy of the veto and his attacks on its opponents in his series of historical addresses and published letters, entitled *Columbanus ad Hibernos*, is probably explained by his close connections with the Grenville party and his disappointment over the bishopric. At least these were among the charges made by those who answered him. It was also pointed out that his approval of the schismatic Abbé Blanchard probably explained his anti-popery.

O'Conor denounced what he called the 'untenable claim of exclusive power' assumed by the prelates at their meeting in Dublin in September 1808, and compared their action with that of 'Rinuccini and his club of clerical politicians' in the seventeenth century. Like them, according to O'Conor, the nineteenth-century prelates took advantage of the 'ignorance and credulity of the people'. They were 'the foreign influenced intriguers who argued that Ireland was in temporals the property of the Holy See'. They had, he asserted, 'furnished an armoury of poisoned arrows against ourselves, and excluded us from the blessings of a constitution the most perfect that was ever known'. There was nothing, said O'Conor, that the 'ever faithful catholic gentry of Ireland' could do to counter this influence. The bitterness engendered by the controversy served to accelerate the aggressive spirit of the catholics. It also helped to increase protestant fears; and the resurrection of the seventeenth-century papal nuncio, Rinuccini, whether as Milner's hero or O'Conor's villain, struck terror into the Orange breast. It was in this same fighting spirit that O'Connell's friend, Hugh Fitzpatrick, publisher to Maynooth, reissued Curry's *Review of the civil wars of Ireland*. Curry's book, first published in the mid-eighteenth century, was an apology for the catholics and had blamed the protestants for the massacres of the seventeenth century. Fitzpatrick's edition of 1810 encouraged the catholics to press on in their awakening spirit, offering them the *Civil wars* as 'your code, your political bible, your magazine of arguments, your depot of authorities'. 'England is again in duress', proclaimed Fitzpatrick's edition, 'and experience and Mr Grattan have informed you that duress alone is the season of her liberality'.[14] The writings of Fitzpatrick, Lawless, Taaffe, Scully and others, not only registered and reflected this new aggressiveness, but also helped to foster and mould these new developments in public opinion. Taaffe, in *A history of Ireland*, written as a tract for the times, had referred to the dreaded 'resurgency of Milesian power'[15] under native leaders in the seventeenth century. Parallel with the veto controversy there was indeed a kind of 'resurgency of Milesian power'. The aggression in historical writing and interpretation was contemporaneous with the resolute stand of the Irish catholics on the question of the veto, and the whole vigorous mood helped to sweep aside catholic aristocratic leadership and carry a new middle-class captain, O'Connell, into command.

The middle-class leadership, which the veto controversy had helped to create, sought to involve the people in ways that had not been attempted before by the Catholic Committee. It was claimed, for example, that an address of thanks to the bishops for their repudiation of the veto in 1808 was signed by forty thousand laymen. The first post-union petition submitted to parliament in 1805 on behalf of the catholics of Ireland had appended to it a total of ninety-one signatures of whom six were peers and three baronets. Early in 1811, when another petition was being organised, a correspondent in Mayo wrote to O'Connell that he had collected in that county alone upwards of seven hundred signatures. This was an indication that the movement for catholic emancipation was being turned into a countrywide popular agitation. At a meeting of the Catholic Committee in July of 1811 it was resolved to procure signatures to petitions in all parts of Ireland. The leaders were quick to see the benefits that might be derived from an extension of the petitioning movement. The same Mayo correspondent urged O'Connell

> for God's sake endeavour to expedite the procuring of signatures *particularly in the country* for ... I have felt since I came here ... that it generates a very strong feeling of independence among the peasantry. I assure you it is scarcely credible how much it had diminished the terror of the petty tyrant in this wretched county ... I trust the hour of redemption is nigh ...[16]

Another way in which the new leadership involved more people was through the introduction of subscriptions. In the initial stages, and before O'Connell and his friends had thought up the idea of the penny a month from the masses of the people, these subscriptions were taken from the middle classes. Money was needed in the first instance to send members of the Catholic Committee to London with the petitions. The commoners who were sent along with Lord Fingall and the other peers needed to be subsidised. When O'Connell was angling to be sent to London with the first petition in 1805, he suggested that a fund be established to which he himself was prepared to contribute for the maintenance of petitioners in London. As the committee grew more professional and the petitions were presented more frequently, it became necessary to collect money on a more regular basis. Suggestions were made from time to time like that in June 1810 from a wealthy merchant who proposed a scheme for collecting money from each parish, in order to help place petitions before parliament with the propriety which they deserved. O'Connell on circuit in the south-west of Ireland was directed by Dublin to collect subscriptions in order to defray the expenses of the 1810 petition. A barrister like O'Connell was in a position to make contact with the men of money in the rural areas.

He reported to his wife on one occasion that he had collected eighty guineas in one day in Killarney and that he was having considerable success also in Tralee. The barristers on circuit were useful for making and maintaining contact with potential subscribers. They had access to many sources of income throughout the country as the movement grew in strength.

Unlike the original aristocratic leadership who could fund themselves, the new leadership needed subvention. The secretary, Hay, might find himself in London for as long as a month at a time in connection with the petitions, and in London, the delegation was expected to live up to certain standards. One gentleman, who offered to become a member of the delegation presenting the petition in 1811, did so on the grounds that he was personally acquainted with the prince of Wales and his friends. He said that he could be relied upon not to degrade the people that sent him, by living in coffee-houses in a shabby manner. He argued that persons sent over on occasions of this kind should have both the ability and inclination to keep up the respect of the catholic body by living in a splendid manner. The group which went to London on that occasion to present an address to the prince of Wales, and to lay a petition before parliament, included about a dozen well-to-do catholic gentry from Ireland. Apart from travel and subsistence, entertainment was also expected from this Irish delegation. O'Connell's very practical-minded uncle had sent a warning to his nephew not to neglect his professional pursuits by getting involved in such a delegation which was bound to cost him money and eat into his time, even though the objective of catholic emancipation was an honourable one. Such a warning underlined not only the need for subscriptions, but also the need to reimburse people for the services and the time they had given.

Apart from subscriptions to defray the costs of petitioning, a subscription was also taken up in order to present Edward Hay with a gold cup, in recognition of the services which he had rendered to the catholic cause. When an Irish journalist in London, Peter Finnerty, was sentenced to eighteen months imprisonment for a libel on Lord Castlereagh, a public subscription of two thousand pounds was raised on his behalf by his friends in the Catholic Committee. And when members of the Catholic Committee were arrested on a charge of contravening the Convention Act, another subscription was raised, and people showed that they were prepared to subscribe in order to challenge the Convention Act. A meeting in Killarney in 1810, for example, resolved to contribute £500 'to be applied in the defence of our invaded rights'. All of the subscriptions provided a fighting fund and increased the involvement of the catholics in the emancipation movement.

This new spirit among the catholic middle classes also encouraged the use of more aggressive language in the wording of the petitions. The earlier humble petitions from loyal subjects were now replaced by demands that their rights be restored. The parliamentary friends of emancipation considered that the 1811 petition was not 'written in a manner becoming the dignity of the catholics of Ireland'. It was clear that the objectionable phrases represented a shift from the milder language of earlier petitions, and that the strong language used embarrassed friends like Grattan and Ponsonby.

The resolve to procure an increased number of signatures, and to involve more people in the emancipation movement, led to the holding of aggregate meetings in the country. Reporting on such a meeting in Ennis, in March 1812, O'Connell stated that everyone present wanted to press forward, and that there was abroad a spirit that only full emancipation would allay. The direction in which the swelling agitation was moving was foreshadowed in a resolution passed at that same meeting to the effect that those present would not vote for any candidate in the forthcoming general election, who would support an anti-catholic administration. The catholics in pursuit of their objectives were now, for the first time, beginning to think of putting political pressure on parliamentary candidates, and they were beginning to realise that they possessed some real political muscle which might be utilised to give backing to their parliamentary friends. In meetings, such as that at Ennis, democracy was being stumbled upon by the Irish catholics.

The expansion of the emancipation movement can be seen also in the resolve of the committee to make itself more representative of the catholic body. They were hampered, however, by the Convention Act of 1793, which prohibited all assemblies except parliament and chartered bodies, which purported to represent the people under pretence of preparing or presenting petitions to the king or to parliament. Indeed, the government decided to meet the Catholic Committee's intentions head on, and Chief Secretary Wellesley-Pole, in February 1811, issued a circular to sheriffs and magistrates instructing them to proceed under the Convention Act of 1793 against catholics involved in the appointment of representatives to the Catholic Committee. Given its new fighting spirit, the Catholic Committee decided to accept the government's challenge, and test the legality of the Convention Act and the determination of the government to enforce it. A meeting of the catholics of Ireland was held in Dublin, in July 1811, with Lord Fingall in the chair. It was resolved: (1) that a committee of catholics be appointed to frame petitions to parliament, and to procure signatures thereto in all parts of Ireland; (2) that the said committee consist of the catholic peers and their eldest sons, the catholic baronets, the prelates of the catholic church of Ireland, and also ten persons to be appointed by the catholics in each county in Ireland, the survivors of the delegates of 1792 to constitute an integral part of that number, and also of five persons to be appointed by the catholic inhabitants of each parish in Dublin. The government responded immediately by a proclamation under the Convention Act, declaring illegal the appointment of county and parish representatives to the Catholic Petition Committee. The catholics proceeded to elect representatives in different parts of the country.

At a meeting of householders of the parish of St Mary's in Liffey Street, Dublin, to prepare a petition, warrants were served on six of the leading participants. The six arrested included three medical doctors, two merchants and one banker. One of these, Thomas Kirwin, a merchant, was found guilty under the act. The attorney-general stated that the government would not continue with the trials of the others listed with him as the law was now clear to all. Kirwin was fined a nominal sum. In the meantime, meetings continued to be held all over the country and representatives were elected. The English catholics, it was reported, were in rapturous amazement with what they called the gigantic stride made in Ireland. A meeting of the general Catholic Committee in December 1811 was dispersed by a magistrate as being illegal. The members withdrew to a nearby tavern and held a meeting at which it was resolved to hold an aggregate — as distinct from representative — meeting of the catholics of Ireland. After the Kirwin verdict, the Catholic Committee became generally known as the Catholic Board, in order to avoid the penalties of the law. The Catholic Board continued to organise petitions throughout the country and presented an address to the prince of Wales.

An attempt by the Catholic Board to have the actions of the attorney-general declared illegal failed. So the government's interpretation of the Convention Act held sway. In all of this flurry of activity, it is clear that the spearhead of the catholic cause had become the legalistic argument concentrating itself on parliament. The cutting edge of the movement was now in the hands of barristers led by O'Connell. The challenge in the courts illustrated the extent to which the barristers had taken over the leadership. The case for emancipation became less emotive and more legal under their control. It was clear, too, that the movement had now become self-respecting and defiant, and demanded rights rather than petitioning for privileges. The arguments of the catholics now emphasised the importance of the treaty of Limerick, rather than concentrating on the religious massacres of the seventeenth century. Resurgent catholic aggressiveness contended that the Irish catholics were entitled to an equal share in the constitution with persons of the established religion. The question that inevitably emerged was: should catholics be permitted to sit in parliament? Emancipators argued that this was not only expedient, but that it was also a matter of right — civil, constitutional and natural. The case for emancipation was based on the grounds of the solemn but violated treaty of Limerick, which had been carved out of the body of general history, and given an existence of its own by the writers, lawyers and politicians. The leaders of catholic opinion regarded the treaty of Limerick as their *magna carta*. According to emancipation propagandists, Limerick was the written civil law which translated their natural rights into a concrete reality, and no subsequent act of parliament could alter that fact. This view was endorsed in the works of parliamentarians like Henry Parnell and John Wilson Croker, and by catholic propagandists like Denys Scully, Matthew O'Connor, O'Connell himself and Bishop Doyle. In the twenty years before the concession of emancipation, the Irish catholics were instructed by their organising propagandists that their demand for emancipation was based upon this solemn legal contract, which guaranteed only rights to which they were entitled by law, and which parliament was bound to ratify, because it was an agreement made by the crown.

Changes taking place in England between 1810 and 1812 had greatly aroused the expectations of the catholics once again. The king's recurring insanity was confirmed and looked as if finally it had become permanent. The prince of Wales was appointed regent in 1811, and a year later the temporary restrictions on his exercise of the full royal power were withdrawn. The Irish catholics had long believed that the prince was their secret friend and they now looked forward to his influence being used on their behalf. When the prime minister, Perceval, was assassinated in the lobby of the house of commons in May 1812, another of the great opponents of emancipation was removed. About the same time as the prime minister's murder, an Irish catholic youth named Byrne had been murdered by a member of an inner Orange circle, the Purple Marksmen. The Orangeman, although convicted of murder, was pardoned by the lord lieutenant on the grounds of insanity. Perceval's assassin although insane was tried and executed. The contrast in the treatment of the two murderers suggested to the catholics and their parliamentary friends that there was one law for the great and another for the lowly Irish catholics. So incensed was O'Connell at the contrast that he publicly described the assassination of the prime minister as a providential visitation on the head of the government for the unpunished murder of an Irish catholic peasant.

The death of Perceval and the incapacity of George III seemed to leave the way open for a more liberal policy. Instead, Lord Liverpool, another opponent of emancipation, became prime minister (1812-27), and Robert Peel, who supported the policy of Perceval and Liverpool on the catholic question, became chief secretary for Ireland (1812-18). What the catholics resented most, however, was the apparent change of heart and policy on the part of the regent. His failure to promote their cause led to a great sense of disillusionment. O'Connell accused him of breaking his pledge to remove their disabilities as soon as he had power, and he had thus in the eyes of the catholic leader thrown away the Irish people's love. O'Connell was later to express the opinion that there had never lived a greater scoundrel than the prince. The indignation felt by the catholics was given expression by the national bard, Thomas Moore, when he had Ireland address the prince:

> I saw thee change — yet still relied
> Still clung with hope the fonder
> And thought, tho' false to all besides
> From me thou wouldst not wander.
> But go! deceiver! go! —
> The heart whose hopes could make it
> Trust one so false, so low,
> Deserves that thou shouldst break it.

At a meeting in Dublin on 18 June 1812, the catholics ascribed the prince's change of attitude on emancipation to the evil influence of a mistress, Lady Hertford, and to the 'blandishments of a too luxurious court'. They stated that they had learned 'with deep disappointment and anguish how cruelly the promised boon of catholic freedom has been interrupted by the fatal witchery of an unworthy secret influence ... To this impure source we trace but too distinctly our baffled hopes and protracted servitude.' And they asserted that 'equal constitutional rights — unconditional, unstipulated and unpurchased by dishonour ... can never be abandoned by men who deserve to be free.'[17] The language was widely resented: naturally by the prince himself, by the lord lieutenant, Richmond, and by many politicians, and it could hardly have helped to persuade these to look more kindly on emancipation. But official resentment did not eliminate the belligerence of the Irish catholics nor of their spokesman, O'Connell, in particular. He made no secret of his contempt for the murdered prime minister whom he denounced as an 'intolerant bigot' and a 'contemptible little creature'. His description of Chief Secretary Peel was even less restrained: 'Orange Peel'. 'A raw youth, squeezed out of the workings of — I know not what factory in England ...'[18]

Many in his own time, and not a few since, have condemned O'Connell's use of scurrilous and virulent language in his attacks upon the great of the land. And while it came naturally enough to one with so fluent a tongue, it also had a purpose. O'Connell calculated that if a native Irish catholic like himself treated royalty, the aristocracy and officialdom as equals or even in ways, as inferiors, then the catholics, who had been treated so oppressively that they almost came to believe in their own inferiority, would learn to develop a self-respect and hold their heads up proudly and stand up to their oppressors. The personal attacks on the mighty and on those who disagreed with him, the harangues of the demagogue, and the employment of what appeared to his critics as the tactics of a gutter politician were used designedly and incessantly by O'Connell to promote his cause.

It was the language, too, which he found won favour with his Irish audience, increased his own popularity among them and advanced the cause of democracy and nationalism in Ireland. The boldness with which he attacked the great in the land won him popular acclaim and the admiration of a people long accustomed to accepting their inferior station. It was all part of the propaganda war which O'Connell employed so successfully to rouse the spirit of the Irish catholics and to lead them to victory over their oppressors and to improve their political and social status. He believed sincerely in religious liberty, and in freedom of conscience, and he had found in his catholic countrymen a powerful weapon, once they were organised, for the achievement of his ends. He set for his people a living example, for he was personally very ambitious in the legal as well as in the political sphere. And he displayed all of the driving energy, hard work and talent necessary to succeed, and the sheer determination and political imagination to overcome the many obstacles that stood in his path.

The dashing of the hopes of the catholics in 1801 and 1804 under Pitt, in 1806 under Grenville and again in 1812 under the prince regent only steeled the determination of the Irish catholics to press for full emancipation without any securities. It had also made them suspicious of the purity of the motives of their parliamentary friends and wary of any proposals that might seek to embarrass the formidable new alliance of O'Connell and the bishops. In 1813 an Emancipation Bill, proposed by Grattan and seconded by Ponsonby, passed the early divisions in the commons, but security clauses were added which proposed a veto and a commission to examine papal bulls and briefs to insure that they contained nothing of a political nature. The Irish bishops denounced the bill as schismatic, and the majority on the Catholic Board also indignantly rejected it. The bill, nevertheless, was only narrowly defeated.

O'Connell's objections to the veto were based largely on very practical considerations. He made the point that if the veto were allowed, the nomination of Irish bishops would be in the hands of an administration notorious for making bad appointments. Since hostility to the Irish was the criterion for all other appointments, he asked how could they be confident that in this one area only people of virtue and moral fitness would receive the approbation of Dublin castle. He poured scorn on the idea of giving the right of veto to government commissioners who might include some of the most bigoted enemies of the catholics. Who could say that the commissioners might not be as hostile to catholicism as the king who appointed them? Their recommendation could produce results that would be even worse than the schism feared by the bishops — they were likely, he asserted, to create a prelacy that was corrupt, profligate and subservient to Dublin castle. The doom of Ireland would then be sealed forever. To expect to be allowed to interfere in the religious discipline of the catholic church, he described as a gross and glaring presumption on the part of the administration. Catholics, said O'Connell, did not desire nor would they accept any kind of interference on their part with the protestant church. He declared solemnly a stronger repugnance to catholic interference with the protestant church than protestant interference with the discipline of his own religion. He was prepared to sacrifice his life, he said, for the principle of universal and complete religious liberty. He denied that protestants had a right because they felt a need for securities — he denied both the right and the need. He drew attention to the implication of the government's logic: that Irish catholics were excluded from the constitution in order to ensure their loyalty, whereas if admitted fully to the constitution they were expected to destroy it. The demand for the imposition of securities was in his opinion an insult to the loyalty of the Irish people. He pointed to the fact that the English exhausted their blood and treasure in the Napoleonic War for the papists of Spain; that they had long cherished a close alliance with the papists of Portugal; that they had emancipated the papists of French Canada and that German papists in his majesty's army were allowed to rise to military command over Irish and even English protestants. O'Connell argued from all of this that the English did not dislike papists as such, but that they had a great horror of the Irish variety. 'We fight their battles, we pay their taxes', declaimed O'Connell, 'and yet we are degraded and insulted while the papists of Spain, Portugal, Canada and Germany are courted and promoted.' He concluded: 'the English do not dislike us as catholics — they simply hate us as Irish.'[19]

On the surface the veto argument was no more than the question of what best practical arrangements could be made for citizens of the United Kingdom who belonged to a particular denomination to alleviate the fears of fellow citizens. It had got completely out of hand, and in the debate that ensued it was blown up into a confrontation between Irish nationalism and British imperialism. There is no question but that O'Connell and his allies were sincere in their opposition to the veto on grounds of both pragmatism and principle. But it is also true that O'Connell saw in the veto controversy an opportunity for advancing his own political ends. At what precise point in his career he purposely set out to organise the people into a democracy may not be clear. But the continuing debate on the veto allowed him to denounce the catholic aristocracy and finally cut adrift from them. It enabled him to consolidate his personal leadership over the Irish catholic cause. It allowed him to form a firm alliance with a powerful backing in the future. And through the bishops and the priests it helped him to draw ever greater numbers to his banner.

During the years of the veto controversy, O'Connell appeared more and more in the role of the agitator. When denounced as such in the press and in government circles, he publicly admitted the charge, and took pride in the title. He argued, however, that an end to agitation would come when their rights were restored to the people. Conciliate the Irish nation, he replied to his critics, and the power of the agitator is gone in an instant. Otherwise, he said that his intentions were to rouse the Irish people from one end of the island to the other, both catholic and protestant. In his attempt to organise the masses he made use of the church and its large congregations; the court room as a forum for addressing the people; the circuit court as a communication link with the movement's headquarters in Dublin; his aggregate meetings as a reservoir into which came streaming the various grievances of the entire country until the Catholic Board took on the role of a people's parliament — led by the 'Man of the People' — the 'King of the Beggars'. In all of this activity O'Connell was the great political artist at work moulding the people of Ireland into his own image.

In contrast with the Irish Catholic Board, the Catholic Board of England took the view that the veto was a reasonable security to grant to their king as a guarantee of the loyalty and allegiance of English catholics. They appealed to Rome for a pronouncement to the effect that the veto was not schismatic or hurtful to the discipline of the church. The pope was at the time a prisoner of Napoleon, and the cardinals were banished from Rome. Monsignor Quarantotti, secretary to the Sacred College for the Propagation of the Faith, sent a rescript, 16 February 1814, stating that the veto ought to be agreed to so that prelates acceptable to the king might exercise their ministry without any doubts about their integrity. The rescript also accepted the inspection of correspondence from Rome. Quarantotti was convinced that 'so wise a government as that of Great Britain' while providing for public security did not wish on that account to compel catholics to desert their religion.

O'Connell resolutely denounced the rescript proclaiming: 'I would as soon receive my politics from Constantinople as from Rome'.[20] The Irish bishops sent Dr Murray as their delegate to Rome where the pope, with British support, had taken up residence again following the fall of Napoleon. The vetoists also continued to make their representation at Rome. From the altar of Clarendon Street chapel in January 1815 O'Connell announced: 'I am sincerely a catholic, but I am not a papist.'[21] He denied that the pope had any temporal authority in Ireland, or that he could be party to any act of parliament, and reminded his audience that catholics had renounced that authority on oath. He believed it impossible that the bishops would become 'the vile slaves of the castle'. But should they be prepared to do so, he warned them to look to their masters for support, for the people would despise them too much to contribute. The people, he said, would then communicate only with some holy priest who had not bowed to the Dagon of power, and the castle clergy would find themselves preaching to even thinner numbers than attended the services of the reverend gentlemen of the established church in Munster or in Connaught. O'Connell's sensational defiance was an open threat of schism.

The Quarantotti rescript had meantime been recalled and referred to the Congregation for the Propagation of the Faith. Its decision was communicated by Cardinal Lita, prefect of the Congregation, on 26 April 1815. The proposal to grant the crown the right to examine papal documents was condemned as an interference with Rome's supremacy in ecclesiastical matters, but the pope had no objection to a scheme submitting the names of candidates for vacant dioceses to the crown for approval. A synod of the Irish bishops in August 1815 resolved that any power granted to the crown of interfering directly or indirectly in the appointment of bishops 'must essentially injure and may eventually subvert the Roman catholic religion in this country', and that they would at all times and under all circumstances deprecate and oppose in every canonical and constitutional way any such interference. Though they venerated the pope as visible head of the church, they were not prepared to accept that the agreement of his holiness to the veto would allay their apprehensions. Not only was the pope's action without their concurrence but, they pointed out, it was in direct opposition to their repeated resolutions and the representations made on their behalf by Bishop Murray. Dr Murray, they said, was more competent to inform his holiness of the interests of the Roman catholic church in Ireland than any other with whom the pope was said to have consulted.[22]

The laity thanked the bishops for their resolutions, and reiterated that the pope had not and ought not to have any temporal jurisdiction within the realm; that they could not consent to any civil arrangement which the British government might derive from Rome; that their resistance to Rome on this matter ought to convince the politicians that catholics deserved liberty, and prove that they distinguished between the spiritual and temporal authority of the pope. In an address to Pius VII, the catholics of Ireland, making the same points, protested against the interference of his holiness or any foreign potentate in their temporal conduct or their political concerns. So, the address said, it was therefore unnecessary to outline the many objections of a political nature which Irish catholics felt to the proposed obnoxious measure; and it solemnly declared that they would prefer their present degraded state in the empire to any barter of their religious fidelity. This address was brought to Rome by Richard Hayes, a Franciscan friar, who was expelled from that city because his tone was said to be intolerable. The pope replied (1 February 1816) to the resolutions of the hierarchy that their apprehensions were destitute of all reason and foundation; that the veto only proposed to concede the power to remove from the list of episcopal candidates those whose loyalty was suspect; that this was in accord with the rule of the Vatican never to promote to vacant sees persons known to be displeasing to the temporal powers; and that such a concession might well be made to the friendly British government which was so powerful for good or evil throughout the whole church.

There, however, the matter rested. Successive emancipation bills — Grattan's in 1819, narrowly defeated in the commons, and Plunket's in 1821, defeated in the lords — incorporated a veto clause. The defeat of these bills meant that the Irish catholics never did have to face the veto as the actual law of the land; that the government did not have the trouble of enforcing it; and that the pope did not have to deal with a potentially schismatic situation. When Lord Wellesley was appointed viceroy in 1821, the hopes of the catholics revived. Wellesley, the first Irishman in years to be appointed to the post, was a strong supporter of emancipation. Since the new administration also involved the substitution of the emancipationist, Plunket, for O'Connell's enemy, Saurin, as attorney-general, the catholics were willing to re-open negotiations with the government. In these negotiations O'Connell, in a very characteristic mood, showed that he was not a doctrinaire even on the matter of the veto, but that he was ready to seek a compromise with government officials he could trust. He proposed to allow the government the power of objecting to episcopal candidates on grounds of disloyalty. But he insisted that the enquiry into the charges of disloyalty would be conducted entirely by two catholic bishops whose judgement was to be decisive. He was also prepared to allow that any correspondence of a political nature between the clergy and Rome should be submitted to the examination of the government. He was not in reality giving much away, and was indeed relieved when the government rejected the proposals.

The veto discussions had helped to weaken the Catholic Board: the gentry, some of the richer merchants and some of the lawyers — notably R L Sheil — seceded in 1813. The government took the opportunity to proclaim it as illegal in June 1814, and Grattan and other friends of emancipation approved of its suppression. During the decade 1813 to 1823 the catholic movement centred around O'Connell. In place of the old aggregate meetings he was reduced to sending out invitations to individuals to join him as guests in Capel Street, where Fitzpatrick, the publisher, had provided rooms for the impoverished catholic organisation. Aggregate meetings almost ceased. But it did mean that O'Connell had come to the fore as the unquestioned catholic leader, and that it was he who had the confidence of the people and the powerful support of an alliance with the clergy. All that was needed was a revival of the catholic agitation to sweep him to the head of public affairs in Ireland. The government by granting emancipation anytime up to 1823 could have pulled the rug from under him. Of this O'Connell was himself quite conscious, and he deliberately made use of the government's withholding of emancipation to promote his 'ulterior object' — the repeal of the union. In one of his speeches in 1813 he had said:

> Desiring as I do the repeal of the Union, I rejoice to see how our enemies promote that great object. Yes, they promote its inevitable success by their very hostility to Ireland. They delay the liberties of the Catholics, but they compensate us most amply because they advance the restoration of Ireland. By leaving one cause of agitation, they have created, and they will embody and give shape and form to a public mind and a public spirit.[23]

The government had left the initiative with O'Connell to renew the agitation on his own terms and to bring it to a pitch of democracy such as had never before been reached.

The years 1800 to 1823, therefore, had witnessed a great shift in Irish politics. As the century opened the catholics were ready to be absorbed into full citizenship of the United Kingdom. Repeated disappointments and delays over emancipation had created in them a more independent and defiant attitude which the recurring argument about the securities issue brought to a head. Legally emancipation meant little more than the admission of a few upper-class catholics to the parliament of the United Kingdom. But the emancipation struggle had been conducted in such a way, by O'Connell in particular, as to begin to call the sleeping power of the masses into operation. The veto question had thrown the bishops into his camp. A latent anti-English feeling in Ireland was linked gradually, but decisively, with the prolonged emancipation struggle. By the time that the pope had pronounced in favour of allowing a veto to the crown in the appointment of Irish bishops, catholicism and nationalism in Ireland had become so entwined that the ancient connection with Rome seemed to be less sacred in Irish eyes than that the Irish national church should be independent of England. So, as O'Connell stood poised in 1823 seeking to launch a massive attack on privilege and to win finally the emancipation of the catholics without any security strings attached, he found himself at a particular point and place where the streams of democracy, catholicism and nationalism converged, and threatened, given proper regulation and leadership, to become a mighty flood.

3 Secret Societies and Agrarianism

Threshers
In the autumn of 1806 disturbances associated with the secret society known as the Threshers erupted in the five counties of Sligo, Mayo, Cavan, Leitrim and Longford. It was a district of bogs and illicit poteen-making and rack-rents. Even in the best of times the peasantry of the area found extreme difficulty in discharging their rents and in maintaining their families. Unexpected demands made upon them for road building increased their misery. The addition of surcharges of tithe and of dues for the clergy left them desperate and drove individuals into illegal combinations in an effort to resist financial ruin. The principal grievances publicised by the Threshers were the priests' dues and the ministers' tithes. The incomes of the catholic priests were derived from dues paid at Christmas and Easter and from contributions made for specific services — weddings, baptisms, masses and funerals. Not since the Rightboys in the mid-1780s had there been such an organised and extensive opposition to priests' fees. And only occasional charges of avarice and extortion were made against individual priests during the rest of the nineteenth century. This campaign by the Threshers and that by the Carders in 1813–16 were the only widespread and persistent cases of opposition to priests' charges.

Disturbances had been first reported in the barony of Tyrawley, Co. Mayo, in the last months of 1805. Then in August 1806 they spread to the barony of Gallan, and then to Claremorris and other places in the same county. While the main object was the reduction of tithes and priests' dues, other grievances complained of were the insufficient wages paid to farm labourers, weavers and others involved in local industry. Assemblies of 'Threshers', sometimes called 'Shakers' (the names were taken from the practice of threshing and shaking out the tithe proctor's corn), began to appear in different parts of the country. Meeting at night in disguise they attacked houses for arms, terrorised the countryside and swore others into their ranks to obey the commands of every outlaw who called himself Captain Thresher. Written notices were posted warning people to refuse the payments of tithes of corn and flax and other crops, and of priests' dues except in a manner and to the amounts approved by Captain Thresher. When these notices were torn down by the magistrates, and rewards offered, the Threshers had their messages delivered in person in the catholic chapels by persons who claimed they had been taken from their homes in their shirts and threatened with carding unless they obeyed the instructions of the Threshers. Priests were warned that if they did not lower their dues they might as well have their coffins prepared. Those people who did not heed the Threshers were warned that the flesh would be torn off their bones with a comb for carding wool.

By September the disturbances had spread to Co. Sligo. On the night of 2 September ten houses were 'visited' in the district of Carton Watt, or Windy Gap, a couple of miles from Sligo town by a group of about thirty Threshers. They were dressed in white shirts or frocks over their clothes and white scarves or handkerchiefs over their hats. The hats were in some cases made of straw or covered with straw. The handkerchiefs were pulled down over their faces. Some were armed with rusty swords or bayonets and one had a gun. They were led by Captain John the Thresher (McDonogh) and William the Shaker (Kearney) and they responded to the commands of a drillmaster.

Money was demanded to refresh Captain John and his men, and some of those 'visited' paid a 10 pence piece or two as a kind of tax exacted for the support of the secret society. All were sworn to follow the regulations laid down by the Threshers regarding tithes and priests' dues. According to the evidence given at the trial of the leaders only one of the householders visited on that occasion was bodily assaulted. This man, O'Neill, had been drinking with one of the leaders on the previous Sunday night, and had been accused of laying out his tithe of oats before any others in the area had done so. O'Neill allegedly replied that he would continue to pay the dues he was accustomed to pay, and would not be dictated to by the Threshers. Two nights later he was taken naked from his house. His back was excoriated with a wool carder, he was given six or seven blows with sticks, beaten back to his house, struck in the small of the back with a gun as he re-entered his home and two of his ribs were broken. He reported the incident to the magistrate, identified the two leaders, and then felt it safer to give up his lease of four acres and a bog to the landlord and leave the neighbourhood. (The accused also belonged to the same class of small farmer.) The beating which O'Neill took was probably not unrelated to the fact that, during the trial, evidence was given that he was feared by some of his neighbours and distrusted by others as a man who had the reputation of stealing beasts and grass and meat on different occasions; of trying to withhold change at a transaction at the fair; and of not paying his bills. The punishment he suffered at the hands of the Threshers was a kind of rough justice inflicted on him as much, perhaps, for past misdeeds as for his readiness to pay his tithes. (It was the evidence against his character which enabled the jury to bring in a verdict of not guilty against the two accused.)

Later in September the Threshers were striking terror into the neighbourhood of Lugnadiva, Co. Sligo. In other instances in the same county in November houses were broken into and firearms demanded and taken. In one such incident the house of a family called Brett, near Tubbercurry, was attacked, the father was wounded and his two sons returned the fire. When the assailants threatened to burn down the house the sons surrendered three guns and one pistol. The chapel in this same parish was shut, and the priest was prevented from entering it.

Meanwhile in the neighbouring county of Mayo the heightened activities of the Threshers had attracted a great deal of attention. Many were arrested in mid-September as a result of information obtained from a former Thresher named Thady Lavin.

In mid-October about forty Irish-speaking Threshers from the district around Minola visited the house of a man named McPhadeen and swore him to inform the priest of the maximum amounts of the voluntary offerings approved by them. McPhadeen who was afraid for his soul on the one hand, and his back on the other, thought it best to comply. At the end of mass, which was celebrated in a private house because Minola was a half-parish without a chapel, McPhadeen told Fr Patrick Nolan precisely how much he was to charge for his services: weddings 10s6d (52½p) which was the usual offering, baptisms 1s7½d (8p) instead of 5s5d (27p), masses 1s1d (5½p) not 2s6d (12½p), and any house to which he came for confession, if he got hay and oats for his horse to take it, but if not, to go away on pain of suffering for it.[1]

The tithe exacted for the support of the established clergy continued to be a major grievance. The Threshers had laid down that money was not to be paid in lieu of tithe; that certain specified proctors were to be given no tithe; and that no one was to buy tithe collected by certain named proctors. In an incident, typical of those from which the Threshers and Shakers had derived their name, eleven tithe stacks were taken in November from the haggard of a man in the neighbourhood of Ballina and strewn all along the road up to the very town itself.

But the most serious incidents in Mayo were connected with the infamous Thady Lavin. Those who had been arrested in September on his word attempted to bribe their way out of Castlebar jail in

November. A few days later Lavin and his wife, who had been removed for protection to Crossmolina where a military force was stationed, returned to their home at Turneen for the purposes of disposing of some of their property and removing the rest to Crossmolina. After the sale of one item the Lavins went with the purchaser to have a drink in a house where a number of local men were assembled. Among those present were relations of the men jailed on Lavin's sworn information. During the night's drinking five men dressed as Threshers rushed into the house armed with a hatchet and bayonets fixed on poles. Lavin was axed and bayoneted to death with more than thirty wounds. His wife who sprang to his defence was also axed and bayoneted and left for dead. She recovered, however, to give evidence (in Irish) against eleven who were present and had not attempted to intervene and who were later indicted for conspiracy to commit murder.

At the very time of the Lavin murder in Co.Mayo, alarming numbers of Threshers were assembling in Co. Longford. On the night of 13 November 1806 the militia, quartered at Granard, were called out to deal with an assembly estimated to be between 400 and 500 men. They faced the militia for a time, but after some shots were fired at them they scattered in confusion leaving pikes, pitchforks, poles, hats with white bands, and shirts behind them, and the police made four arrests. A form of the oath administered in Co. Longford ran: 'to be true to Captain Thresher's laws: to attend when called upon, not to prosecute Captain Thresher or any of his men ...'

Although the numbers that assembled in Longford were more numerous than those reported for other counties, nevertheless the trouble there was more contained and less violent than in Mayo or Sligo. This was due partly to the fact that the leadership may not have been as effective among the Threshers of Longford. But it was also due to the fact that the governor of the county, Lord Granard, and the leading gentlemen of property held frequent meetings to concert measures for checking the progress of illegal combinations and that magistrates, police and militia worked closely together to prevent disturbances. Among the resolutions passed by the magistrates and gentry under Lord Granard's chairmanship was the statement that collectively and individually they would use every means in their power to bring the offenders to justice; that liberal rewards would be given for information leading to the conviction of offenders; that persons giving information would be fully protected; and that they would not renew any lease, nor let an area of land to any person whom they had just reason to believe had voluntarily and actively been concerned in any of the outrages associated with the Threshers.

Cavan, although showing some signs of Thresher activity, was much less disturbed than the other counties involved. In Leitrim the non-sectarian nature of the movement generally exhibited itself in the form of the oath as well as in the membership. The oath bound members to secrecy; to attend when called upon; to observe the Threshers' laws; to pay tithes only to the rector; and to pay only certain fees to the priests. The most serious incident that occurred in the county was an assembly of about 150 Threshers in white shirts marching between one parish (Clonee) and another (Carnygallan) and swearing in people on the way. They were dispersed in all directions by a peace-keeping force of twelve men who fired on them. Pikes, shovels, pitch-forks and shirts were abandoned at the scene. Three men were arrested and convicted, one of whom was a protestant.

The greater the gatherings of Threshers the less dangerous they were. The smaller gangs perpetrated the more desperate crimes. The bodily punishments were inflicted largely on their own class. Class conflict was not so direct or obvious as in other disturbances. They had no political motivation or objectives whatsoever. They had no connection with the Catholic Committee. They were not a 'French party'. They made no claim to being a revolutionary movement, nor did they aim at any general and organised rebellion. They were, instead, intensely local, and reacted to immediate grievances and sought temporary relief from social and financial burdens. They produced no spokesmen to put their case before the general public. They were the primitive rebels who had responded in the only way they knew to the oppressive social conditions in which they found themselves.

Although the Thresher disturbances were localised, the fact that they had spread to five counties suggested that more than the local peace-keeping agencies and the ordinary courts of law might be necessary to deal with the situation. At first the government tried to keep the disturbances out of the public press. When this failed the more frightened urged the government to proclaim the counties and re-introduce martial law of the pre-'98 variety. Instead, a law officer, Sergeant Moore, was sent to Castlebar to investigate the nature of the evidence collected against more than forty prisoners. As a result of his report the government took the unusual step of sending into the area a special commission composed of the highest law officers, including Chief Justice Downes and Baron George, to preside over the trials, and

Attorney-General Plunket, Solicitor-General Bushe, and Sergeant Moore to prosecute the accused. During December the special commission was held at Sligo, Castlebar, Carrick-on-Shannon, Longford and Cavan successively.

The establishment's attitude to the Threshers was well represented in the address made by the attorney-general, W C Plunket, to the jury at the opening trial before the special commission in Sligo (5 December 1806). Plunket pointed out that the outrages, which disturbed the peace and endangered the safety of the district, belonged to that kind of agrarianism into which the peasantry had been deluded, on and off, for half a century by trouble-makers who were self-appointed leaders. It did not surprise Plunket that the rapid spread of the mischiefs had given rise to calls for the adoption of more summary measures to deal with the problem. The government, however, distinguished between peasant disturbances which were non-political and led by obscure men of no rank, property or station, and the kind of treasonable conspiracy which the United Irishmen had promoted a few years earlier. The Threshers were not composed of multitudes too strong for the ordinary arm of the law, and the feeling of the government was that the laws of the country were best vindicated by those laws themselves and without any suspension of the constitution. Yet the government had taken the disturbances as grave enough to merit the establishment of the special commission, at an unusual season of the year, for the immediate and solemn dispensation of justice. It was calculated that the commission, showing the government's determination and firmness, together with the array of local magistrates and gentry attending the sittings of the commission would be sufficient to impress the countryside with a sense of obedience to the law.

The place assigned to the peasantry in the political, legislative and social fabric was confirmed in the attorney-general's words:

> The business has originated with men possessing no situation — whom nobody knows — a set of men who dare not avow themselves — a description of persons not possessed of any rank — of any property — of any talent — of any education — men who are not placed in any situation, either by the conventions of society or their own fitness, entitling them to dictate to their fellow-subjects, or to take upon themselves the task of reformation and of legislation. These persons have discovered that the existing laws are not to their mind — they have found out that there are errors in the state and in the church, and they have conceived that they are the proper persons to undertake the task of reforming them ... But this task of reformation is undertaken. By whom? By the dregs of

the community — anonymous ruffians, who fear the face of day, whose title is founded in anarchy, and whose pretensions are enforced by robbery and murder!²

That such individuals — or nobodies — should infringe the law in their own persons, was criminal enough, in the eyes of the establishment; but that they should associate for the purpose of saying that no other person in the community should dare obey the law was regarded as an outrageous challenge to authority. As Plunket saw it: 'the first act of those who profess to interfere upon the principles of liberty is to exercise compulsion over the consciences of others, and to say, that no man shall presume to form an opinion for himself, nor act upon it, unless it meet the approbation of those self-created reformers.'

The attack upon tithes, upon payments in support of the established church of the country, was looked upon as an attempt to undermine the principle of all personal property. 'The laws which secure the fruits of each man's individual industry are the title by which the property of the clergy is secured to them.' The property of one part of the community could not be protected while that of another was allowed to be spoliated. And the constitution of the church was so intimately connected with the constitution of the state that any assault on the one was to endanger the entire structure of church and state in the United Kingdom. A liberal and a just man, Plunket was as much concerned about the attack upon the priests' dues as he was about the tithes of the established clergy. He recognised that there was no law to compel catholics to pay dues to their clergy for religious services rendered. The objectionable feature of the Threshers' attack was that they proclaimed that no man who chose to do so dare pay the voluntary dues to his priest. This, in Plunket's view, was on the one hand to deprive the parishioner of doing something that emanated from a sense of religion, and on the other to rob the priest of the voluntary bounty of his benedictions and his prayers. He could not help feeling that the intention was to eradicate all sense of religion, so as to make the members of this secret society ready instruments for the perpetration of diabolical crimes. The attorney-general reminded his audience of the interrelationship between the abolition of religion and the atrocities of the French Revolution not so many years earlier. And he reasserted the conviction of all contemporary establishments that if the principles of christianity prevailed, if a sense of obedience and a belief in a future world of punishments and rewards were to be kept alive, then the people would never become the instruments for the commission of abominable crime. But if these sentiments were to be extinguished then the ties which bound people to earth as well as to heaven would be rent asunder. Plunket was only expressing the obsessional fear of democracy felt by many of his contemporaries when he asserted that those who searched after democratic equality were the foes of religion. It was religion that gave a genuine equality to mankind. It made the poor man content with the lot of his inferiority, 'which is the condition of his nature', and in his last hour of existence it put him upon a level with the highest and most exalted.

All of this was quite revealing about the attitude of the ascendancy towards the peasantry. The laws which incorporated these ascendancy attitudes to the peasants who joined agrarian societies were expressed in the Whiteboy Acts of 1766 and 1777. Assembly with arms, the assumption of any particular name or denomination, the wearing of any disguise, distinctive badges and illegal dress to the terror of his majesty's subjects were proscribed, and though no further deed were done the mere act of such assembly was punishable by law. The magistrates were authorised to disperse such assemblies and apprehend the participants. The magistrates were indemnified if someone were killed while resisting arrest. Magistrates were also given the power to examine any person suspected of having information respecting outrages and to commit those who refused to co-operate. They were also entitled to call for the assistance of every man in the county and to raise a posse, and those refusing to help were guilty of a misdemeanour. Persons not entitled by law to carry arms were liable to have their houses searched. If any person tumultuously assembled should assault or damage the person, house or property of any of the king's subjects he was punishable with death. Every person administering an illegal oath binding the person taking it to a particular society was punishable with death. Any person voluntarily taking such an oath was liable to transportation for life. Confessing to a magistrate that one had taken such an oath would not save one from punishment, unless it could be proved that compulsion had taken place, and that the magistrate was informed immediately. Any person harbouring, concealing or assisting those involved in outrages, or supplying them with arms, ammunition or horses was liable to forfeit his life.

Because of the severity of these laws the attorney-general warned the juries that where the evidence was not clear and satisfactory they should not allow any sense of danger or alarm to induce them to find a verdict against the prisoners. In some instances before the special commission prisoners were acquitted; in others the jury was prepared to find prisoners guilty on condition that they were neither hanged nor transported; in some cases a verdict of guilty with a recommendation for mercy was returned. But in the case of the murder of Thady Lavin seven of the eleven tried were executed. A few Threshers were sentenced to hanging for breaking into private houses. Another received the death sentence for administering the oath. For supplying arms and a gun another was sentenced to death with a recommendation of mercy. The same judgement was passed on three who were found guilty of declaring to the congregation at mass the scale for tithes and dues. Three others charged with assembly, carrying arms and taking an oath were sentenced to transportation for life. Four who were charged with demanding firearms with intent to rob were sentenced to seven years transportation. For perjury two or three witnesses were also sentenced to seven years transportation. For assembly six men were sentenced to be publicly whipped twice and given six months imprisonment.

The punishments meted out under the Whiteboy Acts by the special commission had the desired effect of suppressing the Thresher disturbances. That some of those found guilty were fathers and husbands did not save them from hanging or transportation. Their plight was recognised by the law officers to be a sad one, and the details of their living conditions which were indirectly revealed during the taking of evidence showed up a grinding poverty and oppression. Labourers or small farmers renting a few acres, they had little command of the English language. Some witnesses had to be examined in Irish — one of them admitting that he spoke 'gibberish English' and that only when he was drunk. Another claimed he was no 'scholar', and therefore could not have read notices about rewards for information that were posted on the chapel door. The same witness could only give his age approximately. Details of the overcrowded houses of the peasantry also emerged in the evidence. The twenty-three year old brother-in-law of one of the accused swore that he had slept the night of a particular crime in the same bed as the accused while the wife of the accused was sitting up with a sick child. He admitted to having slept in the same bed as the married couple on a previous occasion when he 'lay against the wall'. In another case a witness, who had been sent for by the prisoner's wife, swore that the prisoner had gone to bed while she sat up minding the couple's dying child. A witness, who was employed for sewing and knitting by another of the accused, said that she slept in the same room as her employer and his wife, near the door with the children. Another servant girl and a neighbouring woman, who had come to the house for safety because her husband was beating her, had slept on a settle bed in the closet where the man and woman of the house slept. The story given for the defence was that if the accused had tried to leave the house that night, he would have had to climb over the wife, the servant girl and the battered neighbour before clambering over the children and the knitting woman at the door.

Although the judges were skeptical of the kind of evidence sworn by a close-knit community the innocence of the revelations only underlined the normality of the primitive conditions in which the witnesses lived. Privacy was difficult in such circumstances. The many direct and indirect references to overcrowding, economic oppression, bad and disputed debts, sick and dying children, petty larceny and fraud among neighbours, intimidation, distrust of the upper classes, confederacies, perjury, cruel and vicious acts of bodily assault and the avaricious attachment to pitiably small amounts of money and of land for survival show up the unpleasant aspect of nineteenth-century peasant society.

The success of the commission in dealing with the Threshers was well summarised by Solicitor General Bushe when he addressed the jury at Clonmel in February 1811. Bushe recalled when:

> the entire province of Connaught, with the exception of one county, and two counties in the north west were overrun by the insurgents called Threshers. Upon that occasion the disturbance was so violent and general that the King's judges, upon a special commission, could only move through the country under the escort of a troop of dragoons. The meetings of the people had been so frequent, numerous and audacious even in the open day, and the outrages so many, that it was doubted, for a time, in the town of Castlebar, whether the execution of six convicts could with safety take place pending the commission. Yet in the short space of less than a month the commission visited five counties and by the firm administration of the laws, supported by the co-operation of the magistracy and gentry, such was the triumph of justice, that the insurrection dissolved before its influence, and from that period [1806] until this hour [1811], so perfect has been the tranquillity then established, that the crown solicitors for those counties have never had one case of public disturbance to prosecute.[3]

Caravats and Shanavests
The disturbed state of the south-east of Ireland merited the establishment of another commission in 1811. As in the eighteenth century, Tipperary continued to be the most disturbed county in Ireland. Between 1802 and 1805 that southern part of the county around Cashel and Clonmel and bordering on Waterford and Kilkenny was greatly agitated by outbursts of agrarianism reminiscent of the whiteboyism of

the eighteenth century. Armed men raided homes at night. Wives and children of victims were beaten, and at least a dozen murders and some attempted murders were reported. The most common offence the victims were accused of was land grabbing, meaning the leasing of land which had formerly been rented to others. Labourers who had been brought in from Kerry, and dairymen who had taken land which had once been tillage were also attacked. The *ad hoc* gangs of the area combined to form the Moyle Rangers, called after the local river of that name. The locality had a tradition of lawlessness which spawned its own underworld: Whiteboys, banditti, smugglers, highwaymen, faction fighters, all rubbing shoulders with each other and sometimes overlapping in membership. A series of mail robberies had been committed on successive nights on the Clonmel-Cashel road. While these crimes were not restricted to the poor, the agrarian outrages were generally perpetrated by the poorer classes on their own kind and on those farmers who were just above them in the social scale.

Out of these disturbances arose two distinct factions, the Caravats and the Shanavests, whose feuding continued down to 1811, when it was found necessary to establish a special commission to deal with the problem. The commission was informed that the Caravats were called after a man named Hanly who was executed during the winter of 1805–1806 for burning the house of a man who had taken land over his neighbour's head. Hanly had been the leader of the group called the Moyle Rangers. The cravat which he was accustomed to wear gave rise to the nickname Caravats for his followers.[4] The Shanavests were an opposing faction led by a man named Paudeen Gar Connors, publican, farmer and part-time policeman known by his old waistcoat (shanavest). It used to be claimed that the Caravats were of a better social class because they were said to be well dressed and wore hats and silk cravats while the Shanavests wore old waistcoats. A couple of lines from a Decies folk poem would seem to support this, although one has to be careful since the poem was probably written by a supporter of the Caravats. A government spy also made the same allegation, but he himself admitted the difficulty he had in obtaining evidence. He claimed that the Shanavests were from the lower class and were sworn republicans, and that the Caravats were a catholic group inclined to loyalty. This claim has been accepted by some modern commentators although it is contrary to views expressed in other recent scholarship on the social origins of the two groups.[5] According to this interpretation the majority of the Caravats whose social status is ascertainable were young labourers, and the Shanavests were a more prosperous class of farmer, including the land grabbers who were suffering at the hands of the Caravats.[6] They were a self-constituted defence organisation which practised vigilantism, informed on the Caravats and engaged them in faction fights at fairs and races. They also, like the Caravats, took the law into their own hands. The Shanavests, too, were alienated by religion and politics from the state, and from the local ascendancy who were associated with the repressive government measures which had been used to suppress the rebellion of 1798. Besides, the police force of the day was ineffectual in providing them with the protection they needed from the Caravats. In the Whitechurch area of Waterford, Shanavests were led by a committee of fourteen. Whether the Caravats or the Shanavests were the superior social class would require more research and more convincing argument than we have been given to date. One thing is clear, they were both powerful factions involved in faction fighting at fairs, races and funerals. Apart from this, both groups were involved in land issues, and at times ordinary whiteboyism took the place of faction fighting. It was this Whiteboy dimension supported by faction that worried the government. Factions were able to call on large numbers of supporters including relations and friends ranging from servants and labourers to better off farmers, publicans (whose premises were frequently used as meeting places and headquarters) and artisans (including smiths who were useful in the provision and maintenance of arms). Besides, in a locality where one group dominated, and where local feeling ran high, it was likely to draw support from different social levels in the community. Because there were land grabbers on one side, it did not necessarily follow that they were always better off than existing tenants who refused to pay higher rents. Socially the two factions were perhaps not all that far removed from each other. The parish priest of Fethard, Fr John Ryan, said that both factions attended mass indiscriminately. He also thought that the feuds were confined to the lower orders, and he was not sure whether any respectable parishioner had joined them. Nor could he say whether one faction was more criminal than the other. Indeed, to define the clash between the two factions in terms merely of a class struggle is to presume an almost Marxian consciousness which the evidence does not support.

Some Shanavests were said to have belonged to the United Irishmen. The Liberty Rangers, which was probably the local name for Shanavests at the time when the Caravats were still known as the Moyle Rangers, were active in Co. Tipperary in 1807. The government spy who was sent to the counties of Tipperary and Limerick to get information on the Liberty Rangers only mentions Caravats and Shanavests in his report and makes no reference to the Liberty Rangers. He had tried to ingratiate himself with a family which had one son in Kilmainham jail (possibly for political offences), and another in hiding. The spy claimed that every mind in the country was poisoned against the government and inclined to rebellion, but that there would be no rising until the French invaded. He said, however, that the people were very wary of a stranger like himself. Although he had avowed himself an escapee from prison and an enemy to the present government and drank seditious toasts, he admitted he was unable to find out anything about their secrets. He had asked to be sworn in as a Shanavest but because he was a stranger this was refused. The spy recognised the factious nature of the two groups, and he could find no evidence of regular political or military organisation despite his efforts to discover it. The duke of Wellington, to whom this letter had been sent, believed that the informer was mistaken in respect of the political objects of the two factions, although he accepted his description of the potentially rebellious disposition of the people in the area.

Apart from faction fighting the main concern of the Caravats was agrarian, while that of the Shanavests was vigilantism not politics. The evidence is much too thin to support the claim that Shanavests were nationalists.[7]

From 1806 to 1811 the districts disturbed by these two factions included south and west Tipperary, east Limerick, Waterford, south and mid-west Kilkenny and north Cork. In February 1811, Solicitor-General Bushe, speaking in Clonmel said:

> and if a small portion of Limerick remains at this moment partially disturbed, I am sorry to be obliged to state that it is that eastern limit which owes its unwholesome state to the infectious vicinity of this unfortunate and incorrigible county.[8]

He was referring to Co.Tipperary where gangs of activists were often drawn from towns and villages — from a colliery town like Ballingarry, or a textile centre like Clogheen. The land in this area was rich and valuable; rents were high; middle men were numerous; agriculture was on a thriving commercial basis. The towns had agriculture-related businesses. The general economy of the area was quite sensitive to fluctuations in the market. Land and food prices, wages and employment were influenced by trends affecting the United Kingdom economy as a whole. The labourers in the textile, colliery and quarry industries often rented small holdings so that any changes involving the market in land affected their economic position also. Tightly-knit communities under economic threat encouraged collectivist reaction in the form of local gangs or secret societies. Individuals were bound to the local gang, and the gangs to each other by an oath which declared that members would be true to one another; attend meetings when summoned; bind themselves to secrecy; suffer death rather than betray a colleague and stand by each other at patterns and fairs. Offenders of the Caravat code were entitled to three warnings — threatening notices, followed by attacks on property, followed by attacks on persons. The threatening letters copied the language of legal notices, and the standard legal pseudonym of John Doe was employed widely by the barely literate authors. The gangs, bound by ties of kinship and community, wore the distinguishing emblem of the cravat, and disguised themselves on their nocturnal raids. Personal vendettas and blatant crime were frequent.

The wartime agricultural boom of 1793–1813, the increase in food prices and land and rent values contributed to the rise of the Caravats. It was a period of relative prosperity for the larger farmers, shopkeepers and others. But for the smallholder, without the security of long leases, for those renting potato land, and for the labourers, times were much more difficult, and the consequences of economic competitiveness much more critical. When, for example, the lease was up on part of the absentee Lord Bessborough's estate in Co. Kilkenny the existing tenants refused to give more than 11s (55p) per acre instead of the 42s (£2.10p) demanded. The new tenants who were prepared to pay the higher rent were attacked. The Caravats tried to reduce food prices and rents, and raise wages; and they attacked those who seemed to be profiting at their expense, or were trying to eject them, or were distraining their goods for arrears of rent. Land-grabbing farmers, and the emigrant labourers from Cork and Kerry whom they employed, were the special targets of the Caravats. In their own way of distributing primitive justice they aimed at providing an alternative system of economic laws to protect the local poor from deterioration in their condition.

In order to provide themselves with the means of enforcing their laws, they raided the property of the better-off farmers for arms and for horses. The horses enabled them to make forays into neighbouring counties, thereby extending their sphere of influence sometimes as far as thirty miles from their base. Occasionally the Caravats mustered a few hundred men. At fairs, during this period, there was frequent faction-fighting between Shanavests and Caravats. As many as twenty persons were killed at the fair of Golden, Co.Tipperary, in May 1807. Traditional musicians commemorated the exploits of these groups by naming jigs and reels in their honour.

By 1810 what the chief justice called 'many atrocities' and 'continuing outrage' had reached such proportions that it was found necessary to flood the area with more soldiers than were present during the rebellion of 1798. Stipendiary magistrates were also dispatched to the disturbed counties. A special commission, held before Chief Justice Lord Norbury and Chief Baron Standish O'Grady, opened at Clonmel in February 1811. In his opening address to the grand jury Norbury referred to the reign of terror which had been let loose by 'a paltry banditti of the lowest description'. This banditti, he said, had inflicted the cruellest regime of torture 'on the peaceable and unprotected peasantry'. They had even usurped the functions of parliament by the promulgation of their own laws and the levying of forces and contributions.

Solicitor-General Bushe, in an analysis of the origins of the turmoil, pointed to the fact that it had taken place 'in a season of the greatest plenty', and in a part of the country that abundantly rewarded the industry of its inhabitants by a luxurious produce. The class of men engaged in the unrest were those who hoped to acquire land on tenures more favourable than was the custom of any other country to grant to persons of the same order. Those, however, who believed the propaganda of the incendiary press that poor wretches had been goaded to madness by poverty and suffering had only to look at how well-dressed and comfortable the prisoners were. No country in Europe could exhibit a peasantry better clad or fed than the prisoners of the three counties (Tipperary, Waterford and Kilkenny). Only their crimes allowed them to be called unfortunate. Evidence was given that one prisoner was prepared to give £100 if a charge of robbery of arms were dropped. This prisoner, at least, was not without some financial resources, and held in fact a property worth £300 per annum in rent.

Explaining the state of lawlessness created by the Caravats and Shanavests, Bushe argued that the trouble had begun to get out of hand when people temporised with the disturbers of the public peace in the hope of securing their own individual safety. Many had turned a blind eye when the 'plunder of the clergy' and the collection of tithes had appeared to be the only object of the agitators — some even considering it venial and justifiable. Few had realised that if the regulation of dues were allowed, then this kind of behaviour would eventually develop into a war against property in general, and to 'dominion by the mob'. Addressing the gentry, Bushe said that the secret associations 'plunder your arms to enforce their commands'. Their avowed object was the regulation of landed property and its produce. They tried to fix a maximum rent and a minimum wage. Labourers from Kerry, where the harvest was late, were forbidden to take part in the earlier harvest in Tipperary. The transfer of property to new tenants was forbidden, and existing tenants were to be retained at old rents. Their mandates were directed against rich and poor. They enforced their laws by torture, burning of houses, murder, by terrorising the highways and by compelling others to join their oath-bound conspiracies. The tithes of the protestant clergy, the dues of the priests and the price of provisions were regulated by their decrees. They did not confine themselves to their original purposes, but were ready to commit any crime until the country would become universally depraved.

The peculiar character of the outrages committed by the Caravats, as Bushe pointed out at the trials, was the plunder of arms, and this had generated many other crimes. It emerged in the trials that stage-coaches were ambushed and houses and other buildings were attacked to obtain arms. Even soldiers were fired on and assaulted in order to relieve them of their firelocks. The arms thus stolen or robbed were used in various crimes of intimidation, including murderous attacks on tithe valuers, land grabbers and informers. The plunder of arms seemed to the law officers to be particularly sinister. For, as the solicitor-general said, it threatened the public peace with all of the formidable consequences of an armed peasantry and a disarmed gentry. He admitted that he had no evidence to suggest that the outrages were in any way political, or that the Caravats and Shanavests were plotting treason or planning to aid a foreign invasion. But he was sure that if political rebellion were to erupt, or if the French were to invade Ireland, they would find no more well prepared or willing auxiliaries than the armed rabble of Tipperary habituated to crime and familiarised to blood.

Of the forty men from Tipperary, Waterford and Kilkenny tried before the special commission of 1811, nineteen were sentenced to be executed, seventeen transported, flogged or imprisoned and four were acquitted. This had the effect of crushing the secret societies temporarily, though they maintained some sort of presence at least up to the famine, and hereditary feuds between certain families kept the faction fighting alive. Blue Belts, Bootashees and Bogboys, Three Year Olds and Four Year Olds (in Co. Limerick), Moll Doyles, Coffees and Ruskavellas (in north Tipperary), Black Hens and Magpies, Whitefeet and Blackfeet were the regional names for gangs that continued the tradition of the secret societies and of the opposing factions throughout Munster and Leinster.

Threshers and Caravats (1813–16)

The next outbreak of disturbances coincided with the ending of the Napoleonic Wars in Europe and was, to a considerable extent, influenced by the economic depression beginning in the autumn of 1813. Three areas in particular were affected. These were the midland counties of Roscommon, Longford, Westmeath and King's County; the Kilkenny-Queen's County border country; and the Munster counties of Clare, Limerick, Tipperary and Waterford. The issue of priests' fees, which earlier had exercised the Threshers, surfaced again in Co. Roscommon in 1812, and in Co. Westmeath in 1813. Although the major grievance was no longer the dues paid to priests, the name Threshers continued to be employed. Even before the war had ended, however, the high rents demanded for potato land, the wartime inflated food prices and the non-renewal of leases to existing tenants created a good deal of friction between cottiers and the farmers immediately above them on the social and economic scale. Extensive pastoral farming in the midlands made the acquisition of potato land all the more difficult. Once a secret society had been active in an area its label continued to be applied to conspirators in subsequent disturbances. This did not necessarily mean that there was direct continuity or connection between the two groups. So, in the midland counties, the name of Threshers or Carders continued to be used because rebels of that name were already associated with the area, and had been given a kind of official recognition at the trials of the special commission of 1806.

In the Kilkenny-Queen's County border country, and in Munster, the label of Caravats was used to describe the rebels since the Caravats had already existed in these southern counties and had been named in the special commission of 1811. The causes of the problem in the border country of Kilkenny-Queen's County were similar to those that existed in the midlands, and the friction was between the same social groups of farmers and cottiers. More particularly the trouble here was related to the acquisition of at least four farms by a consolidating farmer called Little. One of these farms he had acquired from a landlord when the previous tenant had refused to pay an increased rent. Over the years 1812–14, Little himself was seriously wounded, and had to be protected by two soldiers. His herdsman was beaten and forced to quit. A new herdsman was murdered. His hayricks were burnt and his sheep stolen. Twelve of his workmen were assaulted by a group of Caravats and ordered to quit or be killed. A magistrate, who prosecuted seven persons accused of these outrages, was himself the victim of retaliation. Under threats from the Caravats the magistrate's labourers left, others refused to work for him and he had to use soldiers to save his harvest. Two labourers who had not quit were flogged; his gardener was beaten and his steward murdered; and a fellow magistrate, for dining with him, was badly wounded.

The collapse of the wartime boom affected all sections of agriculture, and with the extension of distress the number of disturbances increased. The price of wheat slumped by about 40 per cent and that of oats and barley by about 50 per cent. The pork and beef prices paid in London for Irish meat were more than halved, and the army's requirements of these products from Ireland dropped to about one-eighth of its peak wartime demand. The price paid for Irish butter on the London market dropped by about one-third. The effect of these falling prices on Irish agriculture meant that unemployment increased and wages were lowered. Those among the town-based poor who were also dependent on the availability of conacre potato land were affected, too, by the post-war agricultural depression. The depression led to disturbances in Limerick and parts of Clare and Waterford. In this last county, where there was a high concentration of agricultural workers and of larger farmers of over thirty acres, attacks on dairymen who hired out cows and land from the larger farmers became quite common. Migrant workers coming in for the harvest were also assaulted. The most notable aspect of the disturbances in Co. Tipperary was the involvement of farmers who were on a higher social scale than the cottiers and labourers normally associated with disturbances. The corn growers of Tipperary, who marketed a large proportion of their produce, were badly hit by the post-war depression. This county experienced the most violence: between 1813 and 1816 nearly thirty agrarian murders were committed in Tipperary. The question of tithe played a bigger role in this county than elsewhere during these disturbances. Until 1824, pasture land was virtually exempt from tithes, and this meant that it was the tillage farmer who suffered most from the tithe system. In Munster and in parts of Leinster, potatoes as well as grain crops were liable to tithe. The slump in war prices left tithe owners more anxious to collect the tithe, and farmers less able or willing to pay it. Since tithe affected all farmers, opposition to it united, as no other grievance did, the lower classes who were normally associated with secret societies and the middling and better off farmers. This explains why a greater number of larger farmers were associated with agrarianism in Tipperary than elsewhere. The neighbourhood of Cashel where a series of murders had taken place became particularly notorious for its lawlessness. So alarming had the situation become that the government found it necessary to introduce two acts of parliament in July 1814 to deal with the problem.

Chief Secretary Peel's Peace Preservation Act empowered the lord lieutenant to appoint to a disturbed area a stipendiary magistrate (sometimes called a police magistrate, or chief magistrate of police), also a clerk, a chief constable and a force of sub-constables responsible to central government but paid for out of local rates. The new police recruits were farmers' sons and ex-soldiers. This police force was a mobile unit at the disposal of Dublin castle and free of local control. Because the burden of expense fell on local rates the force was not always popular with the local farmers. The second act was the Insurrection Act. It enabled the lord lieutenant, on the request of seven local magistrates, to proclaim a county or any part of a county as being in a disturbed condition. It established a curfew from sunset to sunrise in the proclaimed area. The penalty for not observing the curfew was seven years' transportation, which was also the penalty for demanding arms, possessing arms and administering oaths. The trial of those arrested under the act was held not before a jury but before a court of magistrates presided over by a barrister specially appointed for that purpose. In 1815–16 the Insurrection Act was applied to Limerick, Tipperary and parts of Westmeath and King's County.

The practical application of these acts can be seen in the case of a proclaimed area in Co. Tipperary where, in order to protect the peace and afford protection for process servers, rent collectors, landlords' agents, magistrates and tithe proctors, a number of policemen were to be sent and housed in a building in the village of Ballagh. The local response was highlighted dramatically when the projected barracks was demolished by a force of over one hundred men, and a local tithe proctor (William Dwyer), who was particularly notorious for his exactions, was murdered three days later. A number of those implicated in this murder and in the attack on the building were the sons of respectable strong farmers. The leader of the gang was hanged, and another fourteen sentenced to fourteen years' transportation.[9] Out of a total of 328 persons tried under the Insurrection Act in 1815–16, sixty-eight, or about one in five, were convicted.[10] The presiding barristers tended to be lenient in the many cases involving breaches of the curfew where satisfactory accounts for absence from home could be given. For the authorities the disturbing aspect of the 1813–16 wave of agrarianism was the involvement of the better off farmers' sons, especially in the case of Tipperary. This added a dimension which had not been quite so clearly present in the earlier agrarian movements of the nineteenth century.

Ribbonism

The phenomenon known as ribbonism added a sectarian and political dimension to the secret society which hitherto in early nineteenth century Ireland had been predominantly agrarian. Ribbonism was an outgrowth of sectarian rivalry between catholics and protestants in Ulster, and it also carried forward into the nineteenth century faint echoes of the political objectives of the United Irishmen. It was the successor of the catholic Defenders who had opposed the Orangemen in the 1790s. The Defenders had faded from public view with the rebellion of 1798, and when they re-emerged in the nineteenth century it was in the form of ribbonism. Like the Defenders, Ribbonmen were organised for defensive purposes. The aims of both were largely similar, but, whereas the Defenders had been concerned chiefly with land issues, ribbonism was much more pointedly sectarian. Many Defenders had participated in the United Irish movement with non-catholics; the regulations of the Ribbonmen excluded everyone who was not a catholic.

From their homeland in the Ulster border counties, the Ribbonmen spread into north Leinster and north Connaught, and as they did they built up a fairly extensive organisational network. They were strongest in the counties Dublin, Armagh, Monaghan, Westmeath, Kildare, Sligo, Roscommon, Offaly, Galway and north Clare, and were weakest in the counties south of a line from Galway to Dublin. For example, in Co. Tipperary where agrarian outrages were most prolific, the crown prosecutor in the 1830s claimed that there was no such thing as ribbonism in his district. Ribbonism was mainly an urban movement strongest of all in the city of Dublin, but also to be found in Belfast and Derry. Where it was found in the southern part of the country it was usually associated with towns like Limerick, Tarbert, Mountrath, Mountmellick, Cloughjordan and Bandon where orangeism was strong, and consequently, by way of reaction, ribbonism took root. A similar trend became apparent in the British cities where Irish migrants settled. Both orangeism and ribbonism became established in Glasgow, Manchester and Liverpool. Ribbonism also migrated to the United States where it developed into the Molly Maguires and other more respectable hibernian associations. This underground network of the catholic lower classes tended to thrive when sectarianism was aroused. It fed off rampant orangeism. As O'Connell said:

> ... in proportion as the Orange irritation increased ... has that of ribbonism increased ... They act on each other; the existence of ribbonism makes it necessary for one perhaps to become an Orangeman, and the existence of orangeism has certainly created many Ribbonmen.[11]

Both Orangemen and Ribbonmen responded to the increased tempo in the movement for catholic emancipation, as they also responded to the spread of evangelicalism, and the protestant crusade for the conversion of catholics. The various proselytising societies, with their free tracts and bibles and their schools, excited orangeism among protestants and ribbonism among the catholics. Although ribbonism had wider ramifications than local agrarian societies it would be going too far to see it as a national organisation. It had a chameleon-like quality taking on the colour of local circumstances. It meant different things in different places at different times; and much depends on the point of view from which it is being examined. Although too categorical there is a good deal to be said for A M Sullivan's description of it. Sullivan said that in Ulster it was a catholic league against orangeism; in Munster it fought against the tithes; in Connaught it resisted rack-renting; and in Leinster it amounted to a primitive form of trade unionism.[12] In Dublin especially, but also in other towns, it was largely an artisan movement tinged with political pretensions. In the cities it tended to develop trade union practices among its members. A Dublin shipowner claimed that Ribbon societies and trade unions were too often confounded with each other.[13] Like the friendly societies ribbonism also engaged in mutual benefit services.

Ribbonmen were, for the most part, lower middle-class and working-class catholics. Prominent among the membership were publicans whose premises were used for contacts and as meeting places. Also strongly represented were shoemakers, blacksmiths, brewery workers, porters, carmen and canalmen. The catholic middle classes including lawyers, doctors, merchants and land agents were scarcely represented at all. Nor were the artisans who were in any case strongly organised in trades unions, like the builders, bricklayers, cabinet makers and book binders. The northern influence on Ribbonmen was quite evident. Among the leaders of the Ribbonmen in Dublin was the coal porter,

Michael Keenan, who had a northern accent; and Richard Jones, a clerk in Dublin's Haymarket, who was described as grand secretary of the Ribbon Society, was a native of a Ribbon area in Co. Monaghan.

The structure of ribbonism was derived from that of the United Irishmen and Defenders, and it was modelled also on the masonic organisation of their enemies, the Orangemen. Like the latter, the Ribbonmen had initiation ceremonies, oaths, secret passwords, catechisms and distinguishing regalia especially ribbons. The basic unit was the lodge. The theory was that not more than thirty-six men were to be sworn into each unit. The idea was that no one of the thirty-six should know anything beyond his immediate circle. Each lodge had its own master, treasurer and secretary. The master, or committee-man, as he was sometimes called, communicated with the committee-man of another lodge, and so on up through a network of county and provincial delegates culminating in a national committee known in the 1830s as the Board of Érin. A meeting of national delegates, represented by two from each county sworn, met at least once in Armagh (in 1821). Theoretically committee-men from a district would gather quarterly in a centre like Limerick to meet with emissaries from Dublin, when they would be told the changes that had been made in the passwords and signs. In order to ensure secrecy seldom did the same emissary come twice to a district.[14]

Throughout its existence, which lasted all through the nineteenth century, ribbonism was subject to factionalism. In the 1830s a major division existed between an Ulster section known as 'The Northern Union' and the Dublin based section known as 'The Irish Sons of Freedom'. At the trials of the Ribbon leaders in the early 1820s and in 1840, evidence suggested that the leaders had spent much of their time in attempting to reconcile opposing factions. When the two groups clashed in Co. Meath it was noted that the northerners were more of a religious party and the Dublin faction had something of the nature of a trade union. Since it was required that each member should pay 5d (2p) quarterly, the organisation was also subject to a certain amount of fraudulent practice by those in charge of the collections. Despite precautions in the oath and regulations to prevent undesirables from being initiated as Ribbonmen, government spies and police informers found it relatively easy to infiltrate the organisation through the public houses.

Ribbonism was opposed to mere agrarianism. Agrarian issues were of secondary consideration to the Ribbonmen, but they were prepared to use local unrest to advance the cause of ribbonism as long as they controlled it. The urban-based Ribbon organisation sent agents into the disturbed areas of provincial Ireland to advise on the timing of rebellious agrarian activities. Local Whiteboy conspirators who accepted these emissaries from without were drawn into the vortex of the wider conspiracy. The Ribbonmen were annoyed if locals did not take orders or directions or heed the advice of their agents and initiated rural disturbances themselves. The Rockite disturbances in Munster afforded the Ribbonmen their first real opportunity to propagate their organisation among agrarian societies. Between 1819 and 1822 ribbonism was particularly active, dispatching emissaries especially to that disturbed province. In the west of Ireland, too, ribbonism was the label applied to agrarian activity. Archbishop Kelly of Tuam, in evidence before the parliamentary select committee on the state of Ireland, said that the very serious disturbances in 1820 in parts of Mayo and Galway related to payments and fees of all kinds. The disturbers, he said, were called Ribbonmen not Whiteboys, and their efforts were not specifically directed against tithes but against landlords. The trouble in Connaught included the assassination of the magistrate, Denis Browne, who had been actively prosecuting the agrarian agitators. However, the execution of some of the leaders in Co.Galway, and the deportation of others to Botany Bay (including nine from Roscommon) eventually quietened that area.

It was almost impossible for Ribbonmen in the circumstances of the early nineteenth century to be sectarian without also developing a political nationalism, for to be anti-Orangemen was to be almost automatically pro-catholic emancipation, pro-repeal, pro-O'Connell. Given the recent background of catholic Defenders and United Irishmen, it was natural that the Napoleonic war should encourage the spread of the political aspects of ribbonism. Informants reporting to the authorities the incidence of ribbonism were ever on the alert for all references to French aid in the activities of the Ribbonmen. In the decade following the ending of the war with France the authorities were concerned about the attachment of the Ribbonmen to the prophecies of Pastorini (see p. 99). These 'prophecies' were politically dangerous in so far as they indicated an uprising that would put an end to protestantism and its ascendancy. Some of the Ribbon toasts — 'the downfall of heresy', 'the rights of man', 'no king' — had clear political overtones.

Major Warburton, inspector of police for the west, reported that when the Ribbon system was introduced into Co.Clare about 1820, the object was to 'to overturn the government and to destroy the protestants in Ireland'. The evidence produced during the trial of Michael Keenan claimed that the intention of the Ribbonmen was to rebel, throw off the English yoke and put down protestantism. And for these ends they were said to be holding discussions with the radicals in England. Twenty years later, at the trial of Richard Jones, it emerged that he had aimed 'to remove the brand of tyranny from the foreheads of Irishmen'. Among Ribbon passwords was one which prayed: 'May Irishmen be free / From British Tighs and Tiranny' (*sic*). A Ribbon verse from Queen's County (in 1831) linked Bonaparte and O'Connell as the twin saviours of Ireland:

> We'll back the Great O'Connell
> That Nobleman of Honour
> Young Bony and O'Connell
> Will Old Ireland free.[15]

It was claimed that the Ribbonmen assisted in O'Connell's election for Clare in 1828, and helped other catholic candidates in the parliamentary elections following the Emancipation Act of 1829. Ribbonmen in Co. Wicklow threatened to burn down the house of a landlord because he had signed a document against repeal. Some Ribbon leaders liked to hint to their followers, and the more bigoted opponents of the catholic cause liked to suggest to the government, that the catholic leaders, O'Connell and Lord Fingall, were the secret leaders of the Ribbon conspiracy, and this, despite the fact that O'Connell on more than one occasion strongly condemned ribbonism. He recognised that because of ribbonism the catholics in the north were better organised and potentially more dangerous than the agrarian rebels in the south. Catholics in the north, he said, had to be prepared to defend themselves during Orange celebrations. The Ribbonmen, unlike the peasants in the south, he told the select committee on the state of Ireland 1825, did not choose to fritter away their strengths on pointless acts of outrage. If a foreign enemy were to invade the country, he said, the north would be in greater danger from its catholic population than the south. So much did O'Connell fear the damage done to the catholic cause by the spread of ribbonism that he turned informant. In March 1826, he warned Attorney-General Plunket that the Ribbon Society, no longer demanding an oath, was spreading fast and extensively into Leinster, Connaught and Munster; that the Orangemen of Cavan and Fermanagh had armed themselves with daggers which had blades about fourteen inches long, and that the lower orders of catholics were acquiring similar arms and were expecting all unmarried men to join the Ribbonmen. O'Connell had no remedy to suggest except an increase in the number of troops whose very presence might produce a calming effect. He felt he had done his duty in communicating the facts to the attorney-general.

The vapoury underworld of ribbonism was, in one sense, much more formidable than any of the contemporary agrarian societies. It was feared because of its sectarian character. It was feared, too, because of the suspected radical nature of its politics; and it was feared because it was believed to be a conspiracy with a nationwide network which had links with Irish exiles in Britain and America. Its rituals, symbols, signs and passwords, all enshrouded in a mysterious language, added to its threatening aspects. And yet, in another sense — and despite all the frantic reports from police, magistrates, spies and local gentry, and the condemnations by public figures like Bishop Doyle and O'Connell — no secret society was more ineffective in its practical achievements. It was so trapped in self-mystification that any rational programme of practical action was obscured. Even the name, ribbonism, was given by their enemies and not by themselves. They sometimes called themselves 'Sons of the Shamrock', or 'Northern Union' or the 'Knights of St Patrick', although the authorities did not recognise any of these societies as a serious threat. The two trials that publicised their existence and their nature were that of Michael Keenan in 1822 for administering an illegal oath, and that of Richard Jones in 1840 for being a member of a secret society. At the trial of Jones, the attorney-general admitted that he was unable to press any seditious charges such as the provision of arms. Indeed, no trials took place for sedition or for insurrectionary acts of violence. Although a spy reported that a rebellion was planned for July 1817, when the Wexford and Kildare men were to assemble at the Curragh, the authorities took little heed of this information, and certainly no Ribbon rebellions ever actually took place. The local agrarian societies were responsible for far more crime than were the real Ribbonmen. One modern historian has claimed that:

> Whenever we find Ribbonmen engaged in violence, it is either directed against Orangemen or each other, never against the colonial state.[16]

The claim may be exaggerated but, in general, it is true that the Ribbonmen lacked 'all military perception of insurrection'.[17] Apart from a stray reference to the making of pikes, there were no indications of any concentrated attempts to arm themselves. They acted out their conspiratorial drama in a hazy state of political presumption, placing all their faith in a belief in a single spontaneous uprising of the people which would sweep away their enemies and roll back the centuries to a pre-reformation state of religious harmony. Seen in its proper perspective, ribbonism was a conspiracy that made a great subterranean noise without, however, achieving any substantial change in the course of Irish history. It was, however, a rather crude ancestor of those later movements that combined, in varying proportions, agrarian, sectarian and political elements to produce an explosive mix of Irish nationalism. In its political aspects, ribbonism occupied a limbo between the formidable United Irishmen and the Fenians without providing anything like a clear link between the two.

Even in its most active period of the 1820s and 1830s, ribbonism was often confused with agrarianism. A contemporary commentator, W. Steuart Trench, whose book *Realities of Irish Life*, has been used extensively as a source for nineteenth century Irish social history, employed the term 'ribbonism' as a synonym for the older and more accurate 'whiteboyism'. Trench's book carries an illustration of the master Ribbonman's green collar, scarf and belt emphasising the anti-Orange, sectarian nature of ribbonism. The illustration accompanies a chapter, entitled 'The Ribbon code' which, however, merely relates incidents of outrage in Co. Tipperary that are of the simple Whiteboy variety, namely the assassination of a landlord for prosecuting, and the murder of a peasant for taking vacant possession. The Ribbon code, wrote Trench, was used mostly against improving landlords. The spendthrift, on the other hand:

> providing he does not interfere with their honoured customs of subdividing, squatting, conacre and reckless marriages may live in peace and careless indolence on his estate in high favour with the surrounding peasantry and with no danger of being ever disturbed by a Ribbonman ... The tenant, quite as frequently as the landlord, became the victim ... The main object of the Ribbon Society was to prevent any landlord under any circumstances whatever, from depriving a tenant of his land ... The second object was to deter, on pain of almost certain death, any tenant from taking land from which any tenant had been evicted ... it [Ribbon Society] assumed the position of the redressor of *all* fancied wrongs connected with the management of land, or with landed property in any form whatever.[18]

A perceptive modern historian, in a pioneering article on the phenomenon, also employed the word 'ribbonism' with the agrarian significance assigned to it by Trench.[19]

Increasingly, the social and economic aspects of ribbonism did overshadow its political and sectarian nature, and so ribbonism became a portmanteau label to describe agrarianism especially after the famine. All agrarian outrage, called whiteboyism in the eighteenth century, now, in the nineteenth century, tended to be listed under the umbrella of ribbonism. Whiteboyism is generally an appropriate description of the origins, objectives and activities of the successive agrarian conspiracies associated with Whiteboys, Threshers, Shanavests, Caravats, Rockites, Whitefeet and others. They had much in common including their uniforms and oaths. But the Ribbonmen, at least in their earlier phase, had predominant sectarian and political aspects derived from their Defender and United Irishmen ancestry which were not characteristic of those societies which were rooted in the Whiteboy tradition. That is why the jumbling together of all disturbances under one heading of 'ribbonism' obscures the very real distinctions which existed between the various secret societies in the first half of the nineteenth century. The term, however, stuck, and became a useful shorthand to describe all agrarian conspiracy. The general acceptance of the label was a recognition of the impact which the Ribbonmen had made on commentators and government officials alike.

The use of 'ribbonism' in this general, agrarian sense has obscured the relationship between Ribbonmen and Fenians, and makes it difficult to establish the exact connection between the two societies. Michael Davitt claimed that the Fenians were recruited from the Ribbonmen, and that ribbonism influenced the development of fenianism. Against this it has been noted that fenianism originated in the south where ribbonism, at least in its sectarian form, was weakest; and that fenian leaders condemned the sectarianism which was associated with early ribbonism. It is, perhaps, too strong, and stretching the evidence too far to suggest that the Ribbonmen 'served as prototypes for the better-known separatist fenian movement of the 1860s',[20] especially if by 'prototype' we mean 'model' or 'earlier version'. Nevertheless it is true that both societies recruited successfully from the urban artisans, and the schoolteachers; and that the Ribbonmen of the later agrarian phase provided a recruiting ground for the so-called ribbon-fenianism of the 1860s and 1870s as nationalist conspiracy spread into Connaught and Ulster. The reaching out of urban conspiracy into disturbed areas of rural Ireland had been dramatically forecast by the Ribbon society during the agrarian troubles associated with the Rockite movement of the early 1820s.

Rockites
The most widespread of all the pre-famine agrarian movements was

rockism — so widespread and intense, indeed, that at times the Rockite disturbances had the appearance of nothing less than social revolution. The causes were economic. Adding to the general post-war depression was the partial failure of the potato crop which resulted in famine in 1817 and again in 1821. Potato land was already at a premium because of the post-war movement away from tillage to pasture. In Munster where the soil was particularly suitable to profitable grazing, landlords were anxious to squeeze out the cottiers and smaller farmers who rented potato land. Expanding population, added to by the return of ex-soldiers and ex-sailors from the Napoleonic wars, increased the pressure on conacre and consequently on rents. Wages were down, and under-employment had increased. Legislation passed between 1815 and 1818, making it easier and less expensive for the landlords to evict defaulting tenants and to distrain their goods, 'very much increased', as O'Connell said, 'the tendency to disturbance in Ireland'.

The trouble which was later to spread throughout most of Munster, began on the Courtenay estate near Newcastle West in Co. Limerick. Here the agent of Lord Courtenay, a stranger by the name of Hoskins, tried to increase the rent, collect arrears, dispossess the tenants and introduce English methods into the management of the estate. As Barrington, the crown-solicitor for Munster said, Hoskins 'seemed not to understand the management of Irish property enforcing every covenant as he would in England'. In July 1821 in an act of revenge on Hoskins a gang of seven armed men waylaid and mortally wounded the agent's son returning from coursing at Abbeyfeale. The leader of the gang was Patrick Dillane who afterwards turned king's evidence against his fellow conspirators. In his evidence in court Dillane claimed that he was the first to be called Captain Rock, having been 'christened' that name by his old schoolmaster. It also emerged during the trial that Dillane had been hired for £2 10s (£2.50) to commit the murder by 'the middlemen, the under-tenants of the estate who encouraged the lower orders to commit outrages'.[21] A Walter Fitzmaurice, who had lived with Dillane for three years, pleaded guilty in a notorious abduction case, and was sentenced to death, had also assumed the alias 'Captain Rock'. In March of 1822, seven men entered the Goold household in Co. Cork and abducted the fifteen-year-old Honora 'with the intent that one John Browne should marry or defile her'. For three weeks, she was transferred from cabin to cabin to avoid the militia, before being released. O'Connell, appearing for the defence in both trials, described Dillane and Fitzmaurice as felons. Clearly they were the kind of criminals who were hired out to commit crime where initially genuine

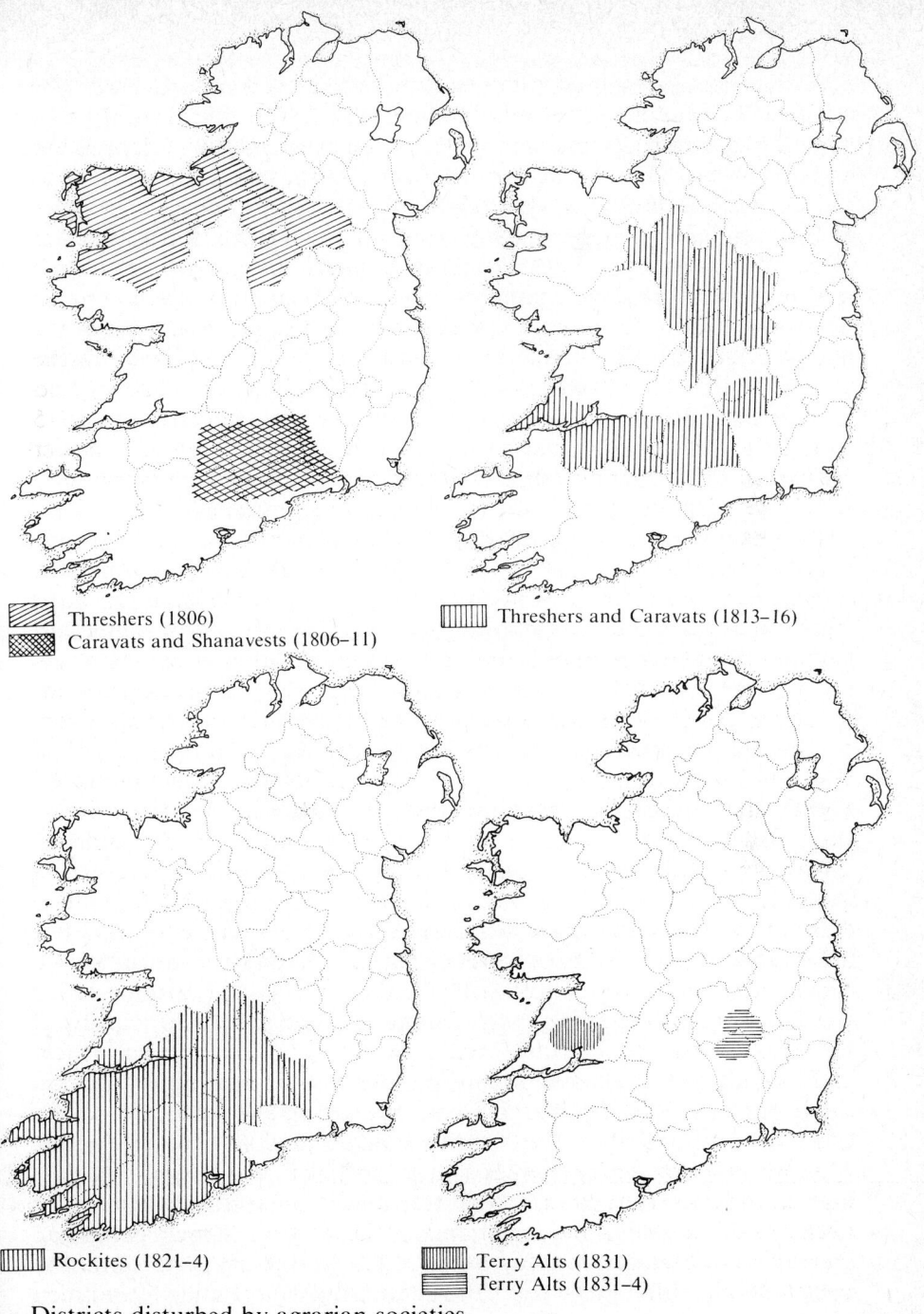

Districts disturbed by agrarian societies.

agrarian grievances might have existed, as in the Hoskins case. The deeds of these two early Captain Rocks were symptomatic of a widespread breakdown of law and order in the latter half of 1821 and the early part of 1822. 'Rockite disturbances' was the general label given to this upheaval. Much of this turmoil, which continued to erupt in Munster and some neighbouring counties down to 1825, had no clear connection whatever with Rockite conspiracies proper, and had nothing to do with any organised rebellion. Much of what was claimed to be the work of 'Captain Rock' was localised crime, and was not the action of any far-ranging secret society like that of the Ribbonmen.

At the time of the murder of Hoskins the magistrate in charge of the Co. Limerick police was a Major Going and he described the situation which had developed as one of rebellion. The *Dublin Evening Post* (23 August 1821), condemning the extreme language of the major, preferred to describe it as a 'rustic riot', and pointed out that it had nothing whatever to do with politics. When Going himself was assassinated (14 October 1821) the *Dublin Evening Post* condemned the crime but still insisted it was not political. It said the assassins were Whiteboys, Rightboys, Ribbonmen or Moll Doyles: they were burglars, robbers and murderers but not rebels. Whatever about politics the trouble in Co. Limerick was soon seen to be not unrelated to sectarian bigotry, the question of tithes for the support of the established church, and the use of the police and military. Major Going had allowed Orange lodges to be formed within the police under his charge, and this led to great hostility towards him. In a notorious tithe affray at Inchyrourke near Askeaton in August 1821 one or two hundred 'Whiteboys' attacked the house of a tithe-proctor and were, in turn, attacked by a party of less than twenty of Going's police. Three 'Whiteboys' and one policeman were killed. To teach the rebels a lesson their dead colleagues were buried in quicklime. It was rumoured that one of the rebels was still alive when thrown into the 'croppy-hole'. Some weeks later Going was ambushed and killed. 'The fate of Hoskins and Going' became a threat of the ubiquitous Captain Rock.

The killing of policemen involved in tithe affairs was reported from other parts of Co. Limerick. The *Dublin Evening Post* reported that in the space of a few days four or five individuals had been murdered. Murder after murder, the paper said of Limerick, was taking place not only in the dark but also in broad daylight in populous villages in the presence of the police and in defiance of the military. Armed gangs had paraded in the villages seizing arms, and all authority seemed to have been held in contempt. A party of 200 wearing white bands round their hats attacked the village of Shanagolden looking for firearms. In Patrick's Well, in the same county, over sixty of the peasantry paraded through the town decked in ribbons and carrying large swords and 'proceeding to a club dinner'.[22] Crown witnesses were also murdered and beaten, and arms were seized from soldiers and the homes of yeomen. By October, said the crown-solicitor for Munster, Co. Limerick 'was in a very desperate state: murders, burnings, breaking houses, outrages of every description'.[23]

Meanwhile from other parts of the country came reports of what might be called the normal or typical kind of disturbances. A representative list from the pages of the *Dublin Evening Post* for the second half of 1821 gives a good picture of the state of the country. In June in the Decies in Co. Waterford, magistrates and soldiers set fire to turf which the country people had claimed the right to cut on a commons that had been enclosed by the landlord. After a confrontation between the people and the soldiers thirty-five were arrested and a boy was killed. A faction fight at a fair in Mallow in August (Twomeys and Swineys against the Mahoneys) involved about 500 on each side in which many were injured. Eventually quelled by the clergy of all denominations, it broke out again in the evening. At a fair in Co. Mayo a soldier was shot when a mob became hostile; another soldier was stoned to death in Co. Cork also in August. A group calling itself the 'Moll Doyles' was appearing in arms in Rathvilly, Co. Carlow, and attacking the houses of tenants who had offended against their agrarian code. A gang of thirty or forty had burned a house in King's County, shot a man, driven a bayonet in the eye of a woman and tried to cut out her tongue — she died the next day from her injuries and her mother died a few days later from shock. The murder of a magistrate was reported from Kerry. Placards appeared in Co. Kilkenny which proclaimed 'no tithes, no taxes, sixty per cent reduction in rent'.

By 1821 the 'Rockite' name had spread from Limerick to the rest of Munster and the neighbouring counties of Leinster. Leaders of local conspiracies assumed the name of Captain Rock, and threatening notices were issued and oaths administered in his name. A notice in Co. Tipperary which was posted in the name of 'General Rock, Major Steel and Captain Ribbon' only emphasises the fact that the agrarian rebels saw themselves as an alternative military system with all of the functions of an organised army of the people.

The grievances, which varied from place to place, were generally related to rents, collections of tithes, quarrels over conacre, grazing and food prices. Putting land on the market when leases were up and renting it to the highest bidder was the cause of much trouble. If Bishop Doyle in 1827 could describe the tithe proctor as belonging to a tribe that was 'less worthy than those who traverse the field of battle to despoil the dead', it can well be imagined the hatred in which this official was held by those who lost their crops to him. The 'tithe farmer', who bought from the clergyman the right to collect tithes in order to make a profit for himself, was equally hated. Tithe-collectors were beaten, and the tithe itself was often destroyed rather than let it fall into the hands of those who were profiting by it. From some parts of Munster it was reported that hardly a night passed that corn or hay was not burnt. Whole areas, it was claimed, had been 'a prey to the incendiaries of the infernal Rock system'.[24] Haybarns, houses and offices were burnt. Elsewhere 'Captain Rock' issued orders about the maximum price that was to be paid for potatoes. Cattle stealing and the houghing of cattle were common occurrences. Fields were turned up; trees were cut. Near Buttevant the peasantry attempted to destroy a furze-brake belonging to the Duhallow Hunt, and when gentlemen tried to prevent this they were attacked by the peasants with stones and clubs. 'The ferocity and fearlessness of the peasantry' on this occasion was remarked on by the *Dublin Evening Post* (3 May 1823). The devastation was so extreme that the grand jury of Co.Cork presented a sum for damages of about £10,000. Near Carrick-on-Suir, Co. Tipperary, the throats of forty sheep were cut on a farm from which tenants had lately been ejected.[25]

Wherever agrarian crime occurred it was being attributed to Captain Rock. When outrage was reported from Down, Antrim and Armagh, it was said that Captain Rock had even made a move towards the north. From Munster the Rockites spilled over into Kilkenny and incidents were reported from a part of King's County bordering on Tipperary, and from Co.Kildare which led to baronies in these counties also being proclaimed under the Insurrection Act during the years 1821–4.

The conspiracy in King's County and Kildare was to prevent anyone taking land from which a tenant had been ejected for rent arrears. In these counties strangers were threatened, as were witnesses. Distress, said the administrator of the Insurrection Act in these counties, made it easier to induce peasants to join the Rockite conspiracy, for they hoped that they would better their condition by joining in the disturbances. Under-employment and over-population were major causes of the distress. In that part of Co.Kildare adjoining the canal there was 'a great proportion of distressed population'. The bishop of Kildare and Leighlin in his pastoral of 19 November 1822, addressing those who had joined the illegal combinations, and noting the futility of the actions to which they had been driven by distress said:

> Some idle tradesmen, boatmen, servants without families and young inexperienced youths of the labouring classes, these have composed your assemblies ... Is it by the breaking of canals, by the destroying of cattle, by the burning of houses, corn and hay and establishing a reign of terror throughout the entire country, that you are to obtain employment?[26]

In King's County, sixty-two persons were charged and sixteen were convicted; in Co. Kildare, 102 were charged and twenty-five were convicted during the period from June 1823 to April 1824. Those convicted 'were with *one* exception persons of the lower orders of labourers or ... cottiers'.[27] The one exception was the son of a once comfortable farmer whose property had fallen in value and was now incumbered with debts. He was a leader of the conspiracy and on his person had been found the Ribbon oath.

The most serious crimes, however, amounting almost to a state of social insurrection with sectarian overtones, occurred in Munster. In north Cork the Rockites were especially active and well organised. In January 1822, in an attack on the barracks at Churchtown, a policeman was killed and others injured, the building gutted and arms robbed. Because of the increasing number of attacks on the police, it was found necessary to build up a big army presence in Munster and in the affected parts of Leinster. One notorious incident which showed the depth of hostility towards the army occurred at Kildorrery, Co. Cork, in mid-February 1822. The wives and children of men serving in the Rifle Brigade, recently transferred to Munster from Britain, travelling in three cars were stopped by a gang of forty Rockites and some of the women were raped. Another infamous event which took place near Kildorrery was the murder of the Franks family. The Franks's home had previously been attacked and arms demanded, and the son of the household had given evidence against a Cornelius Sheehan who was sentenced to transportation. Some time later the home of the Franks was almost destroyed by 'Whiteboys'. The house had been only partly rebuilt when Franks senior, who was an agent for the Kingston estate, had distrained tenants for arrears of rent. Another complicating factor was that Franks junior was engaged to a Miss Kearney whose stepsister's husband was said to resent the possibility of the management of Miss Kearney's property being taken from him by Franks. Four days after Franks senior had distrained his tenants, about ten men rushed into the kitchen, shot and savagely beat to death the father and son, and strangled or suffocated Mrs Franks with a tablecloth. In the resulting trials three brothers, Cremin by name, were found guilty and executed on the evidence of an accomplice; but O'Keeffe, the relation of Miss Kearney by marriage, was found not guilty after O'Connell had discredited the evidence given by a brother of Sheehan the transportee. The savagery of the triple-murder; the complicated motives behind it; the sordidness of the trials where men 'ratted' on fellow-conspirators to save their own necks and evidence was given of police intimidation; and the pathos of the hanging of three brothers aged eighteen to twenty-two declaring their innocence on the scaffold — together portray the distressful state of the country in the early 1820s.[28]

Some indication of the extent to which the Rockites had armed themselves is given in the evidence of Fr O'Brien, the parish priest of Doneraile, before a parliamentary committee. A man named Hickey was Captain Rock of Doneraile district. Before his execution in March 1823 he gave the parish priest in confidence a list of the names of about seventy-five men in the parish who had arms. He said that their aims had been to emancipate the catholics and to get rid of tithes and taxes. The parish priest arranged that the arms could be handed over in secrecy and security, and although twelve 'ruffians' threatened that any man who gave up his arms would be put to death and his house burned, large quantities of arms — pistols, guns, pikes etc. — were surrendered.[29] Earlier in Kanturk when arms had been surrendered to a parish priest, four or five 'Lady Rocks' (i.e. Rockites dressed in women's clothes) carried the whole lot off with them while a detachment of the militia were attending mass in the chapel.[30]

Apart from attacks on the regular police and military the Rockites were also involved in warfare with Orangemen and with the yeomen — a protestant counter-revolutionary armed force established in the 1790s. In July 1821 the Bandon Orangemen during their celebrations killed a woman, and in retaliation an Orangeman was murdered. In late December 1821 and in January 1822 yeomen, who were not as disciplined as regular troops, clashed mortally with crowds in separate incidents in Kerry, Cork and Tipperary. The sectarian element which was present in a number of these clashes with the police, military, Orangemen and yeomen was underlined in the setting fire to half a dozen protestant churches in Munster. This was an activity that had not existed in earlier disturbances. The secret societies which had preceded the Rockites, although opposed to tithes, had not been so aggressive towards the church buildings and churchmen. The sectarianism of the Rockites manifested itself further in attacks on the Palatine communities of Co. Limerick whose ancestors had come from the German Palatinate on the Rhine in the early eighteenth century. In April 1823 over 100 men from Cork attacked the police barracks in the Palatine village of Glenasheen near Kilmallock to get arms. Houses were entered to get fire to burn down the barracks, and a number of houses of villagers who came to the assistance of the police were destroyed by fire. (All tried for the attack on Glenasheen were under 27 years of age.) At Adare, another Palatine village, houses were also attacked to get the arms of the yeomen. Sparling, an Adare Palatine who took land on the controversial Courtenay estate, was murdered. As a police inspector put it: 'There are several detached villages of protestants that have been settled [in Limerick] called Palatines, and they were exceedingly obnoxious to the people.'[31] The Palatines were 'so greatly alarmed and intimidated' that many of them emigrated.[32]

The root causes of the Rockite disturbances, however, lay more in land than in religion, and the outrages perpetrated were by no means directed only against protestants. In December 1821 a catholic priest was nearly murdered in Limerick for expostulating against the proceedings 'of the lower orders'.[33] The parish priest of Doneraile, who had persuaded his parishioners to surrender their arms to him, received threatening letters saying he was as bad as the magistrates, that he was leagued with the government and that he had become a government spy.[34] And a well-to-do farmer in Co. Kilkenny, a brother of Bishop Marum of Ossory, was murdered for taking property for which an ejectment order had been issued. Sectarianism, nevertheless, had emerged as a distinct element in the Rockite troubles. The growth of denominational ill-feeling was related to the noticeable increase in the size of the congregations attending protestant church services, which, in turn, was due to the influx of additional regiments of soldiers from Britain, and to the quartering of large numbers of the new police force in Munster. The additional troops and police soon became associated with the collection of protestant clergymen's tithes and with the protection of the local protestant ascendancy. Temporary barracks were provided by protestant property owners for the additional soldiers. These barracks were burned and threatening notices were sent to those who rendered spiritual or material service to the soldiers. The nature of the work of the military and the police in suppressing the Rockites involved interference with the normal social life of the peasantry — public house gatherings, wakes and dances after sunset were prohibited under the insurrection acts. And the increased numbers of police and soldiers were used more extensively than ever to destroy the illicit poteen stills and to prevent poaching. Numerous cases of undisciplined action and the unauthorised use of firearms by the crown forces and by their allies, the yeomen and the Orangemen, increased hostility of the country people towards them. What initially had been genuine non-sectarian activities on the part of the forces of law and order soon took on, by association, the complexion of blatant anti-catholicism in the eyes of the people. A prophecy in wide circulation at the time referred to the coming of a 'black militia' to Ireland. The police were identified as this black militia because of the dark uniform. One variant of the prophecy said that the 'black militia' would massacre all the catholics; another variant foretold that the catholics would conquer the black militia and regain possession of the island. Either variant only intensified sectarian feeling.

From O'Connell down catholic spokesmen blamed rampant orangeism, and the support it received from government forces and officials, for the intensification of sectarian bitterness. The non-catholic side retaliated by attributing the raking over of religious animosities to the speeches made at meetings of the Catholic Association. This was the opinion of counsel such as George Bennett who administered the Insurrection Act against the Rockites in Leinster, and of Francis Blackburn who administered it in Limerick and Clare, and of the inspector of police for Munster, Major Willcocks. Putting it into the heads of the peasantry that they were oppressed by the established church aroused great bitterness against it. The publication of speeches attacking the established church was 'very injurious' claimed Blackburn, for besides being in themselves a distinct and substantive cause of irritation they also gave currency and effect to the circulation of prophecies which added to the sectarianism. Willcocks explained that the Catholic Association speeches, which 'are generally very violent', were reported in two or three weeklies in Dublin to which the common people subscribed and one person read the offending material to the others.[35] In these speeches at the Catholic Association and elsewhere the whole system and the personnel associated with tithes were condemned in the strongest language. Catholic spokesmen also complained bitterly about the partial administration of the law; and this, it was claimed, had led to a widespread lack of confidence in the legal system on the part of the people. Cases of misconduct by magistrates or by troops and police were given the widest publicity in the catholic press. Sectarian animosities were said to be promoted industriously by persons who hoped to benefit by the confusion. The increasing bigotry of the Rockite disturbances offered fertile ground for the more blatantly sectarian Ribbon society. That is not to say that Ribbonmen and Rockites were one and the same. John Lloyd, sergeant-at-law, the administrator of the Insurrection Act in Cork, maintained that all the insurgents there acted in obedience to Captain Rock and not to the Ribbon society. Major Warburton, inspector of police in Connaught and Clare, was perhaps more fully informed when he said that although a great number of Captain Rock's men were not Ribbonmen, whenever a local disturbance was prolonged the local agitators were likely to be sworn and incorporated into the Ribbon system, and the local grievance given an anti-protestant bias. It was the Ribbonmen who supplied the oaths and the mumbo-jumbo that were fashionable in the contemporary continental secret societies, and the millenialism associated with the Pastorini prophecies.

A document which was found on the person of a Rockite leader in King's County in 1822 illustrated the influence of ribbonism on rockism, and the crude mixture of sectarian animosity, millenial dreams, French revolutionary aspirations and United Irish politics which resulted from that influence and which were all jumbled together in the mysterious language of the secret society.

Millenialism, although never very noticeable in earlier Irish history, was present during the revolutionary 1790s, and reached something of epidemic proportions in the Rockite period of the early 1820s. The famine and the typhus of 1817 encouraged the spread of penny religious tracts sold by pedlars at fairs and dealing with martyrs, heretics, miracles and especially with prophecies — 'the constant resource of a depressed people', as one contemporary phrased it.[36] The distribution of hundreds of thousands of bibles and tracts by the proselytising evangelical societies fuelled enthusiasm for religion, and at the same time provoked response from the catholics who promoted their own brand of religious literature. It was in these circumstances that the prophecies of Pastorini became popular. The book from which the famous prophecies were extracted was entitled *The general history of the christian church from her birth to her final triumphant state in Heaven, chiefly deduced from the Apocalypse of St John the Apostle* (1771). The author's name was given as 'Signor Pastorini'. Pastorini (an Italian word meaning 'little pastor') was a pseudonym used by Charles Walmesley (1722–97), an English Benedictine, titular bishop of Rama and later bishop of York, who had travelled extensively in Italy. The book had wide appeal, was translated into several languages and went through several editions in Ireland. Extracts purporting to prophesy the destruction of protestantism were printed on broadside sheets, and circulated extensively throughout the country with the help of travelling schoolmasters and pedlars. Numerous copies were sold in Dublin at a penny each. Blackburn told the commissioners investigating the nature and extent of Rockite disturbances in 1824 that he had made it his business to inspect every notice and every publication connected with sedition, and that he did not think there was a single instance in which there was not a distinct allusion to the prophecies of Pastorini and the year 1825. The broadsides were not sold openly in the shops, but in the country they were handed from one person to another. It was noted that artisans like smiths and carpenters avidly read the prophecies. It was claimed that where people could not obtain a copy of Pastorini they read instead the Apocalypse of St John in the testaments distributed freely by the bible societies. Although none involved in the commission of enquiry or in the courts could claim that the prophecies had been the cause of any particular offence, all were convinced that they had kept up the irritation in the people's minds. Outrages would have been committed without the prophecies, but their circulation had inflamed the minds, provoked a sectarian spirit, and helped to keep the people in an unsettled and distracted state.

As a result of the propagation of the prophecies it was firmly believed by many among the peasantry that all heretics in Ireland were to be eliminated in 1825. Such a belief made it easier to see the killing of a protestant as an act, if not of virtue, at least of war. That is why some Rockite or Ribbon notices could call for the murder of the 'Palatine devils' or the 'heretick' peelers or why a Rockite oath from Tarbert, where the yeomanry were considered a nest of Orangemen, could call for the murder of protestants, and why one notice proclaimed that it was 'no sin to kill hereticks'.

The excitement of the lower orders was fanned by the prevailing idea that an event and a great change was about to take place. This expectation among catholics engendered a consequential fear among non-catholics. Protestants in Co. Carlow sat up on Christmas Eve 1824 expecting a massacre (many protestants believed that 25 December 1824 was the day fixed for their massacre in accordance with the Pastorini prophecies). In one district in Co. Cork where people faithfully believed in the prophecies it was related how:

> though they may be beat back twice or thrice by the army, yet when, having turned, they will meet a man in the way who comes from heaven, he having sprinkled them with holy water, they will turn round again and the army will fly before them though they [the Whiteboys] should hold up but straws.[37]

It is hardly to be wondered at, therefore, that a people looking so desperately for a saviour should see in the emergence of O'Connell their promised leader and give to him their full confidence and support. In the height of the fever about the prophecies of Pastorini, miracles were ascribed to Prince Hohenloe, a German priest who was visiting Ireland. The miracles (one woman was said to have recovered her speech) were publicised by Bishop Doyle of Kildare and Leighlin and Archbishop Murray of Dublin in whose diocese the miracles were reported. Thanksgivings were offered in the churches, and at Ennis a high mass was celebrated. Reports of the miraculous seemed to confirm the truth of the prophecies. And even when churchmen (including Bishop Doyle) condemned belief in the prophecies, they were not listened to by people who assumed that the priests who rejected Pastorini were only doing so in response to political influence. In these circumstances the government was advised that it would not be safe to remove the application of the Insurrection Act until after the fateful year of 1825, even though it was acknowledged that dispossession, and not prophecy, was the cause of outrage. It was also realised that after 1825 had passed what was described by Blackburn as the ultimate of discontent — 'misery, wretchedness, unemployment, over-population, want of manufactures, subdivision and absenteeism'[38] — would still remain.

Two bishops, Doyle of Kildare and Leighlin, and Tuohy of Limerick, wrote pastorals to dissuade people from belief in the prophecies. Doyle in his powerful pastoral of 1822 against Ribbonmen, acknowledged the motives which had driven men in his diocese into the Ribbon society — 'your distress, your hatred of Orangemen, your love of religion, your faith in prophecies, your hope of seeing your country free and happy'. He analysed each of these motives in turn and the methods employed to promote them, and dismissed them as not being good enough to counter-balance the harm done by joining a secret society. In the section of the pastoral devoted to an examination of Pastorini he said that it was difficult to treat the absurd prophecies with becoming seriousness, and yet he recognised that they had produced the most deplorable effects among his flock. He claimed that Pastorini's *History of the christian church* had been perverted to very different ends from those which the pious author intended. Pastorini's book included conjectures on the meaning of the Apocalypse of St John — a revelation of a vision which the disciple had in captivity. Bishop Doyle explained that even the greatest of the fathers of the church had admitted that John's vision was of such a mysterious nature that it was above their comprehension, that every word and every sentence was replete with mystery. Luther, however, had imagined that in this book he had discovered that Rome was Babylon and the pope antichrist. So, Pastorini retorted that Luther was the star mentioned in the Apocalypse, a star which fell from heaven and which after blazing on the earth for 300 years would then be extinguished (i e in 1825). Lutheranism, Doyle pointed out, was very different from the established church of Ireland, so even if it were to fail it did not follow that the established church would cease to exist. In any case the church had never unveiled the vision called the Apocalypse, and neither of the two zealous disputants — Luther or Pastorini — should be believed. Doyle concluded by urging his flock to lay aside their books of prophecies, to listen to their pastors, and to read, instead, the books provided in the libraries of their chapels.

Doyle's pastoral was welcomed by the authorities. The commander of the forces in the south and some of the magistrates republished the pastoral and had it circulated among the people to counteract Pastorini and the secret societies. An edition was also published in Galway, and printers 'for their own profit' published it knowing that its intrinsic interest would win a wide readership. Doyle, however, said that his pastoral would not have had much effect without the personal exertions of the clergy. He himself 'spent several weeks, going from parish to parish, and preaching to multitudes of people in the chapels, and sometimes by the waysides, against the society (Ribbonmen) in which they were engaged'.[39]

By 1825 the Pastorini fever had subsided, and an improvement in the economic conditions of the people signalised by a rise in agricultural prices had already lessened the distress which had caused the disturbances. Rockism, however, had left its mark on the development of Irish political society. It was during the Rockite disturbances that there had been produced that amalgam of forces which was to be so powerful throughout the rest of the nineteenth century — agrarianism of the traditional Whiteboy variety, sectarianism which was fed by ribbonism and the Pastorini prophecies, and politics with echoes of the United Irishmen on the one hand and the first steps towards O'Connellite democracy on the other. O'Connell had always unequivocally condemned agrarian violence. And yet, as a leading defence counsel on the Munster circuit, he played a prominent role in some of the most notorious of the Rockite trials. O'Connell appeared for the defence in the case of the men charged with the murder of young Hoskins and of Major Going. He successfully defended some of those charged with the murder of the Franks family. In the case of the three brothers hanged for that crime O'Connell always believed in their innocence, and their hanging confirmed his opposition to capital punishment. He defended those charged with the burning of Churchtown police barracks and the killing of a policeman in the incident. He also successfully defended two brothers charged with the murder of a policeman who had gone to a ball-alley to issue warrants for preventing the cutting of a standing crop. He appeared for those charged with the rape of the wives of the Rifle Brigade. This close professional association with the Rockites was to be of great significance for the development of O'Connellite democracy.

The impact of rockism on O'Connellite democracy

Rape, arson, the murder of policemen and killing of land-agents and their families were not, at first sight, the best kind of things to contribute to the making of a political reputation. Yet they helped enormously the rise of O'Connell to the leadership of Irish democracy. Not, indeed, that he approved of these crimes, for he abhorred them. But equally he detested the oppressive social system that made it difficult for the people to obtain justice. He said of the court system that it was 'productive of the vilest perjury, and does more to demoralise our peasantry than all the details of law and religion can be calculated to prevent'.[40] He was fully aware of the damaging political framework in which the courts operated, and which accounted for the people's lack of confidence in them. As a crusader dedicated to obtaining civil rights for his fellow catholics he was ready to condemn any policy of the government that seemed 'to pervert the administration of so sacred a thing as public justice'.[41] To the lord lieutenant, in the middle of the Rockite disturbances, he complained of 'the system by which we are governed, the cold system of exclusion and distrust'. He called upon him to ban the 12 July Orange exhibitions, and pledged his professional reputation to prove their illegality before any impartial jury.[42]

O'Connell was as energetic in the defence of the Rockites as they were active in the perpetration of their crimes. The pressure of business was great. He was, as he wrote himself, 'at the top of the wheel'[43] and even before he had appeared in the most famous cases he could write that he had had 'a great and glorious assizes'.[44] He had already 'a larger professional income than any man ... ever had at the Irish bar'.[45] His tirelessness was phenomenal as he travelled his circuit. He was grateful to providence 'which has given me so strong a constitution as to enable me to resist *all* fatigue'. And he tried to reassure his wife who was worried for his safety while he was in Limerick at the height of disturbances there. He travelled, he assured her, at hours when no attacks were made and besides 'the military force is immense'.[46] But most revealing of all, he told her that 'the people attack only their enemies'.[47] Clearly he did not consider himself an enemy of the Rockites. After a day in the courts, addressing public meetings in the evenings, he was, as a contemporary then described him, 'riding in the whirlwind, and directing the storm of popular debate'.[48]

O'Connell, therefore, was the chief political beneficiary of the Rockite disturbances. By his appearances as defence counsel in so many of the trials held before the special commissions and the regular assizes he won the loyalty not only of those whom he had successfully defended but also of their families, neighbours and priests. The name of O'Connell was associated with some of the most dramatic Rockite events to catch the attention and imagination of the public. He now offered in his new Catholic Association (formed in May 1823) a genuine democratic and constitutional alternative to the blind, violent responses which their frustration had hitherto provoked. Despite the savage crimes and the primitive protests of the agrarian societies they had been, in their own way, a preparation for participation in O'Connellite politics and democracy. The agrarian societies had provided a real if rather crude experience of organisation aimed at the attainment of very basic objectives. Feeling as a people excluded from the official state system they offered at local level an alternative government with an alternative military and police system to enforce their laws. They aimed at providing a democratic regulation of leases, rents, tithes, priests' dues, food prices, wages and employment. They arranged an alternative or peasants' legal system, which made its own awards and handed out swift retribution and penalties for violation of their code. The members of the agrarian societies gained elemental experience of assembly, decision-making, united action, and the regulation of relationships within society. The experience thus gained would soon be turned to the advantage of the more sophisticated organisation provided by O'Connell for political purposes.

It was the general community in which the agrarian societies operated, and not just the members or their families, that formed the raw material for O'Connell's organisation. The widespread ambience of the secret societies has to be understood in order to appreciate something of their significance for O'Connellite democracy. The persistence and strength of the Irish agrarian societies made them perhaps unique among contemporary peasant protests. The geographical spread and the frequency of the outbursts testify to the prevalence of agrarian discontent in Irish society. The large numbers of Whiteboys or 'Rockites' that from time to time assembled were impressive; and the swearing-in ceremonies which took place after mass, or on intimidating nightly journeys from village to village, could involve a considerable part of the local male population. The secret societies could not have survived so long, nor with such numbers, without the tacit support at least of the countryside. This local support was often evident in the court-room where hundreds of alibis were sworn in defence of those on trial. Less numerous, but also significant, were the character references that priests provided for the accused. Like guerillas in later times what accounted for the survival of the agrarian societies was their acceptance in their neighbourhoods whether by active assistance or connivance. In poetry, ballad and folklore many of the peasant captains were turned into heroes, their deeds immortalised, and their objectives praised. A favourable environment was therefore created which allowed them to move freely and to operate relatively unimpeded. Whiteboyism could apparently count on mass support. Contemporary commentators rarely distinguished between the law-abiding peasantry and the secret societies. They were all lumped together as 'the peasantry', or 'the lower orders'. Tarred with the same brush they tended to behave as if they were all sworn members of a conspiracy. The secret societies relied upon the sheer power of numbers, and on the public opinion which they had organised to achieve their objectives. This, too, was a preparation for O'Connellite democracy. Violence was the only form of protest known to the poor and inarticulate in early nineteenth-century Ireland before O'Connell had imposed his leadership on the people, and extended his methods of passive resistance throughout the land. O'Connell's huge success in this respect, however, must not blind us to the fact that it was while his massive campaigns were insisting on non-violence that the most violent agrarian conspiracies persisted. It was almost as if the two went hand in hand: that the endemic violence made O'Connell proclaim his constitutional methods and his passive resistance message all the louder, and that the violent peasant protests took courage from the very success of O'Connell's campaigns against the ascendancy and the government.

The pervasive agrarianism and the secret societies underline the extent of the problem O'Connell faced in trying to get the 'people' organised. Their problems were very basic, fundamental, material — for them the issue was economic. O'Connell, on the other hand, was concerned with political issues — catholic emancipation and the internal struggle with Fingall and other gentry for control of the Catholic Committee. But O'Connell had succeeded in getting control of the administrative machinery of the catholic cause by defeating the catholic aristocracy. And as a lawyer defending the people when on trial for agrarian crime, as 'the Counsellor', he had earned the loyalty and love of the people and won over their allegiance. Like the amnesty movement in the late 1860s which won a great deal of public support for the Fenian prisoners, and funnelled fenianism in an acceptable form into Irish political consciousness, so too, did O'Connell's defence of the Rockites win sympathy for their cause, if not for their crimes, and helped to integrate the agrarian secret society into the nationalist tradition. Rockism in this sense, therefore, became an essential part of the political education of the Irish people under O'Connell. It was to be the achievement of Parnell in the New Departure that he would add the physical force of the Fenians and the agrarianism of the land league to constitutional politics. By contrast, O'Connell's achievement was that to the very raw and crude forms of widespread agrarianism, and to the underworld of the ubiquitous secret societies, he supplied the civilising additive of constitutional politics.

The extent to which rockism had entered the public consciousness can be gauged by the fact that four important publications in the 1820s had the name of 'Captain Rock' in their titles. The *Memoirs of Captain Rock: the celebrated Irish chieftain with some account of his ancestors*, was written by the most popular of Irish poets, already famous for his *Melodies*, Thomas Moore; *Captain Rock detected* was the work of a leading religious controversialist, the Rev. Mortimer O'Sullivan; Roger O'Connor was the author of the *Letters to his majesty King George IV by Captain Rock*; and M J Whitty edited the journal, *Captain Rock in London or the chieftain's gazette for 1825*.

The *Memoirs of Captain Rock*, although published anonymously, was widely known to be the work of Moore, and attracted all the attention which a book by an established writer of his reputation was bound to have. According to the literary device employed by Moore, the manuscripts of the *Memoirs* was allegedly given by Captain Rock to the editor (Moore), whom he encountered at the head of hundreds of Whiteboys, while the latter was on an evangelical mission to Ireland, having been sent over by a society of 'pious persons' in the west of England 'directed to the conversion and illumination of the poor benighted Irish'. It was a clever satire, incorporating, however, with a very nationalistic interpretation of Irish history a strong condemnation of English rule. Captain Rock himself appeared in its pages as a cultured, well-read person descended from kings, with exceptionally wise and statesmanlike views despite the education to which he admitted: in history — *Annals of the Irish rogues and rapparees*; in biography — *Memoirs of Jack the batchelor*, a notorious smuggler, and of Freney a celebrated highwayman; in theology — Pastorini's *Prophecies* and the *Miracles of Prince Hohenloe*.[49] The impression which the reading of Rock's manuscript left on the missioner's mind, and which Moore's book was intended to leave on its readers, was 'that it is the rulers, not the people of Ireland who require to be instructed and converted'.[50] The recurring theme, as Moore took his readers through the history of Ireland, was that every succeeding century was but the 'renewed revolution of the same follies, the same crimes, and the same turbulence that disgraced the former', and that whoever might suffer by such measures Captain Rock at least would prosper.[51] 'The plan of pacifying Ireland by exterminating the Irish' had been tried under almost every government.[52] 'But the only virtue which the Irish Government has been the means of producing in the people is fidelity to each other in their conspiracies against it.'[53] Moore's book was pro-catholic, and bitterly anti-Orange, and especially opposed to the tithes of the established church and the 'drunken' constables who were employed in the services of that church.[54] Tithes, he described, as 'an exaction unparalleled in the annals of tyranny'.[55] He condemned the proselytism of the time. Rock was seen to be the latest rebel in the honourable tradition of resistance to British rule in Ireland. Moore's book made Captain Rock respectable and even heroic. It justified his objectives, and offered no condemnation of his methods. Moore was delighted to be able to record that in Ireland 'the people were subscribing their sixpences and shillings to buy a copy'; that the catholics of Drogheda had written to thank him for his 'able and spirited exposition of their wrongs'; and that a reader had written to say that the book would do more good for Ireland, 'than any book that ever was published'.[56] A recent biographer has written of the *Memoirs of Captain Rock*: 'It was — for a man in Moore's circumstances — a brave book, and it won him his place at Irish cottage firesides' ... 'as a statement of British misrule it is devastating'.[57]

Captain Rock in London or the chieftain's gazette, published in parts from March 1825 to December 1826, presented a view of Captain Rock not dissimilar to that of Moore's portrait. The periodical saw Rock, not so much as an individual, but as a spirit, as a pimpernel who was the spokesman for the just cause of the Irish peasantry.

> He the dark, the shadowy, the unknown,
> Raised for our times, and for our use alone
> That useful phantom ...
> That fear fraught shadow ...[58]

The magazine asserted that Rock was 'synonymous with Irish patriotism'[59] and described him as doing more for Ireland than even the Catholic Association: 'who has redressed individual wrongs without requiring the aid of penny subscriptions? Captain Rock to be sure'. And it continued:

> Who has made England partially acquainted with the state of Ireland; or who caused the nightly protracted debates in St Stephen's Chapel? Captain Rock to be sure; and nobody else, my countrymen. I have made you known abroad and at home, and have collected on you the eyes of Europe. Many of your grievances have been redressed through my means; and please God, I shall never desist until you cease to complain.[60]

In the eyes of the editor of the *Gazette*, therefore, Captain Rock was 'the advocate of Ireland on the broad principles of right and justice'.[61] He aimed to make the people of Ulster liberal; the people of Connaught wealthy; the people of Leinster contented and those of Munster peaceable.[62] Although the editor may have been too full of his pen's importance when he claimed that 'the name of Rock is as likely to endure as that of Alexander or Ferdinand'[63], nevertheless his phrase had underlined something of the significance of the agrarian captain for the development of Irish politics. This literary 'Captain Rock' in London, wishing to take the agrarian agitation in Munster a stage further along the road to democracy, agreed with O'Connell that although the education given in the schools was useful it was by no means sufficient, and that 'political science should be taught to the boys with their religious catechism'.[64]

Roger O'Connor's use of the word 'Rock', in *Letters to his majesty King George IV by Captain Rock*, had something to do with the fact that the initials, R.O.C.K. also stood for 'Roger O'Connor, King'. O'Connor, the brother of the United Irishman Arthur, and the father of the Chartist leader, Feargus, had himself been jailed as a United Irishman. He had also been arrested for heading a band of retainers who robbed the Galway mail in 1817. This raid, it was asserted, was to recover a packet of love-letters written by his friend, Sir Francis Burdett, which were likely to be used in a case against Burdett for criminal intimacy. Although O'Connor was acquitted, the incident attested to his own Rockite tendencies. He addressed George IV as a brother king, *de jure*, if not *de facto*. He asserted that Ireland's independence had been usurped by England; that the lack of respect which Ireland had for the law was justified; and that the concession of 'one pitiful item', catholic emancipation, could not balance 'the account of all the spoilations, massacres, degradations and insults heaped on the Irish people'.[65] The assumption of the name of Captain Rock illustrated the link forged between political radicalism and the Rockite movement.

The growing tendency to politicise the Rockite movement was noted by observant supporters of the establishment. Rev Mortimer O'Sullivan in his book, *Captain Rock detected, or the origins and character of the recent disturbances*, censured the author of the *Memoirs of Captain Rock* for the encouragement his work gave to the robberies, disturbances and murders committed by his countrymen. And Robert Southey, the poet laureate, agreeing with O'Sullivan, held that Moore had 'indeed laboured to inflame the vindictive passions of an ignorant and ferocious people most industriously; and he has exulted in the display of their ferocity'.[66] He also condemned the radicalism of Roger O'Connor. The critics of Captain Rock in all his literary forms pointed to the connections between rockism and the policies and statements of O'Connell and Bishop Doyle. The attempt now launched by O'Connell with the support of the clergy to organise the people into a mass emancipation movement only confirmed the critics' worst fears.

4 Emancipation and Reform, 1823–40

The Catholic Association

On 25 April 1823 O'Connell proposed the establishment of a new association for the twin purposes of organising the people and pressurising the government into conceding catholic emancipation. In his address at this preliminary meeting he said that since the dissolution of the Catholic Board 'the people had been left to themselves — to their own sense of grievance and to their own mode of redress'. He noted how outrageous excesses had desolated Limerick and other parts of Munster; how poverty and local tyranny had produced a local insurrection; and how military law and penal statute had been necessary to quell it. The disease, however, he said, 'was not expelled but chased through various parts of the system'. He continued:

> The new Association would apply a new secret of healing — that wonderful power of sympathy with the sufferer, of fellow interest in the grievance, which would do more than statutes or armies to restore tranquillity. It was dangerous to leave the people without some body of recognised friends to whom they could at least vent their complaints.[1]

To keep within the law the Catholic Association disclaimed any representative character, and to avoid any suspicion of secrecy reporters were admitted to all its meetings. It was to be an open club to which individuals would be admitted on the proposal of any member, and the annual subscription was one guinea. Priests were given *ex-officio* membership. Early in 1824 O'Connell proposed the admission of associate members who would contribute to the catholic rent by a subscription of a penny a month. It was this penny-a-month scheme that transformed the Catholic Association from a small middle-class political club into a mass movement which politicised the countryside. The rent was first collected in the cities and towns, then spread gradually to the neighbouring parishes, and finally extended to the remote parts of the country. Volunteers made the first collections; then committees were formed; local offices were rented; meetings were held; and the newspapers, which gave the subscription lists and reported the speeches given at the association's headquarters in Dublin, were eagerly read and debated. As the rent spread, so too did political discussion among every class of society, and an interest in politics became universal. An

Irish public opinion was created and concentrated in the Catholic Association under O'Connell's leadership.

In his characteristically exuberant way O'Connell announced that the rent would bring in £50,000 a year. How he proposed to allocate it indicated something of the character and objectives of the association. £15,000 per annum was to be spent on gaining favourable press coverage; £15,000 was to be spent on 'legal protection for the catholics against Orange oppression'. For the use of catholic schools and the purchase of books he would allow £5,000. Another £5,000 was to be set aside for the education of catholic priests including those for the missions. £5,000 was to go to the purchase of seats in parliament for the supporters of emancipation, and for the establishment of an agent in London. The remaining £5,000 would be used for the purchase of land, and the building of chapels and houses for the priests. Although little of the money collected may have gone on the education and housing of priests, the declared intention was not only indicative of the character of the association but was also a useful political tactic for winning clerical support. In the event the target set was never reached, but the income was nevertheless significant. £58,000 was collected between 1824 and the dissolution of the association in 1829. The rent made possible the establishment in Dublin of a pro-association newspaper, the *Morning Register*. The stimulus of election contests, especially Waterford in 1826 and Clare in 1828, increased the enthusiasm for collecting. The rent enabled the association to send legal aid and reporters to assizes in cases relating to tithes and local oppression. An extensive premises, the Corn Exchange, was purchased as headquarters for the association, and financial support was given to evicted freeholders who had voted against their landlords on the instructions of the association.

The rent, therefore, made available a fighting fund for the emancipation movement, and was a useful barometer of popular support. While the rent in itself was of the utmost material benefit, what was of even greater significance was the involvement it provided for the people. By 1828 churchwardens, one appointed by the parish priest, the other elected by the parishioners, were organising the collection of the rent on the first Sunday of each month in the churches. The churchwardens, apart from forwarding the rent, reported from all over the provinces to the Corn Exchange in Dublin on the registration of voters, evictions, tithes, proselytism and grievances of all sorts. The publication of the subscription lists supplied propaganda for the cause and a sense of belonging for the contributors. The rent, as it has been remarked, initiated one of those movements which from time to time whips up enthusiasm, takes hold of a whole people and makes them less selfish and more idealistic. The poor gave up snuff, lawyers voluntarily taxed themselves at a penny a case, and jobbers handed over the 'luck-penny' to the catholic rent. A most significant psychological effect of the rent was that it gave contributors a strong sense of proprietary interest in the politics of emancipation. The Irish people were thereby enrolled in what was arguably the first mass movement of organised democracy in Europe, and gradually became aware that they were an awakening giant of enormous strength. The committees and boards which had preceded the Catholic Association had been dominated by the aristocracy, and more recently by the middle-class lawyers, merchants and doctors. But where the guineas from the gentry had failed, the pence from the people, announcing the emergence of democratic power, were destined to prevail.

Contact between the mass of the peasantry and the middle class catholics for political purposes had been non-existent before the foundation of the Catholic Association. Meetings of the central committee in the Corn Exchange took on all the appearances of what was described by a frightened ascendancy as a native, popish parliament. In this alternative to Westminster was processed and publicised a whole litany of grievances pouring in from all over the country. The bigger aggregate meetings which were open to all of the people took place in the larger churches and had about them the air of popular assemblies. The nationwide network of branches made possible a series of meetings by which the propaganda of the association could filter down to the remotest parts of the country. In all of this organisation the clergy played an important role. They became O'Connell's lieutenants, his local organisers and the supervisors of the rent collection. The accession of Bishop Doyle to the association added a most powerful intellectual influence to the emancipation cause. His widely read publications signed 'JKL' (James of Kildare and Leighlin) vindicated the demand for the civil and religious liberties of the catholics, and warned the government that it could not depend on the hierarchy to prevent rebellion. A number of his fellow bishops, hitherto considered to be conservative and loyal, following JKL's lead also gave the association their episcopal approval and encouraged their priests to participate in its activities. Not that the priests needed much encouragement, for it was noted that the priests, educated at home and especially at Maynooth since its foundation in 1795, were more nationalistic than those who had formerly been educated in the Irish colleges abroad closed by the French revolution. As JKL described them:

> This clergy, with few exceptions, are from the ranks of the people, they inherit their feelings, they are not as formerly brought up under despotic governments, they have imbibed the doctrines of Locke and Paley, more deeply than those of Bellarmine or even Bossuet on the divine right of kings; they know much more of the principles of the constitution than they do of passive obedience.[2]

So, backed by the clergy, united through the rent, and guided by O'Connell and his allies in Dublin, the Catholic Association became an unprecedented organ of democratic power, or, in Lecky's phrase: 'one of the most powerful political bodies known in history'.[3]

The Waterford election (1826)

The most ominous challenge to ascendancy rule from the agent of democratic power — the Catholic Association — came during the Waterford election of 1826. One of the parliamentary seats in Co. Waterford was virtually the private property of the Beresfords. Between the union and 1826 only one contest in eight general elections had taken place for the two Co. Waterford seats, and that was in 1806 after the death of the Right Honourable John Beresford who had held the seat for forty-five years. He was so powerful that he was described in 1795 by the lord lieutenant, Fitzwilliam, as 'virtually king of Ireland'. Local magnates saw the possibility of grabbing something for themselves in the scramble for power. The Beresfords, however, retained the seat without too much difficulty. Their influence in the county and elsewhere was based upon the ownership of extensive property. In the late nineteenth century the Beresfords still owned some 40,000 acres in Waterford alone. Wakefield claimed in 1812 that 'one quarter of all places in the Kingdom are filled with their dependants or connections'.[4] To challenge their supremacy in Waterford was a task of herculean proportions, and had radical and revolutionary implications.

Although the national emancipation issue was significant for the 1826 election, it was not the sole cause of all the excitement in Waterford. Local politics played a major role. The revolt of the catholic freeholders on Beresford's estate began in fact with an upper middle-class demonstration of loyalty to the crown. It was not in its origin a democratic protest at all, nor was it specifically a catholic protest. In 1822 when Wellesley, the viceroy, was assaulted in a Dublin theatre by a member of the Orange faction, a group of Waterford gentlemen requested a county meeting to protest at this public insult to the viceroy. The sheriff of the county, directed by Beresford, refused to requisition the meeting. 'Twelve honest magistrates' were then found to requisition a meeting at which Beresford was roundly denounced, and it was agreed to examine the best method to ensure a more popular representation of Waterford in parliament in the future.

Local sectarian questions ensured that the Waterford branch of the Catholic Association would play a committed role in the assault on the Beresford political ascendancy. From the start of the Catholic Association in 1823 Waterford had been prominent. Within three days of the establishment of the penny-a-month catholic rent, eighty Waterford tradesmen had formed a committee to manage local finances. O'Connell visited Waterford in August 1824 when he was engaged as counsel in a case concerning the validity of a lease held by a catholic from a protestant family. He was incensed that not a single catholic was left on the jury, and claimed that Orange feeling had prevented a catholic from getting justice. 'I never was more disgusted by the vileness of the bigotry which crushes the catholics in every step' — he wrote to his wife. His reception by the catholic people of Waterford helped to compensate for the bigotry; his coach was dragged by the people a half mile to his lodgings, and a public dinner was given in his honour in the town hall at which leading emancipationists were among the speakers.

The question of challenging Beresford's supremacy brought together liberal protestant and catholic gentry. As early as August 1824, the possibility of Villiers Stuart standing as a liberal candidate against Beresford was already being canvassed. Villiers Stuart was then just twenty-one years old. His family owned seven thousand acres in Waterford, and he was politically well connected in England. He threw himself into the political game in Waterford by the creation and registering of forty-shilling freeholders on his estate.

In the summer of 1825 a Villiers Stuart election committee was formed, composed initially of protestant liberals, well-to-do catholic gentry, and business and professional men with Thomas Wyse as chairman. The committee was fortunate to be able to use O'Connell's Catholic Association, as well as the clergy and the mass of the people that were gathering into O'Connell's agitation. The election committee employed existing structures which had been set up for the purpose of collecting the catholic rent. Parish committees controlled by the priests were established. Each committee kept a register of electors, and recorded disposition particulars against the name of each person. The catholic bishop, Patrick Kelly, gave his full support. So too did Fr John Sheehan, later parish priest in Waterford, who became one of the strongest activists in the area, and was, perhaps, O'Connell's most faithful link with Waterford over the next quarter of a century.

The election committee's headquarters was established in Shanahan's Commercial Hotel in the Mall in January 1826. The entire hotel was rented for two hundred pounds for the duration of the election. A fancy dress ball, at which Letitia Bonaparte, niece of Napoleon, and wife of Thomas Wyse, was the star, and other entertainments kept enthusiasm alive. The committee members and local parish priests addressed each parish in rotation on Sundays. As Wyse said, 'shame and emulation' were used as stimulants in the campaign. Appeals were made to women to pressurise their menfolk into doing the right thing. Speeches during the campaign stressed that the issue was one of conscience against landlord-tenant loyalties; the wrongs of the Beresfords to catholics; the electoral power of the forty-shilling freeholders and loyalty to one's country and religion. Chapels were used throughout the county as meeting houses. When the chapel at Portlaw, near the Curraghmore estate of the Beresfords, was refused by the parish priest, Bishop Kelly ordered it to be opened. Beresford, in an attempt to gain support, reduced rents and remitted arrears. Villiers Stuart's address to the electors was approved by the Catholic Association in Dublin. The issue was declared to be between 'Stuart, Freedom and Catholic Emancipation' and 'Beresford, Slavery and Ireland's continued degradation'. The Ballybricken butchers acted as a civic guard to keep the peace during the election campaign. Peace was demanded by O'Connell because he feared that if the military and the police were introduced they would only act as an intimidating influence on the side of the ascendancy.

The Beresfords in their election address to the electors complained of 'a few itinerant orators from a scarcely legal organisation' who were claiming the right to impose a representative on the legitimate electors of the county. The address also deplored the fact that the outside agitators were aided by a portion of the Roman catholic clergy which was subservient to the views of the association in Dublin.

The role of the clergy was admitted by both sides. *Freeman's Journal* claimed 'almost everything is owing to the catholic clergy'.[5] The *Dublin Evening Mail* complained that 'the tenants of his (Beresford's) friends with tears in their eyes, confess their absolute dread of eternal damnation if they vote against their clergy ... the priests are in every booth taking down the names of tenants who vote with their landlords against Stuart.'[6] At the end of the election when Beresford realised that he had been overwhelmed he lodged a formal protest claiming that freedom of election had been violated 'by intimidation and threats of evil censures and excommunication used by the catholic clergy'.[7] For seventy years a Beresford had invariably represented Waterford. In the 1826 election Beresford had received only 527 votes against Villiers Stuart's 1,357 when he conceded defeat with about 700 more votes still to be polled.

The contest in Waterford between Beresford and the catholic emancipation candidate ended the electoral stagnation that had existed down to that date. Election contests, or threatened contests, now became the norm during the second quarter of the nineteenth century. What followed in Waterford as a result of the 1826 election was the disruption and the dislocation of political power, and in due course this would spread to the rest of the constituencies. Although the Beresfords had been decidedly beaten, they were not, as is sometimes assumed, destroyed, but due notice of their final overthrow had been given.

Clare Election and Catholic Emancipation
Waterford was only the most dramatic of the 1826 election victories. In Louth, Monaghan and Westmeath also revolts of the forty-shilling freeholders against their landlords ensured the return of emancipation candidates. Victories for emancipationists in several other constituencies, where liberals had strong support, did not require the same widespread revolt. The 1826 elections marked the first general confrontation since the union on a political principle; earlier elections had been fought on the local rivalries of landlord factions. O'Connell and his colleagues in Dublin had formulated a national policy. The Catholic Association had supplied the political machine, and the catholic rent the finances, for the most significant of the election campaigns. The catholic clergy had shown themselves capable of challenging and even replacing the electoral influence of the landlords. The forty-shilling freeholders had been organised and had displayed their democratic power. And none of these lessons was lost on either the opponents or the supporters of emancipation, or, for that matter, on the authorities. Political organisation and the registration of voters now became the norm, and Liberal Clubs whose existence continued into the 1830s and '40s were established in several counties for these purposes.

It was against this background that the decision was taken to contest the by-election in Co. Clare in 1828. Vesey Fitzgerald, MP for the county, on being appointed by Wellington to the presidency of the board of trade was required to stand for re-election. Although the Fitzgeralds were popular landlords, and the MP was himself an advocate of emancipation, the Catholic Association was pledged to oppose the election of any Irish MP who supported the Wellington administration. What in the case of the Clare contest was even more radical than the challenge to Beresford in Waterford in 1826 was the sensational proposal of a catholic candidate — O'Connell himself. A catholic as such was not debarred from standing in a parliamentary election. But the oaths of supremacy and abjuration which were tendered at the bar of the house to the successful candidate could not be taken by a conscientious catholic. O'Connell was nominated as 'The Man of the People'. The leading orators of the Catholic Association converged on Clare. Thousands of the peasantry attended O'Connell's election meetings. No previous election in Ireland had witnessed such popular excitement. Despite the carnival atmosphere of the bands, dances and bonfires the assemblies were well-conducted and sober. The victory was decisive — 2,057 for O'Connell, 982 for Fitzgerald.

The power of the forty-shilling freehold voters had been demonstrated once again, and there was the threat that Clare could be repeated throughout the country. The prospect of the return of a party of Irish radicals to parliament, the overthrow of the protestant ascendancy and the possible paralysis of the government worried Wellington and Peel. What was also frightening was the threat of civil disorder. The passions of the people, which for the moment appeared to have been diverted by the Catholic Association from agrarian outrage to constitutional politics, might not be controlled indefinitely. To avert these dangers the concession of emancipation seemed a small price to pay.

Following the election of O'Connell on 5 July 1828 it was decided to prorogue parliament and to set up a committee on elections to enquire into whether O'Connell had been duly returned. This breathing space allowed Peel to deliberate on whether to concede or to continue with his hardline policy against emancipation. Ultimately he decided that to yield to the emancipation demand was the wiser policy. When parliament met on 5 February 1829, the king's speech recommended a review of the laws which imposed disabilities on his Roman catholic subjects. This was an indication that an Emancipation Bill was about to be introduced, so O'Connell travelled to London for the occasion. Before

Peel introduced emancipation he brought in a bill on 10 February 1829 to suppress the Catholic Association. But before the bill became law, O'Connell and his colleagues decided to dissolve the association voluntarily. In its final declaration on 12 February 1829, the association recorded its indebtedness to O'Connell and said that: 'he is entitled ... to the everlasting gratitude of Ireland.' On 5 March 1829 Peel introduced the Catholic Relief Bill, and on the same day the committee on elections reported O'Connell duly returned. In the house of lords Wellington explained that emancipation was necessary if civil war in Ireland was to be avoided. On 13 April 1829, the king reluctantly signed the bill, and the Relief Act came into operation the following day. O'Connell presented himself before the bar of the house of commons on 15 May to claim his seat under the new act, as a catholic could in good conscience take the new oath. He was refused on the grounds that the act was not retrospective. A couple of days later he was allowed to present a legal argument for admission, but his claim was negatived by 190 votes to 116. The old oaths were then tendered to him, but he refused to take them. The house then decided to issue a new writ for Clare, and in July 1829 O'Connell was again proposed and this time was returned unopposed. He took his seat under the terms of the new act in the house of commons on 4 February 1830 at the opening of the session.

'An Act for the relief of His Majesty's Roman Catholic subjects', as the Emancipation Act was called, repealed the oaths and declarations against transubstantiation, the saints and the mass as a qualification for parliament. Instead of the Oaths of Allegiance, Supremacy and Abjuration, a simple Oath of Allegiance was substituted, one which declared that the pope had no right to depose heretical monarchs; which accepted the land settlement that had conferred property on the protestant ascendancy in Ireland, and which stated that the person taking the oath would never exercise any privilege to disturb or weaken the protestant religion or protestant government in the United Kingdom. Under this act catholics were entitled to hold all offices except those of regent, chancellor and lord lieutenant. (The restriction on the lord lieutenant was removed in the Government of Ireland Act, 1920.) Roman catholics were also debarred from specified offices attached to ecclesiastical courts and establishments, cathedrals, universities and schools. The titles used by bishops, deans etc. in the established church were not to be used by Roman catholics. (A fine of £100 would be imposed for using such titles.) A Roman catholic holding office, judicial or civil, such as that of mayor, was not to appear in his robes of office at any religious ceremony other than in the established church. (The fine imposed for any breach of this article was £100 and loss of office.) The exercise of Roman catholic rites or ceremonies except in Roman catholic places of worship or private houses was forbidden. (Fine £50.) Another article of this Relief Act said that Jesuits were to be banished from the United Kingdom. (This, although long a dead letter, was not repealed until 1926.) Separate acts abolished the forty-shilling freehold vote in Ireland, and forbade the establishment of any new association in place of the Catholic Association.

On the debit side, therefore, the manner in which the Relief Act had been passed, the meanness of the limitations incorporated in it, and the restrictive accompanying acts earned no gratitude from the catholics of Ireland. On the credit side, this act had none of the 'wings' which had been attached to earlier emancipation bills such as the veto on the appointment of bishops, the inspection of correspondence between Rome and the bishops, or the payment of the clergy. Therefore, an unshackled clergy which had demonstrated its massive influence had emerged. Priests had been O'Connell's lieutenants, and because of the role which the church had played in this political issue 'catholic' had tended to become synonymous with 'Irish', and 'Irish' with 'catholic'. Prince Metternich, chancellor of the Austrian empire, described O'Connell's triumph in 1829 as a revolutionary performance covering itself with a religious mask. Dr Jebb, church of Ireland bishop of Limerick, said: 'in truth an Irish revolution has in great measure been effected'. He was indeed right to the extent that the priests' power had been substituted for that of the landlord. Catholic emancipation might have been graciously conceded; instead it had taught the Irish the lesson that concessions would only be made following massive organisation and agitation. The momentum which the emancipation campaign had engendered was not to be easily halted, but was likely to be carried into further campaigns against the tithes, or for reform, or even repeal of the Act of Union. For the achievement of emancipation was a victory for democracy over the king and his ministers, the house of lords and much of the establishment. The non-payment of the catholic clergy by the state ensured that the priests were left on the people's side. The men who controlled the chapel, pulpit and confessional determined to a large extent the public attitude. The government, therefore, had lost the opportunity which might have gained for it so much had it detached the priests from the people.

Decade of reform (1830–40)

In public letters issued in December 1829 and January 1830, O'Connell called upon the country to diminish irresponsible power, to establish popular rights, to crush aristocratic monopoly and to build up a system 'which shall secure for every man his right to select his representative, and to protect him by the secrecy of a ballot in the exercise of that selection'. He urged the people to create a new party. 'Everything and everybody', he said, 'has a party, save only the people. I go to parliament to form the party of the people. My motto is, and shall be, "For God and the people".' This amounted to a proclamation of a programme of democratic action. But the task he had set himself was a gigantic one of breaking the mould of the old system, of introducing far-reaching parliamentary reform and of creating a party of the people to press for his objectives in parliament.

It was at one time customary to regard the emancipation struggle of the 1820s and the repeal movement of the 1840s as the two great peaks of O'Connell's career. In both phases the emphasis was on extra-parliamentary organisation and on agitation, and there is no doubt about O'Connell's massive impact in these areas. The decade of the 1830s, on the other hand, when O'Connell's energies were concentrated on parliamentary activity in London, were looked upon as the valley years in between the peaks of emancipation and repeal. 'Ten years ... of barren labour', was how Seán O'Faoláin described the parliamentary career of O'Connell during this decade. P S O'Hegarty also stressed the barrenness of the policy of trying to get justice for Ireland in the English parliament. 'Ploughing the sands' is the title of the chapter covering the 1830s in Denis Gwynn's biography of O'Connell. And not one of the *Nine centenary essays*, edited by Michael Tierney, dealt specifically with the decade of O'Connell's parliamentary career. Yet, it is in this decade that the real O'Connell is revealed — the utilitarian pragmatist, the political opportunist.

In parliament O'Connell supported the radicals who did not belong to any party but pressed for various reforms. It is hardly surprising that O'Connell joined this group of independents since he had been greatly influenced by the radical philosophies of Godwin and Bentham. As a utilitarian he always agreed with Jeremy Bentham's dictum that the purpose of legislation was 'the greatest happiness of the greatest number'. He supported, too, the laissez-faire policies of Adam Smith. As a radical reformer, O'Connell gave his attention to all the great questions of the day, and was one of the most widely reported and controversial figures in the British parliament where, in his first year, 1831, he spoke three to four times a day on average during the session. He played an important role in the 1832 Reform Bill, and he advocated triennial parliaments, male suffrage, the secret ballot and an elective house of lords. He championed religious toleration and the abolition of capital punishment and flogging in the army, and he pressed for various reforms of the legal system.

The Act of Union had abolished many of the rotten boroughs that existed in the old Irish parliament, and had reduced the number of Irish MPs in Westminster to 100. Up to 1832 these parliamentary seats remained virtually the private property of individual patrons, and were bought, sold and inherited like any other property. This was particularly so in the case of the thirty-three boroughs. Many of these still fulfilled the function for which they had been originally intended when created in the seventeenth century, i.e. to give the crown or the administration a majority in parliament, or to bestow a reward or favour on friends and supporters. Irish 'pocket-boroughs' continued to be availed of in the early nineteenth century, and were sometimes used to further the careers of ambitious young English politicians including future prime ministers like Lord Goderich, who sat for Carlow (1806–1807), and Peel, who sat for Cashel (1809–12). A landlord's status in his own county depended upon winning the representation in parliament. The interest of the MPs tended to be social rather than sociological. The man who represented his county in parliament had many opportunities of advancing himself and his family. Contested elections were relatively rare and only took place when one landed interest challenged another's hegemony. Contests based on different attitudes to controversial issues were not usual.

The influence of the great landlord over the electorate was the result of a number of factors. Since normally there were no issues to interest the electorate there was much apathy, and the electorate might as well fall in with the wishes of the landlord and vote as required. There is also evidence of some loyalty to the local landlord. Open voting, which lasted down to 1872, tended to keep voters on the side of men who controlled their livelihood. There is not much evidence of eviction for going against the wishes of the landlord. But the custom of the 'hanging gale', which allowed a tenant to be in arrears with his rent, also allowed the landlord to impound cattle and other goods if not paid on demand. The fear of this kind of economic and social squeeze kept tenants in line with landlords' wishes. The returning officers at elections in the counties were the sheriffs, whose appointment in the first instance was due to the influence of the local landlord. The power of the sheriff at election time was considerable because he could accept or reject voters, or prolong or close the poll. In the general election of 1831 it was alleged that the sheriff in Co. Waterford 'a terrible Tory', was fitting out the jail to house or 'coop' (see p. 126) the Beresford voters, and was intending to break a passage between the jail and an adjoining store to facilitate them. Apart from the control which landlords held over the forty-shilling freeholders up to their disfranchisement in 1829, it was also possible for them to create fictitious freeholds, thus giving the vote to people who would be constrained to vote as directed by the landlord. Bribery and patronage were essential elements in the electoral system that survived well into the nineteenth century. The political system which was so controlled ensured what the ascendancy regarded as a certain stability in the constituencies up to the Waterford election of 1826, but which O'Connell would have described as stagnation. It was to change or reform this electoral and representative system that O'Connell threw all of his influence behind the movement for parliamentary reform in 1832.

The Reform Bill (1832), however, did not go nearly as far as he had wished. His intention was that any reform applied to Ireland would increase the representation and lower the qualification for the franchise. He argued that Irish representation at Westminster should be proportionate to the population, and pointed out how in this regard Ireland fared worse than either England or Scotland. A minimum of eleven and a maximum of forty-seven additional seats were demanded by O'Connell at different times during debates on reform. The act, however, added only five. (The boroughs of Belfast, Galway, Limerick and Waterford as well as Dublin University were each given a second seat.) O'Connell's principle of universal manhood suffrage was far from recognised in the terms of the act. Before the 1829 Disfranchisement Act accompanying emancipation, a forty-shilling freehold was the principal qualification for voters in the counties. This had given the vote to 216,000. The abolition of the forty-shilling freehold vote had reduced this figure to 37,000 at most.[8] Before 1832, the franchises in the boroughs were even more restrictive and varied considerably. In some the vote was restricted to members of corporations. In others, freemen and other categories also had the right to vote. But in about half of the thirty-three boroughs the patrons' control was so absolute that no election contests took place. Under the terms of the 1832 Reform Act the vote was not restored to the forty-shilling freeholders in the counties, but the £10 freehold was left as minimum requirement for the vote and extended to certain categories of leaseholders. The effect was to increase the number of electors in the counties to 60,000. The borough franchise was given to householders who held property of at least £10 annual valuation, although in some constituencies freemen and others retained their ancient rights. This produced about 29,000 electors in the borough constituencies. Compared with the English Reform Bill this outcome was disappointing. In England 1 in 24 of the inhabitants in the counties and 1 in 17 in the boroughs had the vote, whereas in Ireland the figures were 1 in 116 inhabitants in the counties, and 1 in 26 in the boroughs. The conservative nature of the reform was described by O'Connell as an 'insulting injustice', and it fell far short of introducing any strict uniformity into the electoral system. Although there was an increase in the numbers of voters the possibilities of bribery, corruption and impersonation remained high.

The result of the Reform Act can be seen in the effects which it had upon the fairly typical constituencies of Co. Carlow and the borough of Carlow. In the case of the county, out of eleven parliamentary elections between the Union and 1832 only three were contested, and the representatives were normally members of the leading landlord families. Out of ten elections held for the county in the twenty years following the reform of 1832, eight were contested. In the case of the borough of Carlow, thirteen burgesses had the right to elect the member of parliament. Many of these burgesses were related to each other, and were controlled by the patron of the constituency, the earl of Charleville. So, before the Reform Act of 1832, election contests in the borough were non-existent. After the Reform Act there were 278 electors for the borough. Lord Charleville's burgesses, who resided within seven miles of the town and were registered, continued to have a vote, and this left a number of votes in his power. But the admission of the £10 householders to the parliamentary vote changed the scene and encouraged contests. Out of the seven elections held for the borough between 1832 and 1852 all but one were contested.

Before 1832, the vast majority of the Irish MPs in Westminster were tory-conservative. After 1832 liberals and repealers were able to challenge the tory dominance. And this gave rise to the creation of very effective party machines in the constituencies, to the practice of the registration of voters, to numerous cases of intimidation and corruption during the contests, and to legal petitions afterwards.

Despite its faults and the conservative nature of the Reform Bill, the new electoral system introduced by emancipation and reform opened up greater possibilities than had been imagined. The liberals who had promoted emancipation in the 1820s became the natural allies of the

Irish catholics in the 1830s and '40s. The Reform Act allowed the alliance of catholic democracy and liberals to break the tory-conservative ascendancy that had held sway during the first thirty years of the nineteenth century.

O'Connell's Party

Following emancipation and reform, O'Connell launched a nationwide attack on the protestant control of the Irish parliamentary seats. In the general election of 1832 his repeal party won 39 seats (liberals 36, conservatives 29). Of the 39 MPs in O'Connell's party 26 were catholic and 13 protestant. O'Connell's own family elected to parliament in 1832 included three sons, two sons-in-law, one brother-in-law and one cousin. A fourth son and a nephew were elected in 1835. So the core of the party consisted of O'Connell's own family, close friends and allies.

The thirty-nine returned in 1832 was the biggest number ever to be returned for O'Connell's party. The number is inflated since it would be difficult to say that all were sincere repealers. The bandwagon of emancipation and reform had carried them into parliament. In 1834 repeal was tested by a vote in the house of commons and was utterly routed (523 to 38), and thereafter O'Connell concentrated on 'good government' as opposed to 'home government' as being the more realistic policy. He said: 'I am opposed to repeal if justice is done to Ireland'; and on another occasion he said he was ready to become a West Briton if justice were done, if not he would become an Irishman again. The representatives who had allegedly supported repeal dropped in numbers. At the next general election in 1835 he headed a party of 32. In 1837 this had dropped to 31, and in 1841 it had fallen to 18. By 1847 it had recovered and was up to 35. Yet it was during this time that his party became more cohesive, its effectiveness if anything increased, and the 'party-machine' functioned throughout the country. The Waterford and Clare elections had been individual or spot victories for democracy, but in the 1830s and '40s party politics involved the whole country, and the party machine was applied in each general election. Many who had been emancipationists separated themselves from O'Connell after 1829. Wyse never even pretended to be a repealer, and ended his career as ambassador to Greece. Richard Lalor Sheil, only nominally a repealer, sat for Tipperary from 1832 to 1841, all the time advancing his career until he ended up as minister at the Court of Tuscany. The propagandist, Thomas Moore, who had advocated emancipation was not prepared to press for repeal. And Bishop Doyle argued that the priority should be an attack on the tithe system rather than repeal of the union. These and liberal protestants showed no concern to press home the victory of democracy over the ascendancy.

O'Connell's more active supporters among the clergy, however, were determined to make no compromise. Fr Sheehan led 'the party of the people' in Waterford, kept O'Connell informed of local political developments and acted generally as his agent. He continually warned O'Connell against the 'miserable wretches' who fawned about him in public, but who were privately trying to stab him in the back, including Wyse and Sheil. When Sheil was campaigning for election in Louth, Fr Sheehan threatened to get the priests there to advise the rejection of a man who had roused the forty-shilling freeholders in Waterford against the landlords and who was now, once emancipation was achieved, ready to enter an alliance with the ascendancy class.

At the time of the general election of 1835 O'Connell was pushing an anti-tory association, and was concerned to form an anti-tory electoral alliance between his own repealers and Irish whigs and liberals. He persuaded Fr Sheehan to support the anti-tory candidates although they were not committed to repeal. 'In doing so', the loyal Sheehan commented, 'I make a very great sacrifice of feeling.' To prevent a return to power of the tories and the reinstatement of tory ascendancy in Ireland, a coalition of national and liberal interests had been brought together in closed ranks. In 1826 O'Connell and his Waterford friends like Fr Sheehan had been elated at winning a single seat from the Beresfords. By 1835 all five seats in Waterford (two in the county, two in the borough and one in Dungarvan) were won by anti-tories, most of whom were catholics. The great strides taken towards reform and democratic representation were perhaps nowhere in Ireland highlighted so clearly as they were in the politics of Waterford.

Although political activity in Waterford had its own local colour what had happened there in the struggle between democracy and ascendancy was not untypical of what was taking place in the country generally. The operation of O'Connell's policy of anti-tory coalition, the effectiveness of the party machine and the role played by the clergy in electoral politics stand out most prominently in local studies. Take the case of parliamentary elections in Carlow during the 1830s. In this county a vigorous Independent Club had been formed to organise support for O'Connell's candidates, and to break the control of the Bruens and Kavanaghs who were related and led the powerful resident tory gentry in the area. The Independent Club chose as its candidates for the county constituency a catholic repealer and a protestant liberal.

Bishop Doyle's priests, especially Fr James Maher, threw themselves actively into the campaign, organising the £10 freeholders. The most interesting thing about the election was the remarkable instance of ticket-voting. O'Connell's candidates got 657 votes each. Bruen and Kavanagh got 483 and 470 respectively. These figures could only mean that the freeholders had voted strictly according to plan, and rigidly along party lines. This end product of the party political machine was reproduced again and again in later elections. (See Table 1).

County Carlow carried out this practice of ticket-voting more successfully and rigidly than any other constituency in Ireland. This kind of closely contested election demanded thorough party organisation and commitment. In the 1841 election, for example, O'Connell, the local priests and repealers from headquarters toured the county, holding public meetings in every town. O'Connell advocated that a Liberal Club be established in every village. He requested that his election address be read to every voter and a copy left for his perusal. All who had votes were to be registered, and those who had none were to canvass voters incessantly. Anyone who persevered in supporting Bruen was to be treated as a 'black sheep' even in the church, avoided like a pestilence, scorned by his neighbour and no honest young man was to marry the daughter of a 'black sheep'. During his tour of the constituency O'Connell was reported to have been escorted by as many as fifteen or sixteen thousand horsemen, met by temperance bands, clergymen and deputations from neighbouring towns and counties. Public confessions were stage-managed at which former supporters of the tories asked O'Connell's and God's forgiveness. The pageantry, carnival atmosphere, excitement and political involvement were captured in the procession into Carlow town on fair day. The parade headed by a band included a large, jolly, well-dressed and well-fed fellow carrying a pole with a very large loaf and a banner with the motto 'O'Connell — Peace and Plenty'. A starved-looking, miserable dwarf held a pole with a very small loaf and a banner which read: 'Bruen — Starvation and Desolation'. The big fellow was carried in triumph into the town, the dwarf was carried on a stretcher.

The ticket-voting that took place in the constituency throughout the 1830s gave rise to the practice of 'cooping'. This meant that supporters of the rival parties had to be cooped up safely together for days before election day, and then herded under escort to the polling booths. Upwards of 200 voters who were tenants of Bruen's father-in-law, Kavanagh, were 'kidnapped' and housed secretly in Borris House. A second group was also locked up in the vicinity and protected by

Table 1

population 1831 72,564	CARLOW COUNTY (2 MPs)		electorate 1832 1,246
year	candidates	political affiliation	votes polled
1832	Walter Blackney	R	657
	Thomas Wallace, K.C.	L	657
	Col. Henry Bruen	C	483
	Thomas Kavanagh	C	470
1835	Col. Henry Bruen	C	588
	Thomas Kavanagh	C	587
	Maurice O'Connell	L(R)	554
	Michael Cahill	L(R)	553
	On petition Bruen and Kavanagh unseated and new writ issued		
1835	N. A. Vigors	L(R)	627
	Alexander Raphael	L	626
	Thomas Kavanagh	C	572
	Col. Henry Bruen	C	571

On petition Vigors and Raphael unseated and Kavanagh and Bruen declared elected, 19 Aug. 1835; poll amended and 105 votes for Vigors and Raphael struck off

1837	on death of Kavanagh		
	N. A. Vigors	L(R)	669
	Thomas Bunbury	C	633
1837	N. A. Vigors	L(R)	730
	J. A. Yates	L	730
	Col. Henry Bruen	C	643
	Thomas Bunbury	C	643
	Despite a petition the result was allowed to stand		
1840	on death of Vigors		
	Col. Henry Bruen	C	722
	Hon. Frederick Ponsonby	L	555
1841	Col. Henry Bruen	C	705
	Thomas Bunbury	C	704
	J. A. Yates	L	697
	Daniel O'Connell (jun.)	R	696

R: *repealer* L: *liberal* C: *conservative*.
Source: Brian Walker, *Parliamentary election results in Ireland, 1801–1922*, p. 256.

infantry from going off to listen to O'Connell. Bruen held a third group in the club house in Carlow where, according to the repealers, they were feasted with the best and offered every temptation to break their teetotal pledge. The repealers organised the wives, daughters and sisters of the 'kidnapped' to remove their shoes and stockings and converge on Borris House, and there to 'caoin' night and day until their menfolk were released. One woman tried to intimidate her husband by returning her children to him. The women prevailed; and one report stated that 'the sepulchre opened and the morally dead were restored to life while O'Connell was talking in Carlow'.

The repealers, too, practised 'cooping' on a large scale. For three weeks before the 1841 election 120 freeholders were housed in a Kilkenny brewery by O'Connell's allies. During the day they were entertained by temperance bands, at night they were harangued by political speeches, and at all times they were wined and dined most sumptuously. Strong Kilkenny lads provided a guard which prevented both invasions and desertions. Then on election day the 'caged birds' were brought to Carlow in a procession which was headed by the leading agitator, followed by a band, and then the voters followed by a guard. On each side of the procession was an escort.

O'Connell's pragmatic approach to politics was well illustrated by his involvement in the Carlow elections. To break the stranglehold of the local ascendancy, he was prepared to make use of every human weapon to hand. He used local liberal protestants, he promoted repealers from outside the county, and he imported English whigs. As the government had used the Irish boroughs to place their English supporters in parliament during the early decades after the union, O'Connell in the two decades after reform was often prepared to introduce Englishmen into Irish constituencies in his battle to defeat the powerful Orange faction. Elections and post-election petitions were costly, and this was one reason why O'Connell had to come to an arrangement with English liberals who could afford the contest. Some idea of the kind of money involved in putting forward a candidate can be gauged from the case of Alexander Raphael, who ran for the county in 1835. The arrangement made between O'Connell and Raphael was that Raphael would put up £1,000 before the election and another £1,000 after it, provided he was elected. Although he won the election, Raphael was slow to pay the second £1,000 because the validity of a number of votes was to be investigated. Not only did Raphael eventually pay over all of the £2,000 which went on election expenses, but he was faced with further legal expenses in defending his election against petition. To add to his trouble, Raphael was unseated as a result of the petition, and to rub salt into his wounds, O'Connell failed to procure for him a baronetcy from his whig allies. O'Connell, too, had left himself open to the charge which his enemies were quick to make, i.e. that he had virtually sold a seat in parliament to an outsider. Elections in Carlow cost O'Connell, personally, a good deal of money, for he had sponsored his two sons, Maurice and Daniel, unsuccessfully as candidates for the county in 1835 and 1841 respectively.

The human instruments which O'Connell had used to break tory landlord control in the Irish constituencies may not have been the most ideal; and the methods used during elections may have been no more virtuous than those which were employed by O'Connell's enemies. But they worked. No Bruen was elected for Carlow borough after 1839, and in the county constituency, although Bruen was not routed, his monopoly was challenged and indeed broken. As Fr Maher put it after one election in the 1830s:

> it is now evident that the people have the power in their hands of choosing their own representative. The road to a seat in the legislature is henceforth open to the best friend of the people. It is closed against all others. The key to the House of Commons is now in the hands of the people, which key had too long lain in the breeches pocket of the aristocrats. This is a mighty advantage. The highest court in the realm shall no longer be encumbered by a cohort of aristocratic incapables; or polluted by the presence of boroughmongers, or placemen, or the nominees of any party ... The reform bill has conferred upon the people the power of sending their friends to parliament and of leaving their conservative neighbours at home ... The difference ... between an aristocrat and a popular member of parliament is that the former is always for things as they are; the latter seeks a change for the better ... The victory ... establishes the fact that the people can send whom they please to parliament [and this] has shaken this vicious system, and laid the foundation of a better order of things.[9]

So, behind all the petty squabbles, the intimidation, the venality and corruption and the ballyhoo of local electoral politics, great issues were indeed at stake, and great forces of conservatism and change in Irish society were contending with each other for supremacy — even though the participants in the local skirmishes were generally unaware of all that was involved. Two opposing concepts of politics had been at loggerheads with each other. There was the older view represented by the ascendancy that parliamentary seats were the private property of the local aristocratic families. And this view was opposed by the more novel, reforming and radical notions which insisted that representation should be based upon population figures, and civil rights, and upon democratic ideas of liberty and equality. The local aristocracy defending the *status quo* found itself challenged by extraneous ideas and outside agitators aided by the local catholic clergy organising those who felt themselves oppressed. It was this confused and far from clearly defined conflict of ideas about private property and representative government that influenced local electoral politics in the early nineteenth century.

The onslaught on Waterford and Carlow in the 1830s and 1840s was not just an attack on the private property of the Beresfords and Bruens in the form of their hereditary seats. Victory over them was seen as no less than a most significant capture of a citadel of the old political order. It was the defeat of entrenched aristocracy by the new democracy. The country had experienced, through these elections, the first landslip in the move from aristocratic government to democratic representation. In all this fever of electioneering can be seen the emergence of the habit of democratic politics, and the gradual, uneven and complex transformation of catholic peasants into citizens and Irishmen.

Terry Alts

Two of the most disturbed counties in Ireland in the early 1830s were Co. Clare, shortly after it had returned O'Connell in the historic by-elections of 1828 and 1829, and Queen's County, much of which lay in JKL's diocese of Kildare and Leighlin. Was this simply ironic coincidence, or a case of direct cause and effect due to the close connection of O'Connell with Clare and Doyle with Queen's County? The fresh outbursts of organised crime in these two counties were associated with the emergence of new secret societies — in Clare the Terry Alts, sometimes known as the Lady Clares, and in Queen's County the Whitefeet and Blackfeet.

'There is but one real enemy to Ireland and that is the man who violates the law', O'Connell had declared in January 1827. And he continued to condemn the crimes of secret societies throughout the emancipation campaign, the tithe war and the repeal agitation. The fact that O'Connell's moral force campaigns made vast progress did not necessarily mean that agrarian crime and secret conspiracies totally disappeared. In fact the moral force campaigns and agrarian violence seemed at times to add strength to each other. Almost by way of compensation the more agrarian violence spread the greater the efforts

O'Connell made to substitute moral force. And there was little doubt in the minds of O'Connell's enemies that the greater his success over the ascendancy the more daring became the peasantry as if reflecting his glory in their own violent way.

Disturbance in Co. Clare was threatening to erupt since 1827 and even during the election years of 1828 and '29. It eventually became widespread throughout the county from January to June 1831. There were those, therefore, who rushed forward with the suggestion that the peasant disorders were a direct consequence of extravagant expectations being unfulfilled in the wake of the emancipation victory. Orange spokesmen, frightened magistrates and tory newspapers attributed the disturbances to O'Connellite politics. The *Dublin Evening Mail*, (with which the conservative *Clare Journal*, 28 February 1831, agreed), complained that from the hour that O'Connell and his baneful principles gained a footing in the county, from the moment that magistrates became powerless and priests politicians, a revolution was wrought in the minds of the peasantry, and they were called upon to break every tie that bound them to the gentry, the landlord and the magistrates. The Catholic Association, the priesthood and the press, it was said, had taught them to believe themselves as slaves, their landlords as oppressors, and their liberation to lie in their own hands. Was it surprising, therefore, following their disappointment that they should have resorted to rebellion? Supporters of the popular movement saw it differently. In this view the peasantry had been provoked into a desperate revolt by the backlash of a protestant ascendancy, determined to punish the peasantry by ejectment orders, non-renewals of leases and increased rents for having transferred their political allegiance to the priests and O'Connell. Although both interpretations of the Terry Alt disturbances were too extreme, each contained elements of truth.

An enthusiastic agent, by the name of Edward Synge, sought to introduce into the Corofin area of Co. Clare improvements in cultivation and protestant schooling. With the help of the London Hibernian Society he opened three schools for the purpose of proselytising the children of his catholic tenants. He also recruited preachers for his evangelical crusade until bibles, it was said, became as plentiful as blackberries in this county. This led to a confrontation with the parish priest, which convulsed the parish and beyond for years in the late 1820s and into the 1830s, with the tenants caught in the middle of this battle for souls between their land agent and their priest. The schools were burnt, shots were fired into the agent's home, quit notices were served on tenants who refused to send their children to the schools, those who did were ostracised by their neighbours and attacks were made on individuals sometimes with fatal consequences. An attack was made on one of Synge's servants coming from church on a Sunday in 1829. It was said that the only description of the attacker was that he was wearing a straw hat. The next man on the scene wearing a straw hat was an inoffensive shoemaker by the name of Terry Alt. It became a standing joke that 'Terry Alt' was not only responsible for this assault but also for the increasing number of conspiracies then taking place in Clare. More familiar names (Ribbonmen, Whiteboys, Rockites) were occasionally associated with this new outbreak in the county. Contemporary names (Whitefeet) were also transferred from other areas (Queen's County). 'Lady Clares' was an imaginative local variant for those who were disguised in female dress. But the name of 'Terry Alt' became the most popular label for the agrarian activity which culminated in the general disturbance in Clare in the first half of 1831.

The initial sectarianism of the situation around Corofin was soon caught up in the politics of emancipation and of the county elections. As it happened the parish priest was also one of the foremost clerics in the Catholic Association, so the association was used to mobilise public opinion against Synge and to provide legal aid and financial compensation for those who suffered hardship in the struggle. Medals of the Order of Liberators, which O'Connell had first conferred on freeholders who had suffered because of their resistance to Beresford in the Waterford election, were awarded to those who promised to keep their children from Synge's schools. The sectarian and political aspects were further complicated during the excitement of registering voters for the three Clare elections in 1828, 1829 and 1830. O'Connell's electioneering visits to the county increased this tension.

Although the widespread peasant violence which erupted in 1831 had this sectarian and political content it was largely the result of economic and agrarian causes. The price of corn and of livestock had slumped simultaneously in 1830, and traditionally agrarian unrest had coincided with troughs in prices as in the early 1820s. The labour involved in grain-growing was expensive to the farmer, so he tended, when prices were low, to concentrate on grazing instead. In a region like Clare where impoverished smallholders formed a greater percentage of the rural population, and where the population grew more rapidly than elsewhere, the pressure on potato land was greatest. Non-agricultural work was particularly scarce in the county. Spinning, which had helped in the rural economy, had declined, and whereas there had been between 50 and 100 legal licensed malt houses at the end of the eighteenth century, none of these was in existence by the 1820s.

There were acute shortages of food in 1830. Want and destitution made the peasantry desperate. Neither the warnings of the magistrates nor the pleas of their priests could calm their discontents or control their fury once aroused. The demands of the peasantry arose quite clearly out of a land hunger for the potato garden. The most general cause of the violence was the scarcity of conacre, or where this was available, the inflated rent demanded for it. Other causes were not unrelated to this and included under-employment, dispossession, high rents and the desire to regulate wages.

Between January and June 1831 it seemed as if the entire county was in a state of rebellion. Over twenty murders were committed in those six months. Among them was a magistrate, William Blood, who was battered to death. Edward Synge whose sectarianism, politics and oppression had made him a natural target, narrowly escaped death when a bullet intended for his heart was deflected by a bible! His servant, however, was fatally wounded. Five policemen were surrounded and killed. And hundreds of crimes in less serious categories were committed — beating, robbery of arms, attacks on houses, illegal assemblies, administering of oaths, illegal notices and damage to property. Among the most prevalent and revealing crimes associated with the Terry Alts were the turning-up of grazing land and the levelling of fences. Hundreds of peasants were organised for these large scale diggings, which emphasised the scarcity of conacre, and were intended to ensure that the land would be used only for the tillage of potatoes. These desperate peasants felt that they had a better right to the land than had the cattle or sheep of the graziers. The levelling of walls and fences, the injury done to stock, the churning up of pastures and the assaults on herdsmen indicated the social nature of an insurrection which was the worst and most widespread in the county since 1798, and aroused similar fears among the ascendancy. Although men of property were the object of the Terry Alt attacks, it was their servants who were the more vulnerable. Many of the victims were herdsmen. Much of the hostility of the Terry Alts was directed against the payers of heavy rents rather than against the extractors of them. As in much of the other early nineteenth-century agrarian disturbances the struggle was between the labourer and the farmer rather than between the landlord and farmer as was to be the case in the later nineteenth century. No direct hostility to the government was exhibited by these social rebels. And tithes, which were then a chief grievance in much of Ireland, caused little disturbance in Clare. A special commission dealt swiftly with those arrested on criminal charges, and executions and many transportation sentences dealt effectively with the perpetrators of violence, even if little was done to remove its causes.

O'Connell acted as counsel for some of the insurgents on the grounds that everyone had the right to be defended. He also felt that as counsel he would have the opportunity to go among them, induce them to surrender their arms (which some of them did) and persuade them to return to the ways of law and order. During a parliamentary debate (April 1831), O'Connell emphasised the contribution which absentee landlords had made to poverty in Clare, and suggested that the relief of the poor might be financed out of a tax on absentees and on the property of the established church.

Tithe War and Whitefeet
Coinciding with the Terry Alt trouble in Clare was the Whitefeet violence in Queen's County and Kilkenny. This was in an area closely associated with the origins of the anti-tithe agitation, and the Whitefeet, unlike the Terry Alts, listed tithes among their grievances.

In most of the agrarian uprisings from the time of the Whiteboys in the 1760s down to the Whitefeet in the 1830s tithes had been a permanent cause of agitation. It bore heaviest on tillage farmers since pasture and its produce were exempt. Tithe was levied throughout Ireland on wheat, oats, barley and hay (except in Galway). In Munster, Connaught and four counties of Leinster potatoes were also subject to tithe. And in Leinster sheep and lambs also came under this tax. Ulster got off lighter than the southern provinces. Middle-class catholics, like O'Connell and Bishop Doyle, objected to the payment of tithe mainly on religious and liberal grounds. They objected to the inequity of catholics having to pay an additional tax for the upkeep of the 'heretical' but richly endowed established church which catered for a minority. O'Connell told the government: 'You take from the poor man often in time of scarcity his tenth potato for that church'.[10] Dr Doyle argued that when tithes were first established by the Anglo-Normans in Ireland one third of their produce was set apart for the support of the poor. Now, commented O'Connell, not a single shilling was appropriated for that purpose.[11] In his campaign against tithe O'Connell liked to highlight specific examples of glaring inequity. Pointing to the bishopric of Derry, which he claimed was worth £25,000 or £30,000 per annum to the incumbent and possessed as well 96,000 acres of arable land, he commented: 'It was enough to breed discontent to see this immense wealth poured into the lap of one clergyman while thousands of the poor peasantry around were starving'.[12] On another occasion he named six parishes where not one protestant lived and yet 17,000 catholics, he claimed, in these same parishes were billed for tithe. In another speech in parliament he said that in one parish near Dublin there lived a single protestant who was happy to attend church in nearby Maynooth and got on well with his catholic neighbours. Despite two petitions from him to parliament stating that he did not need a new church, one was forced on him at the expense of the catholics.[13]

The objections of the catholic farmers to tithes were essentially on agrarian and economic grounds. In this case tithes were seen as an extension of rents, and the opposition to one often involved opposition to the other. Tithe, according to the law, had to be paid before the landlord's rent, and in Ireland those who failed to pay either usually had their stock and goods seized. Tithe was thus seen to be very much part of the oppressive land system. Nor did it ease relations between the people and the established church that some of the clergy in attempting to get their tithes were seen to act like tyrannical magistrates and landlords. Many too were absentees who paid curates a portion of the tithe to perform their duties in a parish so that curates, tithe proctors and tithe farmers resembled all of those middlemen who stood between a tenant and the landlord with each having to have a commission. That some of the resident clergy were proselytising evangelicals only served to arouse the hostility of the local catholics. And when the Tithe Composition Acts (of 1832 and 1834) allowed for a money payment to be substituted by parish agreement, it was felt by those with whom money was in any case always scarce that the opportunity was taken to demand an increase in tithe prices, especially where the value had been determined by averages based on years of good harvests.

The anti-tithe agitation of the 1830s began in Graiguenamanagh on the borders of Kilkenny and Carlow. Here a proselytising protestant curate, acting as tithe proctor, distrained the cattle of the catholic priest. By November 1830 the priest's bishop, Dr Doyle, had organised resistance to the payment of what he condemned as an unjust tax. In neighbouring Queen's County, Doyle's friend, Patrick Lalor of Tenakill, supporter of O'Connell and father of James Fintan Lalor, announced his refusal ever again to pay tithe. When his sheep were driven away, he had them branded with the word 'Tithe' so that no one would buy them. This system of passive resistance spread widely especially through Queen's County, Kilkenny and Wexford at first, and then throughout the rest of Ireland, and as it did it was closely related to agrarian conditions.

Lalor argued that since the law stated he should pay the tithe or suffer the consequences of distraint of his goods, he had been given an option, and he elected for distraint rather than voluntary payment. This method of resistance also had the backing of O'Connell. He argued in parliament that people could refuse to pay tithe and refuse also to buy goods taken as a penalty for the refusal and still not break the law. And he defied parliament to make a law compelling people to purchase what they did not wish to buy. This policy forced the government to use both police and military in the collection of tithe. Over 11,000 decrees were issued against defaulters in Queen's County alone in the year from June 1832 to June 1833; 43,000 decrees were issued throughout the country, and only £12,000 was collected at a cost of £26,000. By 1833 more than half (over £800,000) of the total amount of tithes demanded was owed in arrears since 1831. The most extensive passive resistance took place in the south-east and the south of the country although all parts were affected by this policy of non-payment.

Where police and military were used on the side of what was generally regarded as an unjust tax, and where the resistance had the strong backing of a wide range of liberal and anti-nationalist politicians and catholic church leaders, there existed only a very thin line between moral and physical resistance. And indeed, that line was soon crossed. In June 1831 at Newtownbarry in Co. Wexford, twelve people were killed when a force of yeomanry fired into a crowd of peasantry who were protesting against the sale of cattle seized for tithe by a local rector. This massacre was followed by serious collisions between police and peasantry in Westmeath and Kilkenny. At Carrickshock in Kilkenny, a party of police and soldiers was ambushed and eleven or twelve killed. These were only the most dramatic incidents in what had now become a tithe war. Impartially, O'Connell condemned the peasant violence and accused the government of murder. Many of the traditional features of the secret societies reappeared — threatening notices with pictures of coffins, intimidations, attacks on property, houghing of cattle, burnings and assaults on tithe proctors. So much so that it became very difficult to separate traditional agrarianism from tithe resistance. This was particularly evident in the case of the Whitefeet and Blackfeet in Queen's County.

In the early 1820s when Rockites and Ribbonmen were active it was not easy for a town like Maryborough, situated as it was between Dublin and Limerick, to escape being infected by the travelling organisers of the secret societies. The men who had come in with the new canals and the miners in the populous plateau in the Kilkenny/Queen's County/Carlow border-area were also regarded as carriers of infectious insurrectionary ideas. This colliery district of the Leinster coalfield was an area of about fifteen miles by ten, lying on the high ground between the towns of Carlow, Castlecomer, Abbeyleix, Portlaoise and Stradbally. The population of the plateau had grown rapidly since the first decade of the nineteenth century when the canal companies and other private owners began working their collieries in the area. Newtown, in the heart of this district, was built by the Canal Company and had streets with cabins where the colliers lived. Cabins were studded thickly all over the entire district which was sub-divided into numerous small holdings by bad fences. A local magistrate believed that the area possibly had a greater population density than any other part of rural Ireland known to him. There was a tradition of violence in the area especially in hard times. Two gentlemen who had opened a colliery here took a farm by outbidding the local undertenants. One hundred persons assembled and burned down their premises. And an overseer from England, named Potts, had been murdered in 1831 because he had tried to introduce economies and new methods of working. In the evidence given before a select committee it was claimed that numerous people in the colliery district had been sworn into the Whitefeet. (The amazing figure, 9,000, was printed in the report. Even if this is a misprint for 900 the figure is still a staggering one.)

A strong tradition of sectarian trouble also existed in the towns of Mountmellick and Mountrath where orangeism was strong, and provocative parades were held. And in a county in which the liberal Henry Parnell was senior MP and Doyle was the bishop, there was bound to be much political activity and excitement.

The situation in Queen's County, therefore, was compounded of economic depression among the colliers, agrarian grievances mixed with sectarianism and heightened political activity. In 1827, twenty-seven families were evicted for not attending a Kildare Place school, and further ejectments from other estates turned people towards secret organisations. At a meeting of one of these secret societies white stockings were worn by the leader of the group. White stockings, therefore, became an emblem of the society which was initially called 'Whitelegs' and later became known as 'Whitefeet'. Their activities were characteristically Whiteboy as distinct from Ribbon in that they were essentially agrarian and not sectarian or political. Even the name which they adopted was reminiscent of the Whiteboy tradition. The principal object of the Whitefeet, according to Fr Nicholas O'Connor, was to keep possession of their lands. Matthew Barrington, who had seventeen years' experience as crown solicitor on the Munster circuit, agreed and said that he regarded the outrages committed by the Whitefeet as belonging to the same tradition of agrarian violence going back to the Whiteboys in the 1760s. The objects, he said, had always been connected more or less with the land. 'I have traced the origins of almost every case I prosecuted, and I find that they generally arise from the attachment to, the dispossession of, or the change in the possession of land'.[14] Among the subsidiary reasons he gave were: hatred of the tithe proctors, high prices, want of employment, lack of potato ground, and the introduction of migrant workers. He emphasised that the origins of these disturbances were simply agrarian, or arose from the misery associated with unemployment. He stated that those engaged in the outrages were the lowest occupiers of land and farmers' sons. Fr O'Connor made the interesting comment:

> I have often heard their conversations, when they say, 'What good did the emancipation do us? Are we better clothed or fed, or our children better clothed or fed? Are we not as naked as we were, and eating dry potatoes when we can get them? Let us notice the farmers to give us better food and better wages, and not give so much to the landlord and more to the workmen; we must not let them be turning the poor people off the ground.'[15]

The parish priest also claimed that labourers who had returned from England provoked the men by saying: 'If you saw the way that the English labourers lived you would never live as you do.'[16] And they were told by a person who came from another part of the country that they managed things a great deal better elsewhere by joining a secret society. They were then brought to a sheebeen and seduced into the Whitefoot system.

The Whitefeet and Blackfeet were considered initially to have been united in a single society against the Orangemen. Then the Whitefeet combined for agrarian purposes to lower the rent and to raise wages. Those who refused to join were known as Blackfeet. They formed two separate factions, and whereas the Whitefeet formed themselves into an oath-bound secret society, the Blackfeet merely pledged themselves to each other. The two groups represented in many ways the continuation of the earlier feud between the Shanavests and Caravats which had spread from Tipperary and Kilkenny into Queen's County.

The feuding was similar, even down to the point where Whitefeet believed that Blackfeet were informers. This latest outburst of outrage coincided with the tithe agitation and, no doubt, overlapped in so far as some of the Whitefeet outrages were committed in connection with tithe.

Dr Doyle's sympathy with the destitute, the hungry and ragged among his people was profound, and he regarded their complaints against the social system as just. He condemned a legislature which had neglected the grievances of the poor, allowing land agents and tithe proctors to descend on them in successive waves like locusts to devour the entire fruit of their industry, and leaving their children a prey to evangelicals. Should their blood go unrevenged, he warned, 'we need no Pastorini to foretell the result'.[17] On the other hand Dr Doyle conducted something of a crusade against secret societies in his diocese, and his condemnation of the Whitefeet was unequivocal. He said they were not only wrong, but harmed the people whom they purported to help. Revenge, he preached to them, was reserved exclusively to God. Doyle's pastoral of 1831 exhorted the Whitefeet and Blackfeet to follow peaceful ways. He held out before them as a model to follow the constitutional and legal means employed by O'Connell in winning emancipation. If, therefore, the objectives of the secret societies were to remove injustice and oppression, he urged them to be sober, to be united by affection but not by oaths, to obey the law, to desist from secret combinations and to seek redress for the evils pressing upon them by constitutional methods. As one remedy for the evils which resulted from rack-rents, evictions and unemployment he advocated a poor law system which would make provision for the poor to protect them against famine and disease. Let every man, therefore, he urged in his pastoral, petition parliament to enact a legal provision for the poor. Tithes, 'this devouring impost', he said, ought to be opposed not with violence or secret societies but, nevertheless, 'with all the means which the law allows'. So, according to Bishop Doyle, the remedy for Ireland's social ills was to be sought by an organised democracy agitating by constitutional means. In this and other pastorals Doyle had given the church's blessing to democracy in Ireland.

There were those, therefore, as O'Connell said, who would always be found to ascribe the causes of outrage to the interference of Dr Doyle and his catholic clergy.[18] A short time later a witness told a select committee on the state of Ireland that: 'Priest Doyle and the demogogues of the country', by exciting the people against tithe, were the cause of the agrarian disturbances.[19] This witness was convinced that, after O'Connell, Dr Doyle was one of the greatest enemies that the country had, and he was certain that the priests had directly encouraged the Whitefeet. Few other witnesses agreed with this view of Doyle, who among all of the bishops had been the most forthcoming in his condemnation of the secret societies in his pastorals and public letters and in his sermons during visitations to parishes throughout his diocese. The select committee in its report acknowledged that not only had the bishop censured the Whitefeet and Blackfeet in letters read on two successive Sundays at all the masses in the diocese, but he had also called for the setting up of an armed vigilante association to protect persons and property in concert with the constituted authorities. The plan was that the well disposed of every class would unite in their own defence, patrol the country by night and day, detect, apprehend or terrify into better habits the evil doers, and that those who persisted could be safely dismissed from their employment. Edmund Burke's well-known dictum had declared: 'When bad men combine, the good must associate else they will fall one by one an unpitied sacrifice in a contemptible struggle'. In a phrase reminiscent of Burke, Bishop Doyle wrote: 'Such union of the good and virtuous ... could not fail to preserve and to re-establish order, and to suppress every unlawful combination'.[20]

Although the bigots misrepresented the role of O'Connell, Doyle and the catholic clergy, Baron Sir William Smith in his charge to the grand jury of Queen's County in 1832 was perhaps nearer the mark. Listing the variety of crimes which appeared on the calendar of 150 cases before him, he pointed out how easily disorder can shift its purpose and course and after threatening one line of outrage proceed upon another. With the leaders of the campaign of moral resistance in mind, he advised them to be cautious lest by encouraging the discontented feelings of the populace they inadvertently raise a force, the direction of which must be uncertain. The point was not lost on Dr Doyle, who a few years earlier in October 1828 in a letter to the parish priest of Maryborough had expressed his doubts about the propriety of establishing a Liberal Club in that town to press for emancipation because of the prevalence of so much hatred and violence, and because a political club might add to an increase of fear and distrust.[21] Baron Smith argued that the lower classes on account of their sufferings and privations were more liable to be excited and misled. And he warned: 'Popular emotion if once excited strongly, while it obeys an order "Forward", will disregard a call to "Halt".' Addressing himself to those who argued that no law was broken by a passive resistance to tithes he said there was a palpable difference between a man's voluntary payment of a just demand and the suffering of it to be wrested from him by the strong arm of the law. In a purple, nevertheless perceptive, passage he made reference to castles toppling on their wardens, and the antique strongholds of aristocracy sloping their heads to their foundations, and political incantation untying the winds of popular fury and turning them loose on the established church. He reminded all those opposed to tithe that the roots of church property and private property were interlaced, and that in pulling up the one they might be found to have interfered dangerously and injuriously with the other. The multitude who cried that tithes were an intolerable burden — 'away with them' — would soon substitute 'rents' for 'tithes' in their cry. He saw the logic of this process possibly ending in a form of socialism. He asked: 'Are we to banish splendours from our community altogether ... and to send our dukes to delve and our duchesses to spin?' The campaign of resistance to tithe was in his view the probable, if indirect, cause of the crimes now crowding his court. In an interesting analysis of the situation he said: 'Between present outrage and the late tithe resistance there exists some unperceived derivative connection, some lurking dark relation of effect and cause.' Opposition to the law had changed its objects and found a different vent. Crime in the Queen's County appeared to have lost its individuality and to have become part of a more general combination. He discerned the beginnings of an *imperium in imperio* and he continued:

> I see edicts and proclamations, illegal notices and ejectments. I see an unlawful criminal code arraying itself against and attempting to supersede the legal one: surrounding itself with disorderly sanctions and seditious terrors; having its oaths and obligations; its ministers of injustice; its secret treasuries and supplies; its magazines of arms, collected by nightly plunder, seemingly to furnish its standing army of insurgent force. I see its capital punishments, its banishings and maimings; its mulcts of property; its domiciliary visits, house-burnings and attacks. I see these things but yet, it is true, in their commencements; perhaps not strong enough to be despised. It is while it is infirm and small that such a mischief should be met ...[22]

Baron Smith was right in pointing to the existence of an alternative legal system among the secret societies; and he was right also in dimly descrying in the forests of Queen's County the first faint beginnings of an alternative regime, trying to 'burst through and shatter the legitimate sphere of government which nourishes and includes it'. But it was too easy to overstate the cohesion of the alternative legal code, while at the same time underrating the permanent influence of the embryonic alternative regime.

As in previous instances the agrarian disturbances in Queen's and neighbouring counties in the early 1830s were ebullitions of local grievances and *ad hoc* remedies and penalties imposed by local combinations. There was no general system under any organised leadership even at county level, and the agrarian code adopted was not necessarily uniformly imposed from one area to the next. Besides, the state with its own police and legal systems was quite capable of suppressing the disturbances when put to the test. With regard to an emerging alternative government, on the other hand, it was true that the power which had resided in the landlords had now slipped to the priests and 'demagogues'. And the more extreme tories among the gentry were convinced that it was a mistake on the part of the government, the magistrates and police ever to make the priests the means of communication with the catholic population, even on matters of violence, because it gave them a consequence they ought not to have. A tory witness told a select committee in 1832: 'Such persons as Lord Killeen or his father [Lord Fingall], or Lord Kenmare and such other gentlemen who are always loyal and well conducted should have been the medium and not the priests'.[23] But that battle had been fought. Aristocracy, whether catholic or protestant, was retreating, unevenly, it is true, before the onslaughts of democracy, and in Queen's County — as elsewhere — it was Bishop Doyle, the anti-tithe propagandist, or Pat Lalor, the anti-tithe organiser, whose influence mattered to an increasing extent. The O'Connellite movement which they represented may have been no more than reformist in thrust: but it was radical or revolutionary in achievement — or so it seemed to the frightened ascendancy. And behind the Dr Doyles, and middle-class catholic farmers like Lalor, lay the independent influence of the agrarian secret societies. They had little to do with religion or politics or tithe. As O'Connell pointed out the major resistance to tithe came from a different class, and Pat Lalor, the initiator of tithe resistance in his own county, had his house and property attacked by the agrarian insurgents. But that was by the way, for in the final analysis the agrarian societies, the priests and O'Connell were on the same side and even working, though in a very uneasy alliance, towards the same objectives.

The situation which had emerged saw an apparent alliance between peasant insurrection through the secret societies and middle-class passive resistance; politicisation of the country through the clubs that supported O'Connell and his party; the blessing of the clergy on the enterprise; and a party of the people in parliament under O'Connell's leadership acting as a spearhead of a multi-faceted reform agitation and directing the gathering momentum of a democratic movement.

The select committee of the house of commons which reported in 1832 on the tithe and Whitefeet disturbances in Queen's County included Sir Henry Parnell in the chair, O'Connell, Wyse and other members of O'Connell's party who were sympathetic to the catholic peasantry. Among the major causes of the disturbances they listed: (a) land clearances because of over-population (clearance was effected when leases were not renewed); (b) vagrancy and mendicity which resulted from this and from the lack of any alternative employment; (c) the immoderate use of cheap liquor which was readily available because of a defective licensing system. The remedies for the abuse of drink were stricter licensing laws and a temperance campaign, for it was generally agreed that to be acceptable and workable, democracy had to be sober. The social problems caused by vagrancy and mendicity were often alluded to in the evidence given before several parliamentary commissions, and the absence of any Irish Poor Law was constantly noted. It was generally accepted that mendicity could only be mitigated by some form of poor relief system. The select committee proposed a system of landlord and state-aided emigration to relieve the pressures on the land, but the over-population and resultant land clearances required a reformation of the agrarian system much more radical than any that was forthcoming before the great famine imposed its own ruthless solution.

Whig reforms 1835–40
Through the reports of parliamentary committees and from various other official and non-official sources the government was well aware of the ills of Ireland. Not only had agrarian crime to be suppressed and law and order established, but there was also some realisation that the disturbances associated with secret organisations were a symptom of the sickness in society and not its cause. The police, the magistrates, the jury system and the courts had to be reformed and made acceptable to the people. The provocation offered by the Orangemen had to be curbed. A poor law for Ireland had to be devised; something had to be done about tithes; and the unreformed municipal corporations were crying out for attention. Above all, a just and impartial administration of Ireland was needed to ensure that any reform passed would be carried from the statute books to the fields, the market place and the court-

room. In pursuit of these reforms the Melbourne whigs, on attaining office in 1835, came to an understanding with O'Connell. This was known as the Lichfield House Compact. It was an informal and to a certain extent a power-sharing alliance whereby O'Connell and his party kept the whigs in office in return for good government, reform measures and an impartial administration of Ireland.

The most sincere sign that the Melbourne government was serious about reform was the appointment and continuation in office of Thomas Drummond, a Scottish presbyterian, as under-secretary in Dublin castle. Drummond came early to the conclusion that the landlords were 'cold-blooded and indifferent to the sufferings of their tenants', and that the ascendancy was the cause of much of the trouble in Ireland. The spirit with which he dealt with the landed gentry was encapsulated in his famous pronouncement of 1838:

> Property has its duties as well as its rights; to the neglect of these duties in times past is mainly to be ascribed that diseased state of society in which such crimes take their rise; and it is not the enactment or enforcement of statutes of extraordinary severity, but chiefly in the better and more faithful performance of those duties, and the more enlightened and human exercise of those rights, that a permanent remedy for such disorders is to be sought.[24]

He set out vigorously to pursue a campaign of reform. He was determined that the police and military and the legal system were no longer to be used as an arm of the ascendancy. He refused to allow the police or the military to be employed for the collection of tithe arrears.

The hated yeomanry, who had been under the influence of the local gentry, had already been disbanded in 1834, the year before the arrival of Drummond in Ireland. The police system, which earlier in the century was entirely under local control, had also undergone certain reforms — the Peace Preservation Force established in 1814 to assist in disturbed districts was under central control, and the Constabulary Act of 1822 had enabled the lord lieutenant to appoint a chief constable for each barony and also four provincial inspectors. Drummond decided that further centralisation was necessary if the gentry's influence over the police was to be broken. By an act of 1836 the entire police force came under the control of an inspector-general, Dublin castle recruitment was made on a non-sectarian basis, and professional training for the police was begun. Dublin was provided with its own metropolitan police force. Drummond, therefore, played a leading role in the creation of a more acceptable police system.

The stipendiary magistrates, hitherto appointed on request of local justices of the peace to support the forces of military and judicial coercion, were now appointed directly by, and on the sole judgement of, the administration in Dublin. Drummond increased the number and functions of these stipendiary magistrates. A parliamentary commission of inquiry had investigated the penetration of the Orange Order into British and Irish society, and it was also suspected of being involved in a conspiracy to alter the royal succession. This led to the suppression of the Orange Order in England, and to the strenuous application of the law by Drummond against illegal Orange activities in Ireland. The most provocative displays of orangeism were prohibited during his period of office. He employed the police and the stipendiary magistrates — often men with military experience — to enforce his impartial policy. Excessive drinking and faction fighting were dealt with in an equally forceful manner. Exclusively Orange juries in the past had damaged the integrity of the court system: not only was justice not done but was seen in the eyes of the people not to be done. During Drummond's period of office jury lists were compiled under new regulations, and liberals and even catholics were for the first time made judges. Like a man coming into a wild and unreclaimed territory Drummond tried to eradicate the rough and unruly elements in Irish society. This taming of a demi-barbarous society allowed O'Connellite democracy the necessary space and light in which to grow.

Apart from Drummond's administration, the whig government attempted to improve the condition of the country with three major reform acts dealing with tithes, the poor law and the municipal corporations. After several legislative attempts to solve the tithe question an act of 1838 converted tithe into a rent charge payable by the head landlord who passed the charge down to sub-tenants exempting only the lowest class of cottiers and tenants. Arrears were written off. The Tithe Act was accepted by O'Connell despite the fact that it lacked an appropriation clause, which would have benefited the catholics by providing educational and other social services out of the deployment of church funds. The act, despite its limitations, ended the tithe war and the tithe question as such. Before the 1838 act the issue of tithes had supplied fuel to the fires of democratic politics by fostering a combination of peasant agrarianism and middle-class politics in an exercise of Irish democracy. The tithe war against the established church of the ascendancy and its government allies — the magistracy, military and police — was another conflict between the forces of democracy and ascendancy. The slogan, 'No Tithes, no Tories', had helped to give O'Connell his greatest ever electoral victory. The anti-tithe campaign had carried the activist Pat Lalor into parliament as one of O'Connell's repeal party.

The campaign had also aroused political feeling to such a pitch that the popular party rather optimistically decided to run a second repeal candidate with Lalor for the two Queen's County seats in the 1832 election. Bishop Doyle regretted this decision as he feared it was likely to have the effect of excluding the sitting liberal member, Sir Henry Parnell. The bishop 'laboured unremittingly', as he said in a letter to Parnell, to avert this danger. Lalor gave the bishop to understand that he concurred with his wish that two repealers should not be nominated. Doyle assured Parnell that in the circumstances of only one repealer being put forward that the catholic clergy of the diocese would assist Parnell's return, and he hoped that the repealers would also be friendly. Parnell, said JKL, 'should never need an apologist with the people of Ireland — but especially with the catholics'. Despite Doyle's intervention the 'more violent party' and the 'present delusion' and the 'presumption and obstinacy' of the repealers prevailed. It was in his view a disease affecting the public mind.[25] This convinced the sitting liberal member, Sir Henry Parnell, that he had no chance of re-election for the constituency. Ironically, Parnell, although for long the leading champion of the catholic cause in parliament, was excluded by the tithe issue: significantly his politics were not considered popular enough for the new democratic spirit. The political spirit that had been created during the tithe agitation was not abolished by the passing of the Tithe Act. Judge Smith's prediction that the attack on tithes was likely to lead to an attack on rents was proven to be true. Although the act did remove the financial source of conflict between catholics and the clergy of the ascendancy, on the other hand, by making it a rent charge it merely transformed the confrontation into one between tenants and landlords for the rest of the century.

The government also tackled the problem of Irish poverty. The Irish Poor Law Act, passed in 1838, which set up workhouses, was opposed by O'Connell on moral and economic grounds. He argued that a state-imposed system would dispense with the exercise of charity and would destroy initiative and industry. As a supporter of *laissez faire*, he preferred a solution which would include state-aided emigration, public works and a tax on absentee landlords. By 1841 the country had been divided into 130 districts called poor law unions. Each of these was to have a workhouse for the relief of the destitute, and was to be managed by a board of guardians. The boards were to be made up of *ex-officio* and elected guardians in the ratio of one to three. The *ex-officio* guardians were the local justices of the peace. The elected guardians were to be returned by the votes of the ratepayers from the well-defined electoral divisions within each union. The local ratepayers financed the scheme out of the poor law valuation of each holding in the union. Whatever the failings of the poor law it introduced a considerable amount of democracy into local affairs. In Queen's County, for example, where two unions were established, the Abbeyleix union had twenty-four elected guardians, and the Mountmellick union had thirty elected guardians including substantial catholics like the former MP and anti-tithe campaigner, Pat Lalor. Catholic ratepayers all over the country gained their first experience of local government and administration as poor law guardians.

The Irish Municipal Corporations Act of 1840 broke the absolute control of the Orange faction over the administration of Irish cities and towns. The duties of the municipal corporations had included lighting, cleaning, paving and the regulation of markets. Before the 1840 act widespread abuses existed including self-perpetuating cliques, jobbery and money irregularities. The mismanagement and alienation of property had become flagrant. To O'Connell corporations were symbols of Orange ascendancy. They were the strongholds of toryism, and bulwarks against democracy. One of O'Connell's conditions of support for the whig alliance was that there should be a thorough reform of corporations so as to place them under popular control. There were few catholics on corporations before 1840, even though the relaxation of the penal laws in 1793 had allowed catholics to become freemen. Dublin corporation was exclusively protestant. Isaac Butt, then a conservative, and acting as counsel for the tory corporation opposed the admission of catholics to corporations because he said they would tax protestants and bring about the fall of the established church and the end of the union.

Carlow corporation is a good example of the situation that had existed in the governing of many Irish towns. The thirteen burgesses, who were in effect nominated by Lord Charleville, the patron, not only elected the MP for the borough down to the Reform Act of 1832, but also controlled the administration of the town, and enjoyed a monopoly of municipal patronage. The sovereign, whom the burgesses elected annually from among themselves, was a justice of the peace, clerk of the market and presided at the election of the MP. Although he had no fixed salary, he received money from the tolls and from the weighmaster. Freemen, who numbered about twenty, were elected by the burgesses. A freeman elected in the morning might be made a burgess on the afternoon of the same day. Freemen were also eligible to become sergeants-at-mace (who were the corporations' policemen), town clerk, weighmaster and bellman. They were also eligible to participate in the making of the by-laws and were exempt from tolls and customs. No Roman catholic was a member of the Carlow corporation, nor had any been admitted as freemen. Catholics, therefore, were excluded from participation in the administration of the town. As a government commission reporting on the corporation in 1835 said: 'the sovereign and burgesses constituted the ruling body, and as they were all connected with or in the immediate interest of the earl of Charleville, the management of the corporation was entirely in his hands.'

The 1840 act changed all that. Ten of the largest cities and towns were given elective town councils. A £10 property valuation — higher than that in Engand — was the qualification necessary for the elective franchise. The smallest or poorest towns were handed over to the poor law guardians. The centralising tendency of British administration in Ireland took the opportunity once again to assert itself, and the appointment of magistrates, sheriffs and police became crown responsibilities. Although the act was considerably less liberal than O'Connell had demanded, it did have the effect of freeing the corporations from the absolute control of their ascendancy patrons and of enabling catholic citizens to play a role in local administration. The first election for Dublin corporation held after the passing of the act returned forty-seven repealers and whigs and only thirteen tories. O'Connell himself in 1841 became the first catholic lord mayor of Dublin since the time of James II. The office conferred on him, even if we allow for a certain filial exaggeration in his son's description, 'a legally recognised *lordship* from the *people* utterly unconnected with court favour or aristocratic usage — in short a most democratic dignity'. Catholics elected to those corporations gained invaluable experience of government and administration, and in time most corporations were captured by the catholic and popular interests. These municipal councillors provided the local nucleus for nationalist parties of the future.

5 Repeal, Famine and Fenians, 1840–70

In the 30 years following the Act of Union no such thing as an Irish party existed in the UK parliament. Before the parliamentary, municipal and poor law reforms of the 1830s electoral contests were comparatively few, all parliamentary candidates were of the ascendancy and voters were more or less under the sole influence of the gentry. The emancipation struggle and the reforms of the 1830s saw the immediate involvement of the Irish masses in the democratic process. Between 1830 and 1840 O'Connell had succeeded in creating the first influential independent Irish party with about thirty MPs in the British parliament. He had thereby established a force in British parliamentary politics and set the pattern of Irish nationalist behaviour. He had also played a significant role in the van of democracy and of liberalism at a critical stage in their development. The extent of O'Connell's contribution was not always appreciated by the British then, anymore than by his countrymen since. The attitude of the tories to O'Connell was sometimes one of loathing and fear, and always one of distrust and opposition. For them he posed a dangerously formidable challenge which threatened to destroy their establishment, their status and their world. Whigs and liberals, on the other hand, in their reforming endeavours often found themselves on the same side as O'Connell, sometimes desperately needing his support. They were always greatly relieved, however, not to be dependent on him. British radicals wooed him since his objectives and theirs usually overlapped. But in the end O'Connell was too big an oak of the Irish forest ever to be restricted merely inside the tradition of British radicalism. By playing on the stage of imperial politics in Westminster he had raised the political consciousness of the Irish people and drawn widespread attention to the needs of Ireland. The attention he received from abroad encouraged him to redouble his efforts at home.

Behind the Irish party in parliament was a national network of political clubs, municipal councillors, poor law guardians and others, all of whom further contributed to the politicisation of Irish society; and at the base of an interconnected and integrated three-tier political structure lay the majority of the people. This majority, as well as being democratised, was simultaneously being educated, nationalised and catholicised. Emerging democracy was receiving an education in the broadest sense of that word through a school system which was rapidly expanding; through the newspapers and ballad literature which catered for an increasingly literate public; and through the churches of a reorganised catholicism. Schools, literacy, politics and religion were all interconnected. Control over the schools was being established by the priests and the religious orders of brothers and nuns. The voice of democracy was asserting itself in the widely distributed newspapers produced by the popular movement; and as well as being given a blessing from the catholic church, some practical experience of democracy at work was being obtained in the big new churches of revived catholicism, and also in a flourishing ecclesiastical system where promotion and management allowed for the development of an Irish catholic meritocracy. The language which had been associated with an aristocratic Gaelic tradition was rapidly falling into disuse. English, which was being adopted instead by the people in the once Irish-speaking areas of the south and west, made liberal, political and democratic ideas more available throughout the land. Ironically, in order for the Irish masses to become more politically conscious and to be educated into modern Irish nationalism they had first to take up English. For this was the language of Grattan's parliament, of the United Irishmen, of the ballads of '98, of Emmet's speech from the dock, of Moore's patriotic songs, of the emancipation movement, of O'Connell's election addresses and of the *Nation* newspaper.

The illegal assemblies of the secret societies, and the earlier banned meetings of the catholics were by now being replaced by the large gatherings of catholics in the schools and churches, at election rallies and at the monster meetings which characterised the repeal movement. Democracy was gradually taking over from demagoguery, and because of the circumstances in which it developed it was showing a peculiarly catholic and nationalistic character.

A growing volume of newspapers and journals, through their reports and editorial comment, through the publicity they gave to the grievances of the majority, and through the propaganda they provided for the popular organisations fostered and fed the incipient spirit of nationalism. For its inspiration this new nationalism looked more and more to Ireland's past, and enveloped political consciousness in a very distinctive historical frame of mind which not only conditioned the catholic Irishman's attitude to the present, but also made him dream of a happier future for his native land.

Repeal

By the end of the 1830s O'Connell had become disillusioned with the whig alliance and disappointed with the amount of reform which had been won in parliament. As a political realist he recognised, too, that the writing was on the wall for the whigs and that the tories were likely to be returned after the next general election. On a personal level, his popularity had waned in Ireland judging by the drop in the O'Connell Tribute. (This tribute consisted of a voluntary collection at all chapels throughout the country on two fixed Sundays of the year, and it was paid to O'Connell since 1829 so that he could retire from the bar in order to devote himself entirely to a political career.) O'Connell had become convinced that justice would be done to Ireland only in the re-establishment of a native Irish parliament. To that end a Precursor Society was established in Dublin in 1838. This became the National Association of Ireland in April 1840, and was renamed the Loyal National Repeal Association in July that same year, and was organised on the model of the Catholic Association. Its object was the establishment of an Irish parliament. Its principles committed it to an inviolate loyalty to the crown; the total disavowal of physical force or illegality; the constitutional means of organised public opinion; the exclusion of sectarianism; the assertion of equality before the law for all classes; and freedom of conscience. In 1841 when the general election was won by the tories with Peel as prime minister, and O'Connell's party was reduced to a mere 18 MPs, it became obvious that O'Connell's effectiveness in parliament was greatly limited, so he decided to concentrate on extra-parliamentary agitation. Because of the absence of any support for repeal among British MPs O'Connell had to make his extra-parliamentary agitation more imposing than anything he had done before.

The repeal movement gathered momentum when a group of young intellectuals — including Thomas Davis, Charles Gavan Duffy and John Blake Dillon — published the first number of the *Nation* on 8 October 1842. It was priced 6d (2½p), and soon achieved the largest circulation of any weekly in Ireland. It had a readership calculated by Duffy at 250,000. Copies were available in the repeal reading rooms where they were read by many people. Through the ballads, historical narratives and editorial harangues it preached a spiritual and romantic nationalism with a freshness and enthusiasm for the regeneration of Irish society that is difficult to appreciate by a later generation for whom the doctrines of nationality had become trite and enthusiasm had been replaced by cynicism.

In pre-famine Ireland politics had become a very large part of the social life of the masses, and seemed to have become second nature to the Irishman. The repeal of the union agitation brought O'Connell to the zenith of his fame, and the people to the peak of political awareness. He would make a revolution, he said, not as the French had done with blood, but with the moral force of public opinion. To that end he organised the nation behind the repeal agitation which bore many of the same organisational features as the emancipation movement. Like the catholic rent a repeal rent, based on a shilling a year for associate members — men, women and children — provided the finances for the association. The rent amounted to a massive £48,000 and the tribute exceeded £20,000 for the year 1843. Repeal wardens, four in urban and two in rural parishes, paralleled the churchwardens of the emancipation struggle, and their functions were similar: to supervise the collection of the rent and the registration of voters, and to make reports to headquarters in Dublin. It was a sign of advancing nationalism that the repeal wardens were also expected to encourage a 'buy-Irish' policy. Churchmen rallied to repeal as they had done in the days of emancipation. Among the bishops Archbishop MacHale of Tuam gave his public support to the repeal cause from 1840, and most of the other bishops and the lower clergy followed his lead.

O'Connell declared that in the annals of Ireland 1843 would be known as the year of repeal. The most notable characteristic of the repeal movement was the massive outdoor meeting. The first of these was held at Trim in March of 1843, and from then until the banned meeting in Clontarf in October about forty massive demonstrations were held. These gigantic gatherings assembled usually on Sundays and holydays and significantly, at historic sites such as Trim, Casherconlish, Bellewstown, Clones, Rathkeale, Limerick, Kells, Roscrea, Kilkenny, Mullingar, Charleville, Cork, Cashel, Nenagh, Longford, Drogheda, Mallow, Athlone, Ennis, Murroe, Skibbereen, Dundalk, Galway, Donnybrook, Waterford, Tullamore, Enniscorthy, Wexford, Tuam, Baltinglass, Clontibret, Monaghan, Roscommon, Lismore, Loughrea, Clifden, Mullaghmast. They were calculated to rouse the people to a fever of political agitation in favour of repeal.

Although the estimates of the numbers attending were doubtlessly exaggerated the crowds were vast by any standards. What O'Connell referred to as 'a congregation of 500,000 persons' gathered in Cork in favour of the legislative independence of Ireland. The various trade groups with their banners provided much of the colour of the occasion. In Tuam the estimated crowd was 300,000 with 400 gentry and 100 clergy on the platform. The largest of all was held on 15 August on the

Hill of Tara — three quarters of a million, which would have made it the largest gathering ever in Ireland until the eucharistic congress in 1932 or the papal visit in 1979. Over 1,300 vehicles leaving for Tara paid tolls at Cabra, Phibsborough and Blanchardstown. There were forty-two bands, 10,000 horsemen, and women numbered about one fifth of the total. Masses were celebrated at altars along the side of the hill for the vast congregation. The marshalling of the huge processions was carried out by what were called the 'peasant cavalry', or 'repeal cavalry', or 'O'Connell's police'. The discipline and sobriety of these demonstrations were astonishing. The temperance crusade, which Fr Mathew had launched in 1838, contributed immensely to the orderliness of the occasions, and O'Connell was quick to avail of the temperance movement for the advantage of repeal. Temperance, he told his audience at Kilkenny, would bring repeal: Ireland sober would mean Ireland free.

The monster meetings were demonstrations of the massiveness of organised democracy. They were also the hedge schools in which the masses were educated into the nationalist politics of repeal. Forty years earlier the masses had been apathetic and silent about the union. At Tara O'Connell said: 'Let every man who, if we had an Irish parliament would rather die than allow the Union to pass, lift up his hands.' The hands of that vast throng were raised in favour of repeal. The gatherings were imposing expressions of public opinion demanding an Irish parliament. These very efficiently managed demonstrations with the carefully selected historic stage-settings, the processions, the bands, the banners, the religious element of clergy in attendance and spiritual services consecrating the cause, the dramatic moments, the oratorical harangues and the cheering from hundreds of thousands were deep emotional experiences in which both orators and audiences got carried away. At Mullingar Bishop Higgins of Ardagh said that he had formally to announce that all the bishops had declared themselves repealers, and he defied the government to put down the agitation in his diocese. If the government attempted to rob them of the daylight by preventing them from assembling in the fields, then, said Bishop Higgins, they would meet in the chapels and suspend all other instruction in order to devote all their time to teaching the people to be repealers. 'If they bring us for that to the scaffold', concluded the bishop, 'in dying for the cause of our country we shall bequeath our wrongs to our successors.' These immense yet orderly assemblies, according to Lecky, were 'organised with the most perfect skill and inspired with the most unanimous enthusiasm'. And he continued: 'There is, perhaps, no more impressive spectacle than such an assembly, pervaded by such a spirit, and moving under the control of a single mind ... the rapid transitions of feeling as the great magician struck alternately each chord of passion, and as the power of sympathy, acting and reacting, intensified the prevailing feeling ... and men of very calm and disciplined intellects experienced emotions the most stately eloquence of the senate had failed to produce.'[1]

Patriotism, the chief emotion evoked at these assemblies, was fed by the numerous glowing references to the fertile land of Ireland, to the heroes of the past, to the 'finest peasantry in the world' and to the perfidy of the English oppressors. At Trim O'Connell told his audience that nothing but injustice could be expected from an English parliament. At Roscrea, as elsewhere, he asserted that 'there is not a lovelier land on the face of the earth — a more fruitful or fertile land the sun never shone upon'. Ireland was 'the first nation on the earth'. This was simply a prose version of the same sentiment expressed in verse by Davis:

> She is a rich and rare land;
> Oh! she's a fresh and fair land
> She is a dear and rare land —
> This native land of mine.

At Mullaghmast all of the superlatives were paraded again. Among the nations of the earth Ireland was first in the physical strength of her sons, and in the beauty and purity of her daughters. Ireland had, according to O'Connell, the 'richest harvests that any land could produce', hers were 'the sweetest meadows, the greenest fields, the loftiest mountains, the purest streams, the noblest rivers, the most capacious harbours while her water power is equal to turning the machinery of the world'. Such a land was worth fighting for and worth dying for. At Nenagh, as elsewhere, he asked: 'Where was the coward that would not dare to die for such a land?'

> No men than hers are braver —
> Her women's hearts ne'er waver;
> I'd freely die to save her,
> And deem my lot divine.

Those who offered to die for their country during O'Connell's defiant speeches at the monster meetings were so embarrassingly numerous that Ireland seemed to be in danger of becoming a land of blood and carnage. O'Connell, the realist, however, had not quite become the romantic nationalist. He showed that he had lost neither his balance nor his sense of humour when, faced with yet another offer of dying for Ireland, he declared at Skibbereen that 'one living repealer is worth a churchyard full of dead ones'.

A more militant and menacing note than O'Connell had ever before allowed himself swept through the speeches he made at the monster meetings, and encouraged fiery words and reactions from others. At Kilkenny he said that he stood at the head of a body of men who if organised with military discipline would be sufficient for the conquest of Europe; that Wellington never had such an army. At Mallow he uttered the famous 'Mallow defiance', when he said that the time for such speechifying was over and the time for action had come. He defied the government and its troops to suppress them and said that one day the repealers must conquer. 'Have we not the ordinary courage of Englishmen?' he asked. 'Are we to be trampled underfoot?' 'They may trample on me', he added, 'but it will be my dead body they will trample on, not the living man.' In Cromwell's time they were a paltry remnant, but they were nine millions now. At Donnybrook less than a month later he was still claiming that he had behind him more strength and more physical force than had gained the battle of Waterloo. At Wexford he asserted that he addressed crowds which the emperor of Russia himself did not have the power to put down. At Tara O'Connell said that the queen's army was the bravest in the world. But if attacked by them, Ireland, roused as she was, would supply women enough to beat the entire forces of the queen, and he proudly recalled the bravery of the women of Limerick who beat off the besiegers when their men were faltering. In Cork he reminded his audience that if attacked fathers and mothers could be cut down, and sisters become the victims of the ruffian soldiery. If this happened, he continued in language as menacing as any uttered later by the Fenians or Parnell: 'I will ask Mr Peel how many fires would blaze out in the manufactories of Britain?' The response to such incitement was predictable. At Tullamore a banner read: 'Ireland her Parliament or the World in a Blaze'. In these speeches of 1843 there were several references by O'Connell to the battles of the past, and the repeal membership card carried the dates of four of the most famous of these. The old enemy was referred to as the Saxon, and the crown forces as the barbarian and ruffian soldiery. He referred often to Cromwell, the most hated man in Irish folklore, to his massacre of 300 women in Wexford and to his deportation of thousands of Irish as slaves to the West Indies. At Mullaghmast, Co. Kildare, where in 1577 O'Moores and other chieftains were invited to a feast by crown officials and then slaughtered, O'Connell spoke of the massacre as the consummation of English treachery unequalled in the world's crime until the massacre of the Mamelukes by Mahomet Ali. At Clontibret, near Monaghan, Tyrone's defeat of an English army in 1595 under Bagenal was celebrated. At Roscommon O'Donnell's defeat of an English army in 1599 in the nearby Curlew Mountains was recalled. Clontarf was chosen because it was the site of the famous victory of Brian over the Danes in 1014. Enniscorthy and Wexford recalled the '98 rebellion, and Limerick the defence of the city in the Jacobite war. In all of these speeches on such sites O'Connell was, in the words of John Blake Dillon, 'searching the depths of the nation's memory', and tugging at the heart-strings of patriotism.

O'Connell's monster meetings succeeded in bringing together on these historic sites the different and even conflicting causes of the past now presented to the people as the glorious old cause of Irish freedom. Gaelic chieftains, loyalist catholics of the seventeenth century, Jacobites, Wild Geese, protestant patriots of 1782, Defenders and revolutionary United Irishmen — all had the same green flag wrapped around them by O'Connell and his young allies on the *Nation*. The meeting at Tara — a typical romantic nationalistic amalgam of Irish history — said it all: the royal site where Gaelic kings and aristocrats held court, where Patrick had preached the gospel to pagan chieftains and druids, where hundreds of thousands of loyal repealers converged in a massive demonstration and prayed round the grave of the radical republicans of 1798, listened to the harper play 'The harp that once through Tara's halls', and cheered O'Connell as he romanticised about Grattan's Volunteers of 1782 and the defence of Limerick in 1690, or denounced the brutality of Cromwell, and proclaimed that the Hill of Tara was 'stained with murderous blood, and the bones are not mouldered yet of the individuals who were massacred in hundreds upon it'. Neither the orator nor his audience saw any contradiction in his current praise of the croppies and his earlier denunciation of the policies of their leaders, Tone and Emmet.

Despite O'Connell's bluster he also seemed to be anxious to calm the militant emotions which his talk about fighting and dying had aroused. His Ireland was also a country worth living for; and his extreme language was calculated to intimidate Wellington and Peel into repeating the policy of concession they had followed in 1829 in order to avoid the evil of civil war. He was far from preaching republican separatism; and even while prophesying that his peasantry would one day conquer the queen's army, he was in the same sentence proclaiming that the first act of the victors would be to give Ireland back to his 'darling little Queen'. The word 'loyal' — as in '*Loyal* National Repeal Association', or in the 'sober, *loyal*, patriotic people' that he addressed — was bandied about by O'Connell with nearly as much abandon and defiance as by any latter-day Ulster unionist.

The government was worried by the monster meetings. Peel could have decided to sit tight on the union and wait passively for the balloon of O'Connell's promises to deflate as the 'Repeal Year' ended without fulfilment. Instead, he determined to act against the agitation and call O'Connell's bluff, and he showed that he was ready to use force if necessary. He had said: '... deprecating as I do all war, and especially civil war, there is no alternative which I do not think preferable to the dismemberment of the Empire.' Peel meant war, where O'Connell's talk of war was merely tactical brinkmanship. The military language used in the notices for the meeting, which was to be held at Clontarf on 8 October, gave the government the excuse to proscribe it and to send a big number of troops to enforce the banning order. To avoid a potential bloodbath O'Connell backed down and cancelled the meeting. A charge of conspiracy to incite disaffection was brought against O'Connell and other leaders. They were sentenced to imprisonment, but after four months in prison the sentence was quashed by the house of lords.

After O'Connell's release from prison in September 1844 the demand for repeal was renewed, and although further great meetings were addressed by him the wholehearted enthusiasm of the repeal year was never to be recaptured. Repeated assurances from O'Connell during 1843 that there would be a parliament in College Green before the end of the year had an element of millenialism about them — a sort of secular echo of Pastorini. When the prophecy remained unfulfilled disillusionment and frustration were bound to beset the people. In an attempt to pacify Ireland Peel introduced a series of 'good government' measures. The exaggerated claim by Bishop Higgins at the Mullingar monster meeting to the effect that all of his fellow bishops without exception had declared for repeal had created a sensation. It caused the government to initiate a secret investigation into the involvement of the priests in politics, which, in turn, resulted in Peel's attempt to kill repeal with kindness by three measures particularly designed to detach the clergy, but also the catholic middle class, from repeal. These were the establishment of a board of charitable bequests (1844), an increase in the grant to Maynooth College (1845), and the foundation of university colleges at Cork, Galway and Belfast (1845). The Charitable Bequests Act was administered by a board of thirteen of whom five were Roman catholics, and although O'Connell and Archbishop MacHale opposed it, it enabled beneficial bequests to be made to the catholic church and permitted its endowment. The annual grant to Maynooth was trebled, and a generous capital sum was allocated for buildings; but the loyalty of the clergy was not thereby bought. The non-denominational or 'godless' Queen's Colleges were eventually condemned by the Irish bishops and by Rome. Only Queen's, Belfast, which the presbyterians patronised, was to flourish. Peel's attempt, however, opened up the 'university question' that was to remain one of the preoccupations of the catholic bishops for the rest of the century. The Queen's Colleges were also the cause of discord between O'Connell and Young Ireland and weakened the unity of the repeal movement.

Young Ireland and O'Connell
During the repeal agitation O'Connell found himself first assisted and then opposed by one of the most talented groups of young men ever to combine in Irish politics — the Young Irelanders. Their support had raised the movement's intellectual tone. They insisted on educating for freedom, and this they did through the *Nation*, the repeal reading rooms, the Library of Ireland which produced cheap volumes on Irish history, and the *Spirit of the Nation* which made the ballads that were first published in the *Nation* available in a more permanent form. The discordant note which they introduced into O'Connell's movement was partly the result of a generation gap — O'Connell's sons and the Young Irelanders were the same age — which gave rise to criticism of the older politician by the younger idealists. O'Connell criticised the dull rhyming ballads of the *Nation*, and was apprehensive about the militancy of its tone. Young Ireland tended to be a party within a party. On issues of religion and physical force the two sides displayed a difference of emphasis which later emerged as a difference of principle.

In their early days the Young Irelanders sincerely accepted O'Connell as the patriarch of his people. The traces of criticism which they showed were only the natural reactions of thinking young men. When the impulsive O'Connell condemned American slavery outright, or the poor law, or the *Dublin University Magazine*, the Young Irelanders suggested that though they might agree with him he should also consider the consequences of his outspokenness. O'Connell's bombast and exaggerated claims about 'the finest peasantry in the world' did not appeal to Davis whose doctrine of 'educate that you may be free' recognised that the Irish people had a long way to travel before any real progress could be made. Davis was glad when what he called 'the carnival of agitation' associated with the monster meetings was over. After Clontarf Young Ireland suggested that the association could be better employed by becoming the schoolmaster of the nation and educating it to be free. The *Nation* remained silent when O'Connell condemned the Charitable Bequests Bill. O'Connell's newspaper friends in the *Pilot* attacked 'the great ambitions and small morality' of Young Ireland. The non-denominational Queen's Colleges in which Irishmen of all religions or of no religion could be educated alongside each other appealed to the Young Irelanders. O'Connell backed MacHale's opposition to the 'godless' colleges, and preferred catholic control of catholic education. The more doctrinaire Young Irelanders opposed O'Connell's readiness to re-enter a whig alliance (in 1846), and his earlier toying with Sharman Crawford's proposal of federalism (in 1844) which would give an Irish parliament for domestic purposes while continuing with Irish representation in Westminster.

The final break between O'Connell and Young Ireland took place in July 1846 on the issue of moral as opposed to physical force. The so-called peace resolutions stated that the Repeal Association sought its objectives by peaceable and legal means *alone*, and disclaimed *all* attempts to win constitutional liberty by force, violence and bloodshed. The Young Irelanders chose to interpret the resolutions as implying that in no circumstances was force ever justifiable, although the resolutions had specifically allowed for the use of self-defence against aggression. The debate was purely academic, since no side advocated force in the circumstances. One of the odd things about the debate was that we had, on the one hand, the 'party of the sword' professing the most peaceful intentions but clinging to their dogma that force was not everywhere and always wrong, confronted by the advocate of exclusively constitutional action, admitting that under certain contingencies the use of physical resistance might become allowable. In the end, the metaphysicians, Mitchel, Duffy and their friends walked out of Conciliation Hall and the Repeal Association, and established the Irish Confederation. Mitchel, later arrested for treason-felony, was sentenced to fourteen years' transportation, but he escaped after a few years to America.

O'Connell's impact abroad
O'Connell's gigantic campaign, his imprisonment, the failure of the policy to achieve repeal despite his boundless optimism, and his death

in the midst of the great famine captured world-wide attention. It was generally recognised abroad that through the monster meetings O'Connell had introduced the mass of the Irish people to an active democracy, liberalism and nationalism at a time when these were little more than ideological concepts in the minds of intellectuals in other parts of Europe. O'Connell was seen to have fashioned the political identity and consciousness of the Irish and stamped them for good or ill in his own image. Rome had formerly treated Ireland as part of the United Kingdom but as a result of O'Connell's movement the pope began to deal with the Irish church separately. Many would have agreed with Gustave de Beaumont's verdict that 'Ireland is a small country on whose soil a battle is in progress on the greatest problems of politics, morals and humanity.' This interest by Europeans in Ireland was something which O'Connell, with his supreme faith in the force of public opinion, had consciously encouraged. He had told his Clare electorate: 'The discussion which the attempt to exclude your representative from the House of Commons must excite will create a sensation all over Europe and produce such a burst of contemptuous indignation against British bigotry in every enlightened country in the world that the universal shout of the nations of the earth will overpower every opposition.'

O'Connell, of course, had not won universal approbation in Europe. Prince Metternich, presiding over that system which was threatened by agitations such as those headed by O'Connell, led the conservative chorus against the Irish radical. It would scarcely be an exaggeration to label the liberal, democratic and nationalist aspirations of that era as 'O'Connellite'. Before O'Connell's time Ireland's relations with the continent had been passive and receptive in the sense that Ireland was influenced by European movements and never vice-versa. In O'Connell's time winds from Ireland began to make a stir in the world of politics outside of Ireland. The truth of the matter was that O'Connell was very useful on the continent for whatever one's cause happened to be. Democrats saw him as the most successful practical exponent of those ideals of the American and French revolutions which stressed the right of resistance to oppression, and the promotion of popular sovereignty. Other O'Connellite doctrines which appealed to European liberals were those of the total separation of church and state, liberty of conscience, freedom of education, and freedom of the press.

Louis Veuillot wrote, on the occasion of the centenary of O'Connell's birth in 1875, that O'Connell in the modern world 'sprinkled the first drops of baptismal water upon that savage power... which we call democracy'. A free church unhampered by government interference, and an independent clergy uninhibited by secular and financial links with the state were seen to be possible as a result of O'Connell's career. Leading Italian nationalists also commented on O'Connell's significance. Cavour admired the constancy of O'Connell's objective: the elevation of the political status of his countrymen and co-religionists; Mazzini, although he would not describe O'Connell as a nationalist, considered him a reformer; Tommaseo was speaking of O'Connell when he said: 'God does not create a great man for the use of a single age or a single people.' Montalembert, the French liberal catholic, addressing O'Connell said: 'But you are not only a man of one nation, you are a man of all christendom.'

Europeans were correct in looking upon O'Connell's movement as nationalist, but, unlike so many of the continental nationalists, O'Connell was not a separatist, nor republican, nor doctrinaire. His form of nationalism did not stress the romantic cultural ideologies which others associated with distinct national languages and national frontiers. Nor did he hold any romantic notions about the necessity of achieving national liberation through bloodshed and the sword. These views were the prerogative of O'Connell's younger contemporaries, the Young Irelanders. That political freedom was not worth a single drop of human blood was O'Connell's constant message. During the celebrated debate on repeal at the Dublin corporation in February 1843 he had proclaimed: 'Not for all the universe contains would I, in the struggle for what I conceive my country's cause, consent to the effusion of a single drop of human blood, except my own.' His controversial peace resolutions of July 1846 postulated that: 'The greatest political revolution that ever was achieved is not worth one single drop of human blood.' The renunciation of physical force was not acceptable to the militant Young Irelanders of his day, but human life was far more sacred to O'Connell than any political doctrine. That is why 'the sovereignty of the people' was for him no mere political catch-cry, much less a licence for regicide or fratricide. On the contrary, he understood the phrase in a particularly humane sense. Lamartine declared that O'Connell had taught the world the most energetic although wisest means for the people to regain their rights — a peaceful agitation.

A favourite topic with O'Connell at the weekly meetings of the Repeal Association had been the denunciation of slavery. Slavery, in

O'Connell's eyes, was not merely an institution in need of overhaul in an age of reform in Britain, and it was not merely a stain upon the American character: it was universally wrong. Anti-slavery was a moral as well as a humanitarian cause. After his role in the successful struggle for the abolition of slavery in the British empire, O'Connell was largely responsible for directing the force of the British anti-slavery movement into the camp of the American abolitionists. He was, indeed, one of the most significant European accessions to the cause of anti-slavery in America, and American abolitionists appreciated that O'Connell, unlike other notable European nationalists, was prepared to take political risks for the principle of anti-slavery. Ireland and Irishmen wherever they were, he pleaded, should be foremost in seeking to effect the emancipation of mankind. By their memories of Ireland, Irish-Americans should love liberty, hate slavery, and treat the blacks as their brethren. There were times when he had to balance his advocacy of anti-slavery against the consequential loss of support, both financial and political, for his repeal movement. On these occasions he showed himself unwilling to barter his abolitionist principle in return for aid for his domestic Irish cause. When one remembers just how expedient a politician he could be on most matters, his principled behaviour on the slavery issue does him all the greater credit. He returned money to Irish-American allies when it was accompanied by arguments in favour of slavery, as he did when it was accompanied by arguments in favour of physical force to solve the Irish question. He did not want blood-stained or slavery-tainted money. If, because of his advocacy of anti-slavery, he immediately lost many Irish-American friends for his repeal cause, he gained friends for Ireland from among the American abolitionists who, long after the death of O'Connell, continued to befriend the cause of Irish independence. T D'Arcy Magee wrote: 'Whoever may live to see the day when slavery shall cease ... will see the statue of O'Connell in every free senate — and hear in every land the wise and honourable repeat his story with reverence.'

Among the millions of Irish, scattered over the world in America, Britain, Australia, Canada and elsewhere in the British colonies, O'Connell exerted a powerful influence. For Irish emigrants, wherever they settled abroad, it was a source of deep pride and of self-esteem that their nation had produced a man of O'Connell's political calibre. O'Connell, for his part, had contributed powerfully to the development of the idea of an Irish spiritual empire. The fact that he had never been a republican separatist enabled him to think of the British empire as, in a large part, Irish. He had exaggerated the number of Irishmen in the British forces and was proud of the victories they had won. He had recommended his Irish friends to the government for appointments in the colonies. He had insisted that full liberty was not only for the Irish at home, but also for the Irish abroad. He had realised that his influence with the British government on behalf of catholics in the colonies was more powerful than it could ever have been in the American republic on behalf of the Irish emigrants there. He had subscribed to the idea that the Irish nation was one, however far-flung its children might be. He had viewed the empire not only in practical terms as a home for the Irish emigrant, but as something they had helped to create, and in which they could make the progress too often denied them at home. Above all, he had seen the empire as a global mission field where the Irish could fulfil their destiny, which, according to O'Connell in writing to an ecclesiastical friend, was catholicising other nations. Ireland's empire, as conceived by O'Connell, was partly mundane since Ireland was constitutionally an integral portion of the United Kingdom, and it was partly spiritual because of the religious or missionary aspect. It was also, however, psychological insofar as it was a form of compensation for the political frustration at home, and it was also a substitute for the profane imperialism of the ancient enemy. For decades following O'Connell's death the concept of Ireland's spiritual empire could be used to make a virtue out of the grim necessity of emigration.

The changing image
The role played by O'Connell, the legend, was different in many respects from the role played by O'Connell, the man, in his own lifetime. Two of the Young Irelanders, Mitchel and Gavan Duffy, were eventually to devote a vast amount of their talent, energy and time to the demolition of O'Connell's reputation.

Mitchel in a vivid pen-portrait of the leader he had turned against wrote:

> Poor old Dan! — wonderful, mighty, jovial, and mean old man! with silver tongue and smile of witchery, and heart of melting ruth! — lying tongue! smile of treachery! heart of unfathomable fraud! What a royal, yet vulgar soul! with the keen eye and potent swoop of a generous eagle of Cairn Tual — with the base servility of a hound, and the cold cruelty of a spider! ... And after one has thought of all this, and more, what can a man *say*? what but pray that Irish earth may lie light on O'Connell's breast — and that the Good God who knew how to create so wondrous a creature may have mercy upon his soul.[2]

O'Connell's greatest treachery, in the eyes of Mitchel, was that he had called off the Clontarf monster meeting because the government had banned it at the last moment and threatened force against all who tried to assemble. Mitchel agreed that if the troops had fired on the people there would have been a horrible slaughter of the unarmed peasantry, and O'Connell himself might have fallen. 'It were well for his reputation if he had', added Mitchel. And the death of five or ten thousand people at Clontarf might have saved Ireland the slaughter by famine of one hundred times as many shortly afterwards. This stunning assertion was repeated by Mitchel both in his *History of Ireland* and in *The Last Conquest*. Of course, he was never to explain how a massacre at Clontarf in '43 could have averted the slaughter by famine which began in '45. Mitchel, however, had become utterly convinced that Irish liberty could be earned only by the sword.

Mitchel's onslaught on O'Connell was very damaging both to O'Connell's reputation and to the policies which he had advocated. For Mitchel's views not only represented, but also influenced, some of the more idealistic nationalists who came after him. It was, nevertheless, a frontal attack, direct and obvious, and therefore not particularly calculated to destroy O'Connell's standing with the more moderate or constitutional nationalists. The vast credit which O'Connell had accumulated among the constitutionalists was later to be undermined by the far more subtle and insidious methods of Gavan Duffy. Duffy, after nine months' imprisonment, had been acquitted in 1849. He returned to edit the *Nation*, but in 1855, he quitted what he called 'the blind and bitter land', for he could not live in a country where, he said, Keogh and Sadleir typified patriotism and Dr Cullen typified the church. In Australia he was eventually to become prime minister of Victoria. He returned to Europe in 1880 and from then until his death in 1903, volumes of historical comment poured from his pen. More than any other writer, Duffy was responsible for the deConnellisation of Irish history. And this he did largely by a process that might be called the Davisisation of Irish nationalism. He raised his friend of the early 1840s, Thomas Davis, into a giant, beside whose political purity, goodness and wisdom O'Connell seemed vulgar and dwarfish. Mitchel's sketch of O'Connell had been strictly for the converted: his fervid phrases could be used as an armoury for Fenians, Fenian sympathisers and their successors. The pen Duffy used was dipped in a more subtle poison than Mitchel's. The Duffy portrait was ingenious, factually impressive, studiously moderate but all the more devastating for that.

Duffy painted a picture of the Young Irelanders as young men of principle being opposed by an old, scheming, jealous, self-centred, unscrupulous, overbearing, untruthful, rapacious politician. O'Connell was only half the patriot with half the talent of his former self. The reason, according to Duffy, was old age, a generation gap and the deadly influence of that villain of Duffy's piece, O'Connell's son, John. Duffy's Young Ireland friends were made to appear as martyrs; O'Connell's political friends were made to appear as place-hunters. In the 1830s, said Duffy, O'Connell abandoned self-government for good government and equal justice. Several repealers accepted appointments under the system they had recently been pledged to overthrow. This acceptance of office, admitted Duffy, did not outrage public opinion as it would have done at a later period. The admission, superficially just to O'Connell, at the same time managed to suggest that not only had O'Connell got 'jobs for the boys' in his own time, but had also spawned those place-hunters of Duffy's time, Sadleir and Keogh and all their ilk. O'Connell had co-operated with the whig government in the 1830s to the extent of not embarrassing them with demands for repeal as long as they attempted the better government of Ireland. He had toyed with the same idea in the last year of his career. Young Ireland disapproved of the hand he had outstretched to the federalists, and Duffy's comments on these matters made O'Connell's political pragmatism seem like deviation from the principle of independence to which he had pledged himself and his people. The case against O'Connell was all the more powerful, coming as it did, not from a Fenian or even a Mitchel, but from a sworn moderate and constitutionalist. And the criticism lost none of its effect despite the odd circumstance that it was made by a moderate constitutionalist who had been knighted for his services to the British empire. O'Connell, at least, had always remained plain Daniel, while his very skilful critic had meanwhile become Sir Charles.

O'Connell was later criticised by Mitchel's disciple, Arthur Griffith and his Sinn Féin friends, as the father of lies who had invented that great evil, parliamentarianism, the policy of trying to redress Ireland's grievances in the English parliament which, according to Griffith, had won nothing and had turned the eyes of the people away from Ireland. O'Connell's failure to win repeal, and the failure of his 'moral force' policy helped to make rebels out of his successors.

O'Connell has been to Irish historiography what Napoleon is to the French. He is an argument without end. He has been, and remains, the touchstone of Irish political attitudes. When we catholicised him we were as a people pious and devotional. When we condemned his retreat from Clontarf and his moral force doctrine we were in militant, nationalistic mood. When we wrote him off as a mere politician and pragmatist we were in doctrinaire and idealistic mood. And what we omitted to say about him was as much tell-tale evidence against ourselves as what in fact we did say. O'Connell as a European figure introducing French revolutionary ideas of liberty and democracy without French revolutionary republicanism or force was noticeable by its almost total absence from the consideration given to O'Connell in a nationalist age.

The Famine
The material basis of the protestant ascendancy was the possession of the land. At the time of the Act of Union the percentage of the land in Ireland owned by catholics was less than seven per cent. The vast majority of Irish catholics were tenants on short leases. Several social and economic factors combined to impel Irish society to disaster by the mid-nineteenth century. The prevailing system of land-ownership encouraged backward, wasteful and primitive methods of subsistence farming. Because of the large number of tenancies-at-will the peasants who worked the land had little security of tenure. Nor were they legally entitled to receive compensation for any improvements they might make. Tenants, therefore, had little inducement to improve their small holdings. Landlords, generally, were either unable or unwilling to employ capital for improvement. And the government, because of the prevailing economic theory of *laissez faire*, had no mandate to give state aid for agricultural improvement.

To this depressing picture of the Irish land system must be added other grave problems caused by the population explosion. All of Europe experienced a rapid population growth from about the middle of the eighteenth century, but few countries experienced so high a percentage increase as did Ireland. An increased birth-rate and a decreased death-rate are the general reasons given for the phenomenal rise in the world's population statistics. A major reason for this development in Ireland was an abundance of cheap food in the potato.[3] The population growth was also aided by the fact that famine, war and disease were less frequent than in the past. Around the middle of the eighteenth century also, a change in the pattern of Irish agriculture had introduced more tillage in place of pasture-farming. About the same time there occurred a revolution in the Irishman's diet, and the potato, despite the substantial amount of grain-growing, became the staple food of the people especially in the poorer regions of the west. The potato could be grown on soil that was not suitable for other crops or vegetables, and it grew in great abundance. A comparatively small plot of ground was enough to keep a family in food for a year. However, the pressure of population on the land led to an increased amount of sub-letting and subdivision. By 1845 over three quarters of the holdings were less than twenty acres in size. Landlords and their agents, pleased by the prospect of more rents on the one hand and a larger labour force, and therefore lower wages on the other, did little to discourage subdivision. Subdivision encouraged people to marry early. A tiny plot of potato land, a simple mud-wall cabin, a job as a farm labourer on the local landlord's estate or on the land of a more prosperous farmer, and the church's blessing on the enterprise were all that was required to enable a young couple to set out raising another large family in the crowded Irish countryside. The increasing numbers had to be supported off the land, for the industrial revolution with its factories and cities which absorbed the expanding population in Britain had passed Ireland by with the exception of the Lagan Valley area in the north-east. Emigration in the early nineteenth century did little to relieve the pressures on space. Unemployment, under-employment and poverty were chronic. According to a report of 1836 on the condition of the poor it was estimated that 585,000 labourers with about 1,800,000 dependants were unemployed for thirty weeks of the year.

The situation in Ireland, therefore, in the 1840s was one of a teeming population of over 8 millions living on the brink of disaster. About two thirds of the population were living off the land. Four millions were to a large extent dependent on the potato, and about half of these depended absolutely on it for their existence. When the potato crop failed in the years between 1845 and 1849 one of the greatest tragedies in modern European history occurred, and human suffering reached a level of intensity scarcely ever experienced before in the long, sad story of Ireland. The greatest events of history, said Voltaire, turn upon the tiniest springs. A microscopic organism, which gave rise to a fungus since known as *phytophthora infestans*, caused the potato blight, left millions without food and brought about the greatest catastrophe in Irish history.

A system of public works, mainly road building, was introduced by the government to give employment, so that the people would be able to purchase the Indian meal which had been imported from America. But these public works broke down during the spring of 1847 from the sheer weight of numbers and the gross inefficiency in their management.

The very magnitude of the calamity proved to be too much for government organisation, local effort or the charity of religious and other private associations. A census official of 1851 wrote:

> starving people lived upon the carcasses of diseased cattle, upon dogs and dead horses, but principally on the herbs of the field, nettle tops, wild mustard and watercress, and even in some places dead bodies were found with grass in their mouths. Along the coast every description of sea-weed was greedily devoured, often with fatal consequences.

The Irish poor law of 1838 had divided the country into 130 districts called poor law unions. Each of these districts was to have a workhouse for the relief of the destitute. The financing of these workhouses was made a charge on the local rates. Irish property was to be made to pay for Irish poverty.

Kilrush in County Clare was one of these poor law unions. The population of the union was nearly 65,000. The union covered an area which included only two towns, Kilrush itself with a population of around 5,000, and the seaside resort of Kilkee with a population of around 1,500. These towns were eight miles apart. The rest of the area of farmland and bog was dotted with villages of varying size. The numerous, often single-roomed cabins of these villages were built of the local stone. In these cabins lived 'an amphibious race' of peasants who made their living as farm labourers and fishermen. The food they depended on was the potato, grown on a half or quarter acre of rented land. Potatoes and buttermilk were often the only food for the morning as well as the evening meal. It has been calculated that the Irishman ate as much as ten pounds of potatoes on average each day. The rent, instead of being paid in cash, was often paid for by the tenant in a labour-service of one hundred or one hundred and twenty days on the landlord's farm. As late as 1851, nearly sixty per cent of the people of Co.Clare spoke Irish, and the people of the Kilrush area communicated with government officials and visitors in a language that was a mixture of Gaelic and English. Schools in the area were scarce; most people were classified illiterate by the officials, as in other parts of the Irish-speaking areas of the west of Ireland.

During the early famine years, more than one fifth of the entire population of Co.Clare was at one time engaged on the public works. Farms had been left uncultivated by the labourers who had flocked into the public work camps. The camps, however, first broke down under mismanagement and anarchy and then were shut down. After that it was possible to hire a labourer in Kilrush in return for his food alone. Paulett Scrope MP, the chairman of the house of commons committee which investigated conditions in the Kilrush union, complained that too much emphasis had been placed on road building. The failure to build harbours and quays and mooring stations for the security of fishing boats meant that an opportunity had been missed to augment the food supply from the fish which were plentiful in the seas off Kilrush. And a land drainage scheme, Scrope argued, could have greatly improved the fertility of the soil.

Under the terms of the Irish poor law a workhouse had been opened in the town of Kilrush in 1842 to provide indoor relief for the destitute. An extension of the poor law in 1847 allowed for the provision of outdoor relief, consisting of 'a weekly dole of raw meal' to those for whom it had been sanctioned. Thousands of diseased and starving paupers swarmed into Kilrush for food, and there were riots in August 1847. The numbers pouring into the town were swelled by the wholesale evictions taking place throughout the area by the end of the year. The humane and energetic inspector of the Kilrush union, Captain Arthur Kennedy, dispatched a series of frightening reports to the poor law commissioners, published as a parliamentary paper in 1849.

In November 1847, Captain Kennedy reported: 'an immense number of smallholders are under ejectment or notice to quit'. He continued: 'It is really extraordinary and to me unaccountable where or how the evicted find shelter.' Between July and December of 1848 the inspector forwarded returns of the evictions of 6,090 persons. These lists do not include many of those who had taken small bribes to clear out. Mr Coffee, a professional surveyor and a land agent who himself had evicted tenants, attested before a house of commons committee in 1850 that no less than 14,364 individuals had been evicted in the Kilrush union since 1847. Because it was feared that these evictions would lead to what English commentators of the time called 'disturbance', extra troops were brought into Kilrush just before Christmas 1847.

In 1848, as throughout Europe, there was revolutionary activity in Ireland led by the Young Irelanders. Fintan Lalor demanded: 'Will Ireland perish like a lamb, or will she turn as turns the baited lion?' Smith O'Brien MP left the relief work he was doing on his estate in the neighbouring county of Limerick to lead the abortive rising in the south-east. But a starving and diseased people, disorganised and badly led, had little stomach for fighting for the establishment of an independent Irish republic. And Kilrush, like most of the country, and especially that part of it affected by the famine, remained quiet. Quiet, that is, except for the keening of the women and the wailing of children as their homes were 'tumbled' before their very eyes. The stated reason for these 'monster evictions' was the inability of tenants to pay their rents. And the reason the landlords had the houses destroyed was to avoid having to pay the rates for which landlords were directly liable on all holdings under £4 in valuation.

The evicted sometimes found shelter in the overcrowded cabins of relatives and friends. In payment for their miserable lodgings they parted with a portion of the raw meal which they collected from the poor law relieving officers. Sometimes they built themselves makeshift shelters, called *scalps* and *scalpeens*, in bogs and ditches and among the ruins of their old homes. Here, Inspector Kennedy said, 'they exist like animals till starvation or the inclemency of the weather drives them to the workhouse'. On one day alone in March 1848 'three cartloads of these creatures who could not walk' were brought to the workhouse in Kilrush, 'some in fever, some suffering from dysentery, and all from want of food'. Parents, 'scarcely human in habits', were presenting themselves at the workhouse with 9 or 10 skeleton children already beyond any possibility of recovery. Kennedy also wrote: 'Panic-stricken parents frequently send in a donkey load of children in fever a distance of fourteen or fifteen miles for admission. How to dispose of them I know not ... I saw several admitted yesterday, who I am sure, cannot survive many hours.' After describing the make-shift shelters of the dispossessed peasantry, the correspondent of the *Illustrated London News* wrote: 'In such, or still more wretched abodes, burrowing as they can, the remnant of the population is hastening to an end, and after a few years will be as scarce nearly as the exterminated Indians, except the specimens that are carefully preserved in the workhouse. Those whom starvation spares, disease cuts off.'

The workhouse was not much of a preserver. At Kilrush it was besieged by the destitute. In December 1847 it had 500 to 600 more inmates than it had been built to accommodate. Temporary and auxiliary buildings had to be found. In April 1848 the vice-guardians had to remain up night after night admitting paupers. By the end of the year funds had run out, and contractors refused to give further food supplies on credit. And, for a couple of weeks in December 1848, no outdoor relief of any kind was given to the eleven and a half thousand persons on the official lists. Meanwhile, as the chairman of the house of commons select committee reported, the outdoor poor ate 'weeds, shell-fish and some turnips' given to them by their neighbours. And turnips from the garden of the workhouse were fed to the two and a half thousand inmates.

The number of deaths in the workhouse reflected the development of the crisis. In November 1847 there were 21 deaths; in December, 71; in January, 146; in February, 137; and in March, 202. These deaths in the workhouse scared paupers away from applying for admission, and induced them, as one writer put it, 'to prefer the chance of starvation outside to the prospect of death apart from their families within.'

It was not until April 1848 that the food supplies at the workhouse were back to normal. But the numbers seeking relief were not diminished. One relieving officer attended four successive weekly meetings of the Kilrush board before he could get them to consider his list of 840 applicants. Many of these failed to trek the twenty miles from Kildysart to Kilrush on the day that their application was eventually taken and consequently they got no relief. Hundreds of paupers used to stay overnight in the town during the winter huddling together around the market-house. And householders were warned by their landlords not to give shelter to these vagrants. What was called 'famine fever' continued to kill in the workhouse.

Those who managed to get a passage on an emigrant ship to America considered themselves more fortunate than their neighbours. These ships were sometimes called coffin ships because of the numbers who died of fever on board. Statistically, the census of 1851 recorded the havoc of the famine years. Between the census of 1841 and that of 1851 the population of the Kilrush union had declined by more than 13,000 or approximately one fifth. Out of the 27 electoral divisions in the union the town of Kilrush alone showed any appreciable increase in population — no doubt because of the existence of its workhouse. Indeed, the population of the workhouse in 1851 at 4,796 was greater by over three hundred than that of the town itself. The decline in the ratio of males to females in Kilrush was everywhere noticeable. Men had emigrated, men had deserted in search of employment, and men had succumbed more easily than their womenfolk to the rigours of the famine.

Because of eviction, death and desertion, there were nearly 3,000 fewer inhabited houses in the district than there had been before famine struck. Approximately a quarter of all the houses had been either destroyed by the evictor or deserted by the inhabitants, because of the famine. Hunger had proved to be as effectual an evictor as the sheriff himself. Villages were described as looking like 'the tombs of a departed race'. And yet the destruction in the Kilrush union was no different from what had happened all over the west and south of Ireland.

Out of a total Irish population of over eight million at the beginning of the famine, approximately one million had died of hunger and its attendant diseases and another million had fled from the starving land by the time the census was taken in 1851. Those who had died in Kilrush from famine and 'fever' and exposure, or who had emigrated, constitute the vast amount of human misery which lies behind the neat statistics of that 1851 census. The attempts of the governments of Peel and Russell to deal with the grim situation were tardy, cumbersome, restricted by the economic theory of the day and largely ineffectual. In fairness to the government, however, no nineteenth-century administration had the means or the skill to handle successfully a catastrophe of such proportions as the great famine. The poor-houses and fever hospitals that already existed were inadequate for an emergency so vast. The relief works, the importation of Indian corn, the food-depots, soup-kitchens, and other measures taken by the government and private groups were insufficient to counter the magnitude of the tragedy. The famine is the great watershed in nineteenth-century Ireland. Its consequences, both immediate and longterm, were profound and affected the political, social, cultural and economic life of the country.

During the rest of the century each census showed that Ireland's population — unlike most of the world — continued to dwindle. The major reason for this was emigration, for the number of emigrants was greater than the excess of births over deaths. Between 1841 and 1844 an average of 50,000 a year left the country. In 1846 this number doubled to 116,000. In 1847 the figure rose to 230,000 for those going to America and Australia, apart from the tens of thousands more who had settled in Britain. In 1851 the peak was reached with a quarter of a million emigrating to America alone. The emigrants of the famine years suffered under appalling conditions. Those who survived the voyage were held for a period of quarantine on landing in America and Canada, during which time many more died of fever. Immigrants had to undergo long years of struggle, hardship and discrimination before they were assimilated into American society. As these immigrants of the famine years got established, however, they supplied the passage money for relatives back home, and it became easier for later waves of emigrants to settle into Irish communities in American cities.

Together the decline in population and the increase in emigration took some of the pressure off the land. The tiny pre-famine holdings were consolidated into farms of more economic size. The number of holdings of less than fifteen acres that existed on the eve of the famine had been almost halved by its end, and the farms of over fifteen acres became more numerous. Some landlords, too, were ruined economically by the famine. During the next thirty years about one quarter of the land of Ireland changed hands as a result of the working of the Encumbered Estates Act (1849). If the new landlords were more efficient than the old they often tended also to be more severe in evicting tenants who had fallen into arrears with their rents. Eviction after the famine was further encouraged by the tendency to increase grazing land at the expense of tillage. This change in the farming pattern from grain production to cattle raising was due to economic factors related to world markets.

The pre-famine practice of marrying young and of having large families was also affected by the famine.[4] The marriage-rate in Ireland declined until it became one of the lowest in the world, and late marriages became one of the features especially of rural society.

With fewer people, marriages and farms, the cabins and hovels which had dotted the countryside before the famine were no longer required to the same extent for human habitation. According to the 1841 census half of the houses in Ireland had consisted of single-roomed mud cabins. By 1851, however, 70 per cent of these had disappeared. The ultimate outcome of all these post-famine changes was a higher standard of living for those who remained behind in Ireland. The depopulation, emigration, consolidation of farms and the changes in economic and social patterns which the famine either launched or helped to accelerate in Ireland were also influenced by world-wide economic and social trends over the next half century. One has to be careful, therefore, not to attribute all change in Irish society in the second half of the nineteenth century to the famine.

A calamity which had such complex yet deep social, economic and psychological effects was bound to have, also, a big political impact on the shaping of modern Ireland. Under O'Connell in the first half of the nineteenth century the country had been in the main loyal and pacifist. The loyalty and pacifism perished in the famine. English rule was held to be responsible for the catastrophe. Out of the famine graves and the coffin ships there arose phoenix-like a political hatred of England. This hatred was best and most bitterly articulated in the writings of John Mitchel. Mitchel claimed that 'the Almighty indeed sent the potato blight, but the English created the famine'. And Mitchel's interpretation was the one generally accepted in Ireland and by Irish-Americans.

People who held with Mitchel that the government had attempted genocide found it easy to support the fenian policy of breaking totally with England by force, or the land league's aim of destroying landlordism. The hostility felt by Irish emigrants for England was immortalised by Yeats in the lines:

> Out of Ireland have we come
> Great hatred, little room,
> Maimed us at the start.
> I carry from my Mother's womb
> The fanatic heart.

Separatist objectives, and extremist methods for achieving those objectives, re-entered Irish politics largely as a result of the famine. And the land question which had not been a political issue before the famine became one of the chief political issues of the post-famine period. During the second half of the nineteenth century, republicanism, the physical force tradition and agrarianism were to draw much of their inspiration from the remembrance of the terrible famine years.

The Irish language

For centuries, Irish had been the language of the country. It had been not only the ordinary medium of social intercourse, but the repository also of the people's laws, their annals, their genealogies, the lives of their saints, their history, their folklore, their deepest religious convictions and their political aspirations. By the beginning of the nineteenth century, however, the most glorious years of Gaelic literature were long past, and spoken Irish was retreating fast from the linguistic map of Europe.

Census returns can sometimes be misleading due to the subjectivity of replies. In mid-nineteenth century Ireland many with little facility in English liked to be able to boast of their knowledge of it. The figures in 1841 immediately before the great famine show that about 50 per cent of a population of over eight million people spoke Irish. Ten years later, in 1851, this had been reduced to 23.3 per cent, and 5 per cent spoke Irish only.

Remorseless erosion of the language had begun long before the twin nineteenth-century tragedies of the great famine and subsequent emigration increased the rate of change, although the famine powerfully accelerated the process, for the resultant depopulation struck most severely at the poorer, Gaelic-speaking areas of the west. It was once fashionable, but far too simplistic, to put the blame on O'Connell and the national schools between them for the wiping out of the language. Long before a national school was built in any part of the country, and long before O'Connell appealed to the forty shilling freeholders of Waterford and Clare for their votes in the emancipation struggle, the children of the country were eagerly learning English in their own hedge schools and at the insistence of their Irish-speaking parents. One of the most important factors in the decline of the Irish language in the early nineteenth century had been the powerful pull exercised by the English-speaking world. On one side of Ireland operated the commercial and industrial force of Britain, and on the other was the magnetic new world of America. What cannot be overlooked, however, was the increasing encirclement of the Irish-speaking districts by the expanding English-speaking areas in Ireland itself. Some idea of the inroads made by English can be gauged by the fact that if we take Westmeath in the very heart of the country, we find that in the whole of that county in 1851 there was only one person in the total population of 111,000 who spoke Irish only; 920 persons in the county, or 0.8 per cent, claimed to know both Irish and English, and these were in the older age-groups. The other 99 per cent claimed to know English only. Busy marketing midland towns like Mullingar or Athlone, the gateway to Connaught, were English-speaking long before the famine. By 1861, not a single person in all of Westmeath spoke Irish only. And less than 500 (or 0.5 per cent) of the total population of the county claimed to know Irish. Relentless economic laws undermined the foundations of the Irish-speaking world and continually narrowed down its dominion.

What is important to remember is that when people learned English, they did not become bilingual; they simply ceased to use Irish. Bilingualism was a middle-class luxury, or dream, of later and more prosperous times which the struggling peasantry, small farmers and small shop-keepers of Ireland in the nineteenth century could not afford.

With many in nineteenth century Ireland, Irish had become a matter of shame. It was a mark of inferiority to know Irish only, and it even became a matter of pride to some to be able to boast their ignorance of the Irish language. A generation of Irish people went through the saddening experience of being ignorant in both languages. A German traveller in the country stated that everything about the people was 'patchwork' — their clothing, their dwellings, their language. Patchwork, by choice, can be artistic and colourful; patchwork, by necessity, is the outward mark of poverty and degradation. The Irish people had become the poverty-stricken victims of a patchwork culture. Scarcely able to read or write in either language, their Irish, which was becoming increasingly poorer, was being replaced by a smattering of bad English. Because of the speed with which the language was being abandoned, and because parents with little English refused to communicate in Irish with their children, who had only poor English, a vast amount of traditional culture was lost. As far as the Irish-speaking culture was concerned, the great famine was followed by what has been called, appropriately enough, the great silence. A generation of Irish people was being instilled with the lesson that cultural values should not be allowed to stand in the way of material progress. The language, and all that was associated with it, was seen to be cast away by one's parents and teachers and priests as something that was not only worthless, but even damaging. The experience was bound to have detrimental psychological effects.

A priest in Limerick told a traveller from the continent in 1860 that the people had to pull down in order to build up, meaning that they had to pull down the edifice of the Irish language in which they were denied an education, in order to build up educational opportunities for themselves in English. Even in the Irish-speaking districts, English was the medium of instruction in the schools. The sad fact was that people, priests and political leaders co-operated willingly with this system for the benefits which it offered. One educationalist, Sir Patrick Keenan, afterwards chief commissioner of the board of national education, petitioned in vain that Irish-speaking children be taught first their own language grammatically, and then English, through the medium of their own language. Apart from the difficulty in Keenan's time of providing qualified Irish teachers, the plan was rejected on the grounds that the parents did not look for it, and what is often not mentioned is that he made his proposal, not to benefit Irish, but in order that the schoolchildren of the Gaeltacht might acquire a better English more speedily and efficiently.

A state system of anglicising education for an Ireland that had only recently become part of the United Kingdom is perfectly understandable from the official standpoint. It is more difficult, however, to explain why the catholic church, or rather so many of the priests, surrendered the Irish language apparently with so little compunction or cultural sensitivity. While there were indeed many instances of awareness of the value of Irish, and of concern for its preservation among individual priests, there were many other examples of neglect and abandonment. A German visitor to Ireland on the eve of the famine, reported that in the whole of the city of Cork, lying in a district where Irish was still widely spoken, in only two churches were sermons preached in Irish. And the prisoners in Cork jail had to petition the chaplain to preach his Sunday sermon to them in Irish. Although a rich oral tradition of prayers in Irish and of religious poetry still survived, there was a scarcity of devotional literature in the language. And what was even more significant was that where printed books did survive, as in the case of Gallagher's *Sermons*, it was estimated that only 1,000 of the estimated 70,000 Irish speakers in Donegal in 1874 were literate enough in their own language to be able to read it.

It is true that once the proselytising societies began to issue bible tracts in Irish in the crusade to wean the people from catholicism, catholic church authorities became suspicious of religious literature in Irish. But this in itself can hardly account for the neglect of the Irish language by the catholic clergy. The priests, like the people themselves and their political leaders, were merely responding to the utilitarianism of the age. The people who were demanding and, let it be said, acquiring the political and civil rights of nineteenth-century England, and who were aspiring to the social, commercial, and economic status of the English colonists in Ireland were only too eager to imitate their conquerors in the matter of language also, and adopted it as their own vehicle of communication, and as the measure of their advancement. The acquisition of the English language was seen as a victory of urban sophistication over rural backwardness, of 'townie' over 'culchie', of the richer farmlands over bog and mountainside, of the commercial economy of the eastern ports over the fishing villages of the west.

Priests, educated in the new seminaries at Carlow, Kilkenny, Killarney, Belfast, Maynooth, Thurles and Clonliffe, regarded it as fashionable to pretend a lack of knowledge of Irish. The establishment of the largest of these seminaries in the English speaking towns of the eastern half of the country helped to ensure the victory of English over Irish. To minister to the growing catholic middle classes of the towns, English was more than just a symbol of respectability. It had become a necessary tool of office if the faith, which had survived the poverty and persecution of the penal laws, was to survive the comparative prosperity and tolerance of brighter days.

Apart from the Royal Irish Academy, special organisations for the study of Ireland's ancient language and history were established throughout the nineteenth century. The Gaelic Society of Dublin was founded in 1806, followed by the Hiberno-Celtic Society in 1818, the Ulster Gaelic Society in 1830, the Irish Archaeological Society in 1840, the Celtic Society in 1845 and the Ossianic Society in 1853. All of these were associations producing material for scholars. They did not aim at converting the people over to a language policy. Non-sectarian and non-political, these societies encouraged progressive awareness of the value of the Irish language and literature. Among middle-class intellectuals they helped to restore some pride in a culture that was disappearing. A few individuals — like Philip Barron in Co. Waterford in the 1830s — occasionally attempted to promote the spoken language among the people. Richard D'Alton in Tipperary published a paper briefly in the early 1860s, the purpose of which was the restoration of the language. Archbishop MacHale of Tuam advocated the more widespread use of Irish by his clergy, and set the good example himself, by publishing a number of works in Irish. But these individuals could do very little to halt the tide of de-gaelicisation.

Among political leaders and propagandists, Thomas Davis alone advocated an Irish language revival policy. Influenced by what continental romantics were saying about their national languages, Davis asserted in the *Nation*: 'a people, without a language of its own, is only half a nation. A nation should guard its language more than its territories; 'tis a surer barrier and more important frontier than a fortress or river.' Davis's suggestion was that Irish should be preserved and gradually extended. Teachers in Irish-speaking districts should be required to teach through Irish and a newspaper, partly or wholly in Irish, should be established so that the Irish speaker could find in his native tongue the political news and general information he had otherwise to seek in English. The views expressed by Davis made little impact in their own time. Individual Fenians promoted Irish: O'Donovan Rossa spoke it in his shop in Skibbereen and taught it in the Mechanics Institute in Dublin. John O'Mahony translated Keating's *Foras Feasa ar Éirinn*. But official Fenian policies, concentrating on the establishment of the Irish republic, had nothing to say about the language. Constitutional nationalism simply ignored Irish. O'Connell's attitude was typical. As a native speaker he knew a great deal more Irish than did Thomas Davis. Yet he could witness without a sigh the gradual disuse of Irish because he regarded English as the more useful medium of modern communication. Through the speeches, writings, press and propaganda in English of O'Connell, Young Ireland and the Fenians, political nationalism was developed among the people in general and with little or no thought for the language that was being simultaneously abandoned. For the people had first to become nationalistic-minded through English before they could become aware of the political importance of a national language.

Tenant League, Catholic Defence Association and Independent Irish Party

The land question had been brought dramatically into public consciousness by the famine — and it was to remain as one of the major issues in Irish politics during the next half century. The government's effort to deal with the problem only scratched at the surface. The Encumbered Estates Act (1849) cleared the land of debt-burdened landlords over the next couple of decades, but it did little for the tenants. Several bills were introduced into parliament in an attempt to give tenants greater security, but all were defeated. The number of families permanently dispossessed through eviction in 1849 and 1850 was almost 28,000, and between 1851 and 1854 another 21,000 families lost their holdings.[5] This does not take into account the numbers threatened with eviction, or the numbers evicted and then allowed to return to their homes. The tenants realised that they must organise in their own interests.

Tenant protection societies began to spring up locally from 1847 onwards. The best known of these was that founded in Callan, Co. Kilkenny in 1849 under the leadership of two catholic curates, Fr Matthew Keeffe and Fr Tom O'Shea. The example of the Callan society, which was organised to prevent the local landlord from clearing people off the land and to protect tenants against high rents, was soon followed throughout other parts of the south and west of Ireland. In Ulster a custom had grown up which gave security to those tenants who paid their rents, and allowed them to sell their interest or goodwill in a holding to an incoming tenant. This 'Ulster-custom', as it was called, should be given the force of law according to the Ulster Tenant Right Association which was founded for that purpose by William Sharman Crawford and James McKnight.

An attempt was made to link all of these local societies together in one national organisation. The editors of three leading journals, John Gray of *The Freeman's Journal*, Gavan Duffy of the *Nation* and Frederick Lucas of the *Tablet*, called for a national tenant-right conference to meet in Dublin in August 1850. Out of this conference was founded the tenant league. Gavan Duffy, who wrote a history of the league, liked to refer to it as the league of north and south because tenant societies from all over Ireland were involved in its origins.

The aims of the tenant league were to lower the rents, to have the Ulster-custom legalised and extended to the whole country, and to win security of tenure. These objectives were summed up in the phrase 'the three Fs' (fair rent, free sale and fixity of tenure). The chief method by which the tenant league hoped to achieve its aims was by the building up of an independent parliamentary party to press for these reforms.

Meanwhile in parliament Irish MPs became involved in another issue. The pope had restored the English hierarchy and instructed the Roman catholic bishops in England to use their ecclesiastical titles. This, however, was a sore point with many protestants, and so there arose one of those periodic public outbursts against popery which was never far from the surface in nineteenth-century Britain. The public outcry influenced the government to introduce an Ecclesiastical Titles Bill (1851) prohibiting catholic prelates from assuming their diocesan titles. Over 20 Irish MPs (known as the Irish Brigade, or later as 'the Pope's Brass Band'), campaigned vigorously in parliament against the introduction of the bill. They failed to prevent its passage into law. Back in Dublin, however, they set up a Catholic Defence Association, whose leaders were George H Moore, MP for Mayo, William Keogh, MP for Athlone, and John Sadleir, MP for Carlow — a landlord, a barrister and a banker respectively.

Many of the same people were active in both the tenant league and the Catholic Defence Association: the league welcomed the support of the parliamentarians of the Catholic Defence Association, and the latter welcomed the support of the journalists who had organised the tenant league. Thus the agrarian and religious agitations were now formed into an alliance. This alliance worked successfully in the general election of 1852. In post-election conferences forty-eight MPs pledged themselves to act in parliament as an Independent Irish Party opposed to all governments which did not concede their demands on religious equality and agrarian reform. A cohesive party of forty-eight MPs was greater than any that O'Connell had commanded. It was made possible to a large extent by the passing of the Franchise Act of 1850. Largely as a result of the famine the electorate, based on the complicated qualifications of 1832, had fallen from 121,000 to around 45,000. The notion of the possession of property as a qualification for the vote was replaced by that of occupation. Ratepayers holding a £12 poor law valuation in the counties, or £8 rated occupations in the boroughs were given the vote. This effectively conferred the vote on all farmers of twenty acres and upwards, and increased the total number of voters to more than 163,000. This new electorate had compactness and a social coherence unknown before 1850, and the Franchise Act removed from the electorate some of its former fickleness and subservience. (It was essentially this electorate that Parnell later exploited to the full.)[6] A couple of months after the emergence of the Independent Irish Party a coalition government under Lord Aberdeen was formed. Two leaders of the Irish party accepted office in Aberdeen's government — William Keogh as solicitor-general for Ireland, and John Sadleir as a lord of the treasury — despite their pre-election pledges. This caused an immediate and bitter split in the Irish party and among its supporters. Even the catholic clergy engaged on opposite sides. Archbishop Cullen took a grave view of what he regarded as unedifying, political squabbles amongst the priests. Some priests who were active on behalf of the tenant league and vocal in their condemnation of Sadleir and Keogh were punished for breaches of ecclesiastical discipline. Cullen who, unlike some other bishops, had not publicly denounced Sadleir and Keogh, was in favour of introducing ecclesiastical legislation to restrict the political activities of priests, and this was done at meetings of the hierarchy. To men like Lucas and Duffy the order that priests should get out of politics seemed to be a direct undermining of the support of the Independent Irish Party and of the tenant league throughout the country. Lucas appealed to Rome against the archbishop's policy, but got little satisfaction in a quarter where Cullen's reputation was very highly regarded.

The public dispute with the archbishop only did further damage to the Irish party. The party which numbered forty-eight MPs after the election of 1852 had fallen to twenty-six after the Sadleir-Keogh defections, and now, largely as a result of the dispute with Cullen, was no more than 12 MPs strong. Duffy was so disheartened by the failure that he decided to emigrate to Australia. The strain under which Lucas had worked impaired his health, and he died in 1855. Under the leadership of Moore the tenant league made a slight recovery, especially after Sadleir, who had fallen into financial difficulties, committed suicide, and those who had denounced him all along since his defection seemed to have been justified. In 1859 the Independent Irish Party finally disintegrated when six of those who were still associated with it voted with the conservative government on the grounds that the conservatives were making some concessions to Ireland, and five voted against.

So ended the attempt to create an Irish party in Westminster separate from both whigs and tories. The alliance of Catholic Defence Association and tenant league was always an uneasy one. Besides, given the system of open, non-secret voting, it was difficult to get support for candidates who were not approved of by the local landlords, and these were not likely to approve of candidates who demanded land reform in the tenants' favour. Indeed it was often difficult to find suitable candidates since elections were expensive, and MPs were still not paid a salary, and a man had to have the necessary property qualifications and be of independent means before he could consider standing for a seat in parliament. The conditions which initially had given rise to the emergence of the Irish party — religious intolerance and agrarian distress — abated; and as material conditions improved, and no prosecutions took place under the Ecclesiastical Titles Act, the party's fortunes declined. Finally, throughout its career the party suffered from a chronic lack of leadership: it produced no leaders of the calibre of an O'Connell. The attempt to raise the land question to the level of national politics, and to create in parliament an independent party to press for land reform had failed ingloriously. The policy was something in the nature of a false start.

Origins and spread of fenianism
One of the immediate results of the failure of the league and of the Independent Irish Party was that it helped to discredit constitutional politics. Politics of a more radical and violent kind began to have a widespread appeal in the late 1850s and early 1860s. The famine graves and emigrant coffin ships undermined the policy of non-violence which O'Connell had preached in the first half of the century. Bitter resentment against the English administration in Ireland ran deep. The rebellion of 1848 was the desperate reaction of those Young Irelanders who held England responsible for the great famine. Their badly organised and poorly led insurrection had depended for success on the willingness of an unarmed and starving peasantry to rise up spontaneously against their oppressors and establish a republic. In the circumstances the rising of 1848 was easily suppressed. The leaders were either jailed or exiled. Many of the younger participants who escaped from the country were determined to put up a better showing next time. It was these young rebels who, a decade later, organised the much more formidable fenian movement.

Two of these young '48 men were James Stephens and John O'Mahony who had both fled to Paris after the insurrection where they met up with some of those other political refugees from every country where revolution had been attempted in 1848. From Paris O'Mahony went to New York arriving there in 1854. Irish Americans numbered a quarter of the total population of New York. O'Mahony found among them many Young Irelanders and famine refugees who were only too willing to help in any nationalistic enterprise. They were not, however, very effectively organised. And so an appeal was made to Stephens who had returned to Ireland in 1858 to form a revolutionary movement at home which would provide a base and a centre for all future operations and towards which Irish-American aid could be directed. The first meeting of this new movement — the IRB (the Irish revolutionary, or later, republican brotherhood) — took place in Dublin on St Patrick's Day, 1858. The organisation's members became popularly known as Fenians. It was a tightly organised, oath-bound, secret society, modelled on continental societies, and based on 'circles' and local cells. It aimed at the establishment of an Irish republic by force of arms.

A combination of factors proved favourable to the spread of fenianism in Ireland. The great display of nationalist sympathy which was evoked by the funeral in 1861 of the '48 veteran, Terence Bellew MacManus, so successfully stage-managed by the Fenians, brought support to the movement. It was the longest funeral procession in Irish history, from San Francisco to Glasnevin, and outdistanced by far that of Napoleon from St Helena to Paris. Economic depression in the early 1860s, with the inevitable increase in evictions and the rise in the numbers seeking poor relief, provided a favourable background. The promise of Irish-American aid in terms of money, men and arms following the ending of the American civil war in 1865 also encouraged the growth of the movement. Stephens skilfully exploited these circumstances, and was ably assisted by TC Luby and O'Donovan Rossa whose Phoenix Society, a political and literary club founded in Skibbereen in 1856, was merged with the Fenians.

A weekly newspaper, the *Irish People*, was established in November 1863 to propagate the policies and ideals of the Fenians. There were, of course, grave risks involved for a secret society in having a public newspaper office, which also served as the headquarters of the conspiracy. It could, and did, provide the authorities with an identifiable major target at which to strike. But the advantages in terms of propaganda, at least in the initial stages, were also great. Like the *Nation* of the Young Ireland movement, the *Irish People* educated its readers in nationalism. Its patriotic ballads may not have reached quite as high a standard as those of the *Nation*, but its political programme was much more pointed. It stood for the total separation of Ireland from the United Kingdom, and insisted that there could be no compromise with constitutional or reformist agitations. It advocated, instead, the ultimate use of physical force as the direct and only way of attaining Irish independence. 'True national independence', said an editorial in the very first issue, 'never was and never will be anywhere achieved save by the sword.' Discussion of social and economic objectives, although permitted, was not allowed to distract the movement from the single-mindedness of its political course. Through the *Irish People* the Fenian gospel seemed to say: seek ye first an independent Irish republic and all these other social and economic benefits shall be added unto you. The paper which was under the management of O'Donovan Rossa had as its chief editorial writers, besides Luby, two Co. Tipperary men with considerable literary talents — John O'Leary, afterwards immortalised in the poetry of Yeats, and Charles Kickham, the novelist, who was the author of the popular nineteenth-century romances *Knocknagow* and *Sally Cavanagh*.

Membership of the organisation spread rapidly. Middle-class intellectuals made up the leadership, but it was basically a working-class and lower middle-class movement. John O'Leary, in observing that shop-keepers and farmers made very good agitators but very poor rebels, stated that shop-assistants and farm labourers swelled the Fenian ranks. Teachers, artisans and men of the building trades were also prominent among the classes that composed the rank-and-file. The so-called 'Ribbon', or agrarian Fenians, who joined the organisation in the west of Ireland in the late 1860s out of an interest in fixity of tenure, rents and the breaking-up of large farms, were a strong echo of the agrarian secret societies of the first half of the nineteenth century. Fenians were to be found even among the many Irishmen in the British army and the prison service. John Devoy, one of the chief organisers in charge of Fenian recruitment in the regiments stationed in Ireland, stated — probably with some exaggeration — that as many as 15,000 men (more than one third of the total) among the army regiments in Ireland were sworn Fenians. A total Fenian membership in Ireland in 1864 was assessed at more than 54,000.[7] In its hey-day in the USA, 45,000 active members was the figure given for the brotherhood there, which in addition enjoyed the moral support of far greater numbers. The famous 'Fighting 69th' regiment of New York was one of a number said to be composed entirely of Fenians. It was estimated that in March 1866 over 100,000 persons attended a Fenian rally in New York.

By any reckoning fenianism presented a formidable revolutionary threat. The determined opposition it met with, however, was no less formidable. This opposition came mainly from two quarters — the church and the government.

The church and the Fenians

The leadership of public opinion in Ireland which the Fenians sought was a direct challenge to the catholic clergy. The challenge was given precisely at the moment when Archbishop Cullen was the dominant figure among the hierarchy, and was also, allegedly, the grey eminence in political affairs during the vacuum in lay leadership between the passing of O'Connell and the rise of Parnell. Cullen, a great administrator, powerfully influential at Rome where he had been rector of the Irish College, was indeed very much the 'Romaniser' of the nineteenth-century church in Ireland. Appointed archbishop of Armagh in December 1849, he was transferred to Dublin in March 1852 and became Ireland's first cardinal in 1866. Under his guidance the church, emerging from the disintegrating experience of the penal days, was brought back into full discipline with Rome. Contemporaries whispered about the 'Cullenisation' of Ireland. What in effect this meant was that Cullen drew together the individual bishops and moulded them into the Irish hierarchy, a formidable weapon geared to serve the papacy, and strong enough to give politics in Ireland an ecclesiastical slant. Symbolically Roman dress became the fashion among the priesthood during the Cullen era.

At the very moment when the Irish church was being more closely linked with Rome the papacy under Pius IX had developed something of a siege-complex, and this communicated itself to the Irish hierarchy. The temporal power of the pope was under severe attack, while 'liberalism', 'socialism', freemasonry, and the secret societies were all described as anti-religious and condemned in a number of papal decrees culminating in the Syllabus of Errors (1864). It had never been more difficult for a catholic, than in these circumstances, to justify his joining a secret, oath-bound organisation for the purpose of rebellion against the recognised or legitimate government.

From the first stirrings of the Fenian movement in 1858, therefore, the organisation provoked a chorus of episcopal censures led by Archbishop Cullen of Dublin and Bishop Moriarty of Kerry. The basis of these censures was firmly stated and constantly reiterated. In the first place, the bishops maintained, a series of papal bulls had condemned 'occult societies'. It was, therefore, sinful to join such a society, or to try by force to overthrow the legitimate government. It was wrong to swear blind obedience to strangers who might not even be men of religion. It was further stated that the Fenian paper, the *Irish People*, preached socialism and disrespect for all ecclesiastical authority. And it was claimed by the bishops that fenianism only played into the hands of the enemies of Ireland and of catholicism; that it was a hopeless enterprise leading to bloodshed and the ruin of the country.

The bishops' stand against fenianism had the support not only of the constitutional nationalists in O'Connell's tradition, but also of the ex-'48 men like Smith O'Brien, John Blake Dillon and John Mitchel. Cullen's interest was primarily in matters like education. When he did express any political opinions it is clear enough that his views were moderately nationalistic. In the pastoral in which he denounced fenianism he also stated that Ireland ought to be 'great, happy and free'.

What in practice the bishops' condemnation came to was that in the confessionals the question was asked whether one had taken the Fenian oath. Absolution was refused until the penitent had promised to give up the organisation. The church's hostility to fenianism created for many Irish catholics a conflict of loyalties: the love of Ireland appeared to be opposed to fidelity to catholicism. The dilemma was how to be a good catholic and a Fenian at the same time. However, there was many an instance where the interpretation of the episcopal censures by a sympathetic priest left the door open for the man who wanted to reconcile his fenianism with his religious beliefs.

The most celebrated public protagonist of fenianism among the clergy was Fr Lavelle of the parish of Partry in the archdiocese of Tuam who outspokenly attacked landlordism and proselytism in his area. In 1861 Dr Cullen refused to allow a lying-in-state in the pro-cathedral for the body of Terence Bellew MacManus, because he regarded the whole affair as a Fenian publicity stunt. Fr Lavelle publicly attacked the archbishop and the priests of the diocese for their attitude, and travelled to Dublin to preach the funeral oration. A few months later (11 February 1862), Fr Lavelle was back in Dublin's Rotunda lecturing on 'The catholic doctrine of the right of revolution'. In his incessant propaganda Lavelle explained that fenianism was in full accord with the precepts of the catholic church, and he insisted that preparation for resistance to a tyrannical government was not only justified but indeed the duty of Irishmen. On one occasion he argued that the papal bulls against secret societies applied only to those which aimed at the overthrow of church *and* state, and not to those like the Fenian Brotherhood which aimed only at the overthrow of tyrannical governments. Lavelle was also vice-president of the Brotherhood of St Patrick, which was a sort of front-organisation for the Fenians, and membership of which was a reserved sin in some of the dioceses.

Lavelle, protected by his superior, Archbishop MacHale of Tuam, was for long able to thwart not only Cullen and the Irish bishops, but even Rome itself. The Lavelle case was, however, regarded as a great scandal by the majority of the Irish ecclesiastics outside of Tuam, for it led to a great deal of wrangling (at Rome) between the two archbishops — Cullen and MacHale, the latter dubbed as 'His Holiness's opposition in Ireland'. There is some evidence to suggest that privately MacHale may not have approved of fenianism, but he was not going to be bested by Cullen. His stand in the matter, however, had the effect of countering some of the force of condemnation by the other bishops, and, of course, it made very useful material for the Fenian propagandists.

Many Fenians felt that ecclesiastical opinion, whether favourable to fenianism or not, was altogether irrelevant. Perhaps the most constantly reiterated message of the *Irish People* during its two years of existence was that of 'no priests in politics'. In his articles on this topic, the sincere catholic, Kickham, maintained that while one could take as much religion as one liked from the priests they were very bad guides to follow in politics. Priests, said Kickham, were especially unsuited to any form of political leadership. They came straight from a seminary without any experience of the world. Even the most patriotic of them could not be trusted with leadership for they were not free agents. At a moment's notice, as in the case of the '48 priests and the tenant right priests, they would have to accept the ruling of ecclesiastical superiors, and desert the people who had followed their lead. It was, therefore, bad for both priests and people that the clergy should get involved and try to lead in matters which were not spiritual. He wrote: 'We never uttered a word against the priests as ministers of religion. But we challenged and do challenge their right to dictate to the people in politics.' Kickham explained the origins of clerical influence in Irish politics in the following words:

> The Irish priest assumes an authority over his flock which the clergy in other catholic countries never dream of assuming. Yet this is not to be wondered at. The history of Ireland explains it. The fiendish tyranny of England ground our people down to the condition of ignorant slaves. In this state of compulsory ignorance and serfdom the people naturally looked for guidance to the only educated class that cared or sympathised with them. But times are changed. The people are now comparatively educated, and demand the right possessed by the people of other catholic countries of acting according to the dictates of their own judgement in all wordly concerns.

The issue between the clergy and the Fenians was one of political morality. It was largely a question of where politics began and the jurisdiction of the church ended. In this confrontation between the church and the Fenians, catholicism and nationalism, which had been so closely interwoven since the days of O'Connell, now seemed to be breaking apart. The links between the two forces were maintained, however, not only by the kind of arguments used by the *Irish People*, but also by the fact that Rome did not condemn fenianism by name until 1870 — three years after the Fenian rising. That a few priests were sympathetic to them and that Lavelle who argued the Fenian case appeared to have the protection of Archbishop MacHale of Tuam also helped to preserve the link. Although harassed by the catholic clergy in general, the Fenian movement continued to attract recruits, and while engaged in verbal warfare with the catholic church was directing its main efforts at organising rebellion against the state.

For many Fenians patriotism had become one of the greatest of the virtues, and the language of religion was used by them to express their deeply felt patriotism. Their almost religious fervour and obvious sincerity had their effect. The widespread sympathy and the great demonstrations in connection with the Manchester Martyrs, the massive appeal of the Fenian Amnesty Association and the welcoming home parties for the released prisoners — in all of which priests took an active part — helped to heal the threatened breach between Irish nationalism and the catholic church. The dedication, self-denial, suffering and self-sacrifice endured by the Fenians — virtues which the clergy extolled — could not but be admired by the same clergy.

A head-on clash between Irish nationalism and the catholic church had been averted, for in the end neither side had really wanted to fight the other. In the process, however, each had learned to regard the other with a healthy respect. And largely because of the Fenian episode 'catholic' and 'Irish' no longer necessarily meant the same thing. For, in their own often inarticulate and non-philosophical way, the Fenians had insisted on separating the state, which they sought to overthrow, from the church to which the majority of them belonged.

The Fenian Rising and its aftermath

The state papers which include police reports, reports from G Division of the Dublin Metropolitan Police which was responsible for intelligence work, dispatches from consular officials in the USA, and information from informers within the brotherhood reveal the extent to which the authorities had the activities of this secret society under careful surveillance. To combat the threat of fenianism and of political crime secret service work was organised on a more professional basis in Dublin and London, and when the time was ripe the government struck.

Army regiments, whose loyalty in the event of a rebellion was in doubt, were moved out of Ireland and replaced by more dependable units. The *Irish People* was suppressed. In the autumn of 1865 just before the date planned for a general rising, the principal leaders were arrested and jailed. Indecision among the leaders and successive postponements of the date of the rising; the arrest of the leaders and discouragement among those who still remained at large; the failure of sufficient arms to arrive from America due largely to a split in the movement in the United States; the condemnation of secret societies by the ecclesiastical authorities; the well-timed precautions taken by the administration — all contributed to upset the plans for a country-wide rebellion. Minor local risings did take place, however, in various parts of the country. In Cahirciveen, Co. Kerry, a rising broke out prematurely on 11 February 1867. On 5 March other efforts were made in Tipperary, Cork, Limerick, Clare, Wicklow and at Tallaght, Co. Dublin, mostly in severe snow storms. All of these attempts were soon suppressed. As a military operation the rising in Ireland was virtually a bloodless failure; in fact no more than a gesture made by men who did not expect to win. They had acted in the belief that to disband without a fight would have been more demoralising than an utter failure in arms. Fenian activity extended beyond Ireland. Attempts at an invasion of Canada were made. Although the Fenians were tolerated openly in the United States by the administrations of Johnson and Grant because of the importance of the Irish vote, the raids on Canada had little success. It was the activities of the Fenians in England which brought home to the English people on their very doorsteps the deep discontent which was felt with British rule in Ireland. An attack on Chester castle in an attempt to procure arms received wide publicity, as did an attempt to blow down the wall of Clerkenwell prison. During a raid on a police van in Manchester, in a successful attempt to rescue two Fenian prisoners, a policeman was accidentally killed. Three men, Allen, Larkin and O'Brien, were tried for their part in the raid and executed. The execution of the three 'Manchester Martyrs' (23 November 1867) on what was regarded as very doubtful evidence aroused bitter feelings among Irish people everywhere, and a wave of sympathy with fenianism swept Ireland. The ballad, 'God Save Ireland', honouring the bravery with which the three men had faced execution, became the country's unofficial national anthem. It was written by T D Sullivan whose paper, The *Nation*, which represented constitutional nationalism and had been strongly opposed to fenianism, now took up the cause of the Fenian prisoners.

Seen in context fenianism was the product of a range of social, economic, political, cultural and personality factors; and its force was so great that it, in turn, powerfully influenced contemporary Irish society in many aspects. Conspiracy and violence had been used by agrarian societies as the means to remedy local grievances in pre-famine Ireland. Fenianism as a sophisticated version of the agrarian society, and as a nation-wide secret society, introduced the mass of the Irish people to the idea of secret organisation and physical force for the removal of national grievances and the attainment of national objectives. In doing so it simultaneously propagated the idea of republicanism widely among the masses. By embracing Irish emigrants in the USA it added an American dimension to Irish nationalism. The consciousness of the revolutionary tradition which it fostered linked a magical combination of numbers — 1798, 1803, 1848, 1867 and 1916 — in a chain of historical continuity. The longevity of some of its more prominent leaders — O'Donovan Rossa's funeral in 1915 was the occasion of one of Pearse's most stirring orations; and Devoy in New York actively sought German aid for the 1916 rebels — reinsured the survival of the physical force tradition, and the single-minded pursuit of political independence. The row with the church had reinforced the republican doctrines of non-sectarianism and the separation of church and state. The commemoration ceremonies held in connection with the Manchester Martyrs emphasised, on the one hand, aspects of the secularist religion which was nationalism, and on the other, forged an acceptable link between the catholic community and the rebels. The imprisonment of the Fenians, and the massive demonstrations that were organised by the Amnesty Association helped to keep fenianism alive; by that time, however, fenianism had become not so much an organisation as a spirit — an attitude of mind, in fact, no longer restricted to the sworn members of a secret society. Amnesty symbolised redress of the grievances of the whole community. It was in this sense that fenianism pervaded Irish society and influenced all those political, agrarian and cultural movements which came after it. 'It remained', as one historian has written, 'a powerful political force, a rival and a spur to constitutional nationalism, and even, on occasion, its ally'.[8]

Fenianism may not have been the cause and justification of Gladstone's Irish policy, but from it he had received ample lessons of the intensity of Irish dissatisfaction with British rule. When he announced that his mission was to pacify Ireland, that he was committed to a programme of 'justice for Ireland' and that Ireland was to be ruled in accordance with 'Irish ideas', he had before him demands from constitutionalist and catholic Ireland relating to ecclesiastical, agrarian and educational reform. The major remedial measures which he introduced during his first ministry (1868-74) were the Irish Church Act (1869) and the Land Act of 1870. The wealthy established church of the ascendancy had long been a major grievance and an irritant in Irish society. Its disestablishment severed completely the legal connection between church and state, thereby placing all churches on an equal footing as voluntary bodies without state privilege. Disendowment allowed for its property to be used for generous compensation to be paid over to its own clergy, and the remainder was used for the relief of poverty, the encouragement of agriculture and fisheries, the endowment of university education, and for generous sums to be paid to presbyterian ministers and Maynooth College for the loss of their annual grants.

The 1870 Land Act legalised the 'Ulster custom' where it existed, compensated the tenant for improvements, and compensated him for 'disturbance' if evicted for any reason other than the non-payment of rent. The right to compensation was, for the first time, the admission of the principle that the tenant, too, had an interest in the property he rented, and that the state had the duty to regulate the relations between landlord and tenant. The provision for land-purchase in the Irish Church Act as well as in the 1870 Land Act, however limited in scope, was a recognition that peasant-proprietorship might eventually be substituted for landlordism as the solution to the Irish land question. Gladstone's adoption of the National Association's reform programme did much to revive that confidence in parliamentary politics which contributed to the launching of the Home Rule movement in 1870.

The 1869 act put an end to protestant ascendancy in its religious aspect. The 1870 Land Act saw the beginning of the end of landlordism. The dismantling of these two pillars of the union and symbols of Anglo-Irish domination marked an important stage in the victory of catholicism over protestantism, nationalism over unionism and democracy over ascendancy.

6 Epilogue: Society and Democracy

Mass education, the popular press, organised religion, the growing realisation and cultivation of distinct communal identities — each in its own way, no less than popular politics or agrarian agitation, made significant contributions to emerging democracy in nineteenth-century Ireland. Widespread elementary education provided the basic reading, writing and arithmetic skills necessary in an age of the masses. Cheap, widely-read newspapers excited the interests of the people by reporting national and international political events and debates, communicating political ideas, and helping to form public opinion. An expanding middle class demanded educational facilities at the second and third levels. Education had never before been so comprehensively in demand: with land and the union it was one of the biggest public issues of nineteenth-century Ireland. Various religious bodies and orders, as well as the state, committed themselves to the provision of increased educational opportunity.

Primary Education
The great expansion in educational opportunity which took place in the nineteenth century was related to the spread of democracy, although this had certainly not been the objective of the various educational bodies. As the penal laws were relaxed in the late eighteenth century, dedicated men and women consecrating their lives to religion with a remarkable single-mindedness devoted themselves to the education of the catholic poor. Nano Nagle and her Presentation Sisters had already established convent schools in Cork, Killarney, Dublin (George's Hill), and Waterford before 1800. The Presentation sisters were raised to the status of a religious order with papal approval in 1805 and thereafter continued to expand.

Catherine McAuley opened her first house of the Sisters of Mercy in Baggot Street, Dublin in 1828. By 1850 there were 3,000 sisters. The Mercy nuns had soon become the largest teaching congregation in the country, extending themselves to several towns and fully deserving of their reputation as educators. They carried forward their mission into secondary education and eventually into teacher-training.

Other Irish congregations of women devoting themselves to

education included the Brigidine Sisters (like the Patrician brothers originating in the diocese of Kildare and Leighlin); the Loreto Sisters established first in Rathfarnham in the 1820s by Frances Ball for the education of the daughters of the catholic middle-class; the Irish Sisters of Charity; and the Holy Faith Sisters. These native foundations were assisted by Irish houses of Ursulines, Dominicans and Sisters of St Louis.

Edmund Ignatius Rice established his first school in Waterford in 1803. Then followed other Irish Christian Brothers' schools in Carrick-on-Suir (1806), Dungarvan (1807), Cork (1811), Dublin (1812) and Limerick (1816). The Christian Brothers were confirmed as a religious order by the pope in 1820. As with the nuns the formation of christian character in the pupils under their charge was the main objective. The school day opened and closed with prayers in the classroom; on every hour the *Hail Mary* was recited; and religious emblems were displayed prominently in every classroom. From the start, however, the excellence of the secular instruction was remarked upon by observers. Whereas Irish history was excluded from the schools which were under the board of commissioners of national education and from texts approved by the commissioners, the Christian Brothers produced their own texts which were frankly nationalistic, critical of British policy in Ireland, and inculcated patriotism. By 1820 there were 10 Christian Brothers schools in five dioceses. By 1846 there were 16 schools in seven dioceses, and by 1867 there were 55 Christian Brothers schools. The number of pupils kept on increasing and by 1921 there were 24,000 receiving an education in the schools run by the Christian Brothers. Franciscan, Patrician and Presentation Brothers, although not as numerous as the Christian Brothers, also organised schools for the education of Irish catholics. These Brothers' schools for the most part remained separate from the national system so as to retain their denominationalism and independence. (Out of 77 Brothers' schools listed by the Powis Commission [1868] only 3 were connected with the national system.)

In 1824, 50,000 children attended schools provided by the various protestant societies for the conversion of Roman catholics; 46,000 were in catholic free schools provided by the priests, nuns and Christian Brothers. Another 58,000 were attending schools run by the Kildare Place Society — nominally a non-sectarian body established for 'promoting the education of the poor in Ireland'. This society received financial support from the government. A much greater number — nearly 400,000 — attended the so-called 'hedge-schools' or pay schools. These *ad hoc* or voluntary schools varied considerably in the numbers enrolled, standard of instruction, kind of building, qualifications of the teachers, average daily attendance of the pupils, durability of their existence, the availability of suitable texts, and the fees charged. Catholic bishops like Doyle and spokesmen like Thomas Wyse demanded a state-aided, improved system which would be free of any charges of proselytism associated with the schools of the protestant missionary societies. The government, anxious to have a contented peasantry, to inculcate the political and social virtues, to counter the influence of demagogues and agitators and to preserve public order, met this demand in 1831. The national school system gave rise to much wrangling between the government and the heads of the different churches. The regulations, which prohibited the compulsory reading of the bible, allowed the priests, like other ministers of religion, to give religious instruction on one or two days of the week, and excluded children from instruction in religions other than their own, provoked intense church of Ireland and presbyterian opposition. Between 1838 and 1860 the church of Ireland boycotted the national schools to a large extent and established their own Church Education Society. By 1840 a compromise which excluded priests from presbyterian schools and allowed religious instruction during an intermediate hour in the regular school day removed the most major of the objections raised by the presbyterians, and allowed them to associate their schools with the national system. The catholic bishops (with the notable exception of MacHale) initially quietly welcomed the system and availed of its opportunities. But the government's compromises and the consequent fears of proselytism increased catholic suspicions. A papal decision in 1841 allowed each bishop to decide whether the schools in his diocese might participate in the system. Ironically MacHale's opposition to the national schools meant that by 1868 the protestant Irish Church Missions had 53 schools with 1,726 children on their rolls in Co. Galway.

    The attitudes of the churches eventually led, in practice, to denominational schools under the control of clerical managers from the different religious bodies. The national schools themselves, however, went ahead, and despite limitations and weaknesses they provided a free and uniform educational opportunity for children throughout the land in basic reading, writing and arithmetic. The following table shows the expansion in the number of pupils on the rolls of the schools associated with the board of commissioners for national education.

Year	No. of pupils
1833	107,042
1840	232,560
1850	511,239
1860	804,000[1]

This expansion took place against the backdrop of a falling population in the post-famine decades:

Year	Population
1831	7,767,000
1841	8,175,000
1871	5,412,000

The average daily attendance was less than half the number on the rolls during these years. Although attendance was casual, teacher training poor, and education levels low, progress was made. One indication of this was the increase in the level of literacy.

In 1841 more than half (53 per cent) of the population of five years of age and upwards was listed as illiterate. This was down to one third (33 per cent) in 1871, and down to about one sixth (18 per cent) in 1891. (Many of those literate in 1891 had been to school before 1871.) The almost total elimination of the cottiers, and the decimation of the farm labourers in the famine, the increase in emigration, and the drastic decline in the numbers of Irish speakers account in part for the increase in the percentage of the population classified as literate. Despite their shortcomings the national schools' contribution to the spread of literacy accelerated the pace of change. Contemporaries observed that most children left school with the ability to read a newspaper even if 'with difficulty', and they were encouraged to do so to retain their reading skills. The letters from emigrants, the signatures on marriage registers replacing the earlier 'X', and the increase in the number of threatening notices and letters during the land war of 1879–81 were only some of the indications that the national schools had played their part in the advance of literacy.

Secondary Education
The *Catholic Directory* (1865), claiming to give 'the first and only complete list' ever published of catholic grammar and diocesan schools and colleges for boys, listed 60 intermediate schools. (This does not include the 55 Christian Brothers' Schools, which by 1867 were in existence and in the higher classes of which there were some intermediate studies,

including Latin.) The only counties which had no intermediate schools listed were Tyrone, Fermanagh, Leitrim and Wicklow. A committee of Irish catholics published what appears to be an incomplete list of forty-seven intermediate schools and colleges in 1872. Of these twenty were opened in the first fifty years of the nineteenth century and twenty-seven during the two decades 1850 to 1870. Twenty-two of the forty-seven were diocesan colleges, and these included many ecclesiastical students. Of the other twenty-five, five were managed by the Jesuits, six by the Carmelites, three by the Vincentians, three by the Patricians, three by the Marists, two by the Holy Ghost order, one each by the Dominicans, Augustinians and Cistercians. The estimated cost of building these was over £360,000, and the annual expenditure (exclusive of books, travel etc.) was £100,000. These schools were to the catholic middle class what, for example, the Belfast Academical Institution (opened in 1814) was to the presbyterian middle class; or a public school like St Columba's (1843) was to the church of Ireland middle class. This expansion, although notable, still left the catholics a long way behind anglicans and presbyterians in educational opportunity at second level. Out of a total population of nearly 5.5 million in 1871, about 1.25 million were non-catholic. Yet only half of the 24,000 pupils in intermediate schools were catholic, which meant that for every thousand catholics three were attending intermediate schools, and for every thousand non-catholics, nine were attending such schools. The catholic grievance and attempts to remedy it extended also to university education.

University Education
For the first two hundred years of its existence, from its foundation in 1592 until 1793, Trinity College Dublin (Dublin University) was virtually an exclusively protestant institution. Because of religious tests imposed by statutes all students attending the only university in Ireland in the seventeenth and eighteenth centuries had to be anglicans. The Relief Act of 1793 allowed catholics to take degrees there, but they were still excluded from scholarships and fellowships. Despite the abolition of the penal laws, as long as episcopalian protestants had the exclusive control of Trinity neither the catholic majority nor the protestant dissenters felt they were receiving equality of treatment in matters of higher education. In 1845 Prime Minister Peel introduced a bill into parliament proposing the establishment of the Queen's Colleges in Belfast, Cork and Galway which were to be strictly undenominational. Most catholic bishops and O'Connell considered the

Queen's Colleges to be 'dangerous to faith and morals', while a minority of bishops were prepared to accept them, and the Young Irelanders thought they might promote national unity. The colleges were opened in 1848. Out of sixty professors only seven were catholic. Papal rescripts condemned the colleges, and this contributed to the relative lack of success of the colleges in Cork and Galway. The presbyterians made the most of the opportunity provided by the establishment of the Queen's College in Belfast.

In 1850 at a national synod of bishops held in Thurles the condemnation was formally promulgated; the clergy were prohibited from participating in them; and the laity were discouraged from supporting them. It was further decided in response to urgings from Rome to found a catholic university under the control of the bishops and on the model of the catholic University of Louvain. A committee was formed for this purpose, and financial assistance was requested from catholics in Ireland, England and the United States. A collection made in most of the parishes throughout Ireland on the Sunday before St Patrick's Day in 1851 realised £22,840. A further £8,000 was donated from England and the United States. This was the first of the voluntary annual subscriptions from the catholic people for the support of a great experiment. By October 1855 a total of £58,000 had been contributed (more than £28,000 from Ireland, £16,000 from the USA and £4,000 from Britain). In 1854 John Henry Newman was installed as rector, and the Catholic University opened its doors at 86 St Stephen's Green. Newman dreamed that Dublin would be the university centre for the English-speaking catholic world. A few non-Irish students, many of them the sons of friends and admirers of Newman, were attracted to the Catholic University by the rector's reputation, but the university ceased to attract foreign students after Newman's return to England in 1858. The Catholic University had to labour under serious limitations, for as it was without a government charter its degrees were without legal recognition; and without any endowment from state funds it had to face stiff competition from the richly endowed Trinity College Dublin, the Queen's Colleges and the British universities. Neither was the demand for a university education, nor the supply of students from the schools all that great in a struggling economy such as Ireland's was in the nineteenth century. In the twenty-five years of its existence from 1854 to 1879 (after which the Catholic University became UCD, administered by the Jesuits), the average yearly intake of students — excluding evening, affiliated and medical — was about twenty-five. But despite what Newman called a 'struggle with fortune' there had been significant triumphs. O'Curry's lectures on the manuscript materials of ancient Irish history, attended by Newman himself and published by the university, were a milestone in the development of Irish scholarship.

The Medical School which opened in Cecilia St in 1855 was the Catholic University's great success story. Its examinations were recognised by the Royal College of Surgeons in Ireland. The school developed connections with the two catholic hospitals, the Mater and St Vincent's, and with Jervis Street, which ensured the career prospects of its students. (Ten years after its opening, 110 of its graduates were engaged in civil practice, and 57 others had been given commissions in the army and navy and other medical services.) Archbishop Croke boasted when preaching at the university inauguration ceremonies in 1868 that 'it would be difficult to find elsewhere in the United Kingdom a school superior to Cecilia Street'. Archbishop Cullen, its chancellor, liked to point out that when the university was founded people asked what advantage could come from a university in Dublin to the remote parishes of the country and to the humbler classes of the community who were being asked to contribute financially to its support. The supply of medical practitioners alone, he felt, furnished a triumphant answer to such questions, for there was no one whom the advantages of this branch of the university might not reach.

When Newman opened the Medical School he noted that out of 111 medical practitioners in situations of trust and authority (that is, attached to Dublin hospitals, or lecturing in the medical schools of the city), 12 were catholics and 99 were protestants. By the end of the century the number of medical students attending lectures at the Catholic University was greater than in any of the other five medical schools at Surgeons, Trinity, Belfast, Cork or Galway. What had particularly appealed to the Irish bishops was the fact that the country now had not only men highly qualified in the practice of medicine, but also well versed in the tenets and practice of the catholic faith. The university had also produced a number of graduates in the humanities who were to play important roles in the church and in the public life of the country.

The Press

Parallel with the spread of schooling and literacy, and not unrelated to them, was the phenomenal growth of the press in early nineteenth-century Ireland. Newspapers, periodicals and books were purchased in ever-increasing numbers even by the lower orders. It was an age of print. By 1831 the Kildare Place Society had sold or given away one-and-a-half million textbooks in its twenty years of existence. In the year of 1851 alone the commissioners of national education issued to pupils in the national schools 400,000 texts, one third of which were given away free and the rest sold at half-cost. Annually the evangelical societies were distributing hundreds of thousands of bibles and other religious tracts. Earlier estimates of the number of periodicals published in Ireland in the first half of the nineteenth century have been far too low. Nearly three hundred newspapers and periodicals were issued in Dublin alone in the thirty years 1815–45 and although some were short-lived, others were published daily throughout the period. (A figure of between 700 and 1,000 journals has been suggested for the entire country for the first half of the nineteenth century).[2] The reasons for such feverish publication were varied. Apart from the spread of literacy, government controls over the press had been relaxed, techniques in printing had been improved, transportation was facilitated with the coming of the railways and a cheaper post made circulation easier. In an age of rampant democracy, political excitement, widespread popular education, evangelicalism and religious revivalism affecting all churches, and emerging trade-unionism, many individuals, interests and groups felt they had something ideologically worth saying. Apart from public meetings the press was the only means of mass communication. Although much of this expanding press was intended for the middle class a growing proportion of it was aimed at a working-class readership — through trade union journals, religious tracts, political pamphlets as well as through the more regular channels of the newspapers. The many penny journals and magazines (e.g. the *Penny Journal*, *Dublin Penny Journal*, *Catholic Penny Journal*, *Protestant Penny Journal*, *Christian Penny Journal* etc.) were a response to the demand for cheap literature, and an outlet for the great variety of views even within the protestant and catholic communities, and within the camps generally lumped together as either unionist or nationalist. Very few of the proprietors made financial fortunes, but then they were inspired more by ideological than commercial considerations. While the numbers reading this press should not be exaggerated, the sheer torrent of print was bound to have some effect on the direction of public opinion.

The industrialisation of Ulster
Meanwhile the religious barriers that had grown up between the northeast and the rest of the island were strengthened by economic develop-

ments. The linen, cotton and shipbuilding industries resulting from the spread of the industrial revolution to the area accentuated the economic distinctiveness of the north-east. Throughout the eighteenth century linen, however important to the economy of Ulster, was little more than a domestic adjunct to farming. Unlike the Irish woollen industry it posed no threat to English merchants, and it even received encouragement from the government when the woollen trade was being suppressed. Huguenot refugees who had settled in Lisburn brought with them modern techniques in spinning, weaving and bleaching. The domestic linen industry, thus encouraged and invigorated, became the base upon which the industrial revolution in Ulster was built. The farmers who relied on home-grown flax brought their unbleached cloth, which was made by the female members of their families, to the linen markets where it was purchased by the drapers, and the finished cloth was transported to Dublin's linenhall. In Antrim, Down and Armagh small factories for weaving and bleaching were established and linenhalls were founded in Belfast and Newry.

The manufacture of cotton came to Ulster in the late eighteenth century. In contrast with linen, cotton was distinctively a machine industry of the industrial revolution with its imported raw material, steam-engines and fuel. The cotton mills brought the industrial workers in great numbers to Belfast and stimulated the growth of an industrial city. Housing was required for the factory workers, and an engineering industry was needed for servicing the new machinery. Unable to keep pace with the competition from Lancashire the cotton industry of Ulster went into decline in the second quarter of the nineteenth century. It had, however, provided a model for the re-organisation of the linen industry. The cotton mills themselves and the machine techniques that had been employed there were adapted to the linen industry. The machine production of linen which now replaced the hand-loom of the farmer's wife went on apace. By the middle of the nineteenth century Belfast had twenty-eight flax spinning mills with from 600–800 workers employed in some of these. When the American civil war in the 1860s created a cotton famine the Lancashire cotton mills were adversely affected, but this only brought unprecedented opportunities for Belfast linen which reached a peak about 1870 when Ulster became the undisputed centre of that industry in the United Kingdom. In most of the towns of Ulster outside of Belfast the textile trade provided the only or main source of employment.

Shipbuilding, Belfast's other industrial giant, began its phenomenal growth with the arrival of Edward Harland in 1853 as manager of a company which he later acquired. Harland built ships with new designs for Britain's expanding imperial trade. The completion of work on the development of the port of Belfast provided the facilities for shipbuilding and for the importation of the coal and iron necessary for such a heavy industry. Shipbuilding, in turn, stimulated engineering and other related industry. The building of roads, canals and railways assisted in the rapid development of the region, and the new northern banks and joint stock-companies facilitated its economic expansion.

All of these developments created the conditions for the spectacular growth of Belfast. After the famine exodus, one historian has argued, the rise of Belfast was the most dramatic event in Irish economic history since the union.[3] In 1782 it was a little port of 13,000 inhabitants and much smaller than many of the other towns and cities in the country. With the population explosion and the beginnings of the industrial revolution in the area it had grown to something less than 20,000 by 1803. (Dublin was nine times larger with an estimated 182,000 in 1800.) It had sprouted into an industrial city of 100,000 by 1851, and had outstripped all other cities in Ireland except Dublin. Belfast's phenomenal growth continued until it rivalled Dublin with a population of about 350,000 at the end of the century. (Dublin's population actually decreased in the period 1851–91, while the population of the suburbs increased steadily.)[4]

Throughout the eighteenth century the inhabitants of Belfast had been mainly presbyterian. Catholics then constituted less than 10 per cent of the population of the city, but by the middle of the nineteenth century made up about one-third of the total, and although thereafter the percentage of catholics in the city began to decline they remained a substantial element in absolute numbers. Many of the nineteenth-century rural immigrants from mid and south Ulster belonged to the church of Ireland, and methodists and other small sects also added to Belfast's denominational diversity. But the presbyterians, although reduced to about 35 per cent of the total population by 1861, remained dominant.

An industrial city which had experienced such rapid growth and so vast a change in its denominational balance was bound to have all of the usual social problems of the Victorian city. The worst of these problems in Belfast's peculiar circumstances was sectarianism. From the 1830s, and coinciding with an intensive phase of industrialisation, immigration and mass urbanisation, sectarian riots became endemic. Sandy Row, built in the 1840s, was Belfast's first proletarian quarter, largely episcopalian and a centre of the linen industry. Close by was the Lower Falls which was catholic territory. Competition for work added to the sectarian bitterness imported with the rural immigrants. Serious rioting involving confrontation between the two communities took place in every decade from the 1850s. Shankill was the home of the shipyard workers. These 'islandmen', as they were called, were Belfast's labour aristocracy. Because of their skills they had a certain mobility and independence of their employers not enjoyed by the factory hands of the linen mills. The streets of dockland were used only by the shipyard workers so that the Shankill developed an integrated insularity with its own cultural and moral order reminiscent of the rural communities of agrarian secret societies. The shipyard workers saw themselves in the role of democratic representatives whose duty it was to provide vigilant protection for the rest of the protestant population. 'Loyalty' indicated obligations to one's community which took priority over the conditional loyalty to the state. The intimidation and expulsion of the catholic minority were always a possible consequence of this sectarian tension.

The Belfast shipyard became the symbol of British imperialism. The city and its hinterland had an overwhelming economic interest in the preservation of the union with Britain. This, apart from the ethnic or religious causes, was sufficient to separate Ulster protestantism from Irish nationalism. Just as nationalists saw the declining Irish economy as following directly from the union, unionists saw the economic progress of Belfast as springing directly from that same union. While industrial cities elsewhere in the United Kingdom were strongholds of British liberalism, it was conservatism that benefited most from Belfast's sectarian and economic circumstances. Post-union prosperity, the methods employed in the campaign for catholic emancipation; the change in the political and social balance ushered in by the Catholic Relief Act of 1829; the fear of catholic domination in an independent Ireland; the hardening of denominational attitudes among episcopalian evangelists; presbyterians who had undergone 'conversion'; and catholics who had experienced the devotional revolution — all contributed to the widening gulf between the northeast and the rest of the country. There is indeed plenty of evidence to show that liberalism was alive and well in nineteenth-century Belfast, but it had become more a part of British liberalism, very different in fact from the nationalist-tinged variety of the 1780s and '90s, and it was no longer identified with the radicalism and republicanism of the United Irishmen. The *Northern Whig* remained liberal on such issues as catholic emancipation, parliamentary reform and rack-rents, but it was strongly opposed to O'Connell's repeal movement.

The widely-read *Belfast News-Letter* advocated strong conservative views, and Belfast's electoral politics reflected the development of these trends. During the period of the repeal agitation about three quarters of the parliamentary seats in Ulster were consistently held by the tories and no repealer was returned, but then no repeal candidate ever even stood for an Ulster constituency. Repeal found little or no support in the fifteen constituencies of Ulster. Even the liberal presbyterian, Henry Montgomery, refused his support for repeal, and expressed his fear that a Dublin parliament would be sectarian and despotic. O'Connell declined Henry Cooke's challenge to debate repeal. Cooke had declared to O'Connell: 'Look at Belfast and be a repealer if you can ... when I was myself a youth I remember it almost a village. But what a glorious sight does it now present — the masted grove within our harbour — our mighty warehouses teeming with the wealth of every climate ... all this we owe to the union.'[5] During the 1850s, '60s and '70s not even a liberal — not to mention a repealer, was returned for Belfast, except in 1868, and then only because of a temporary split in conservative ranks. This did not mean that Belfast politics were lacking in all of the outward trappings of expanding democracy. As elsewhere with the pocket boroughs the Belfast corporation had been the tool of the absentee Donegall family whose nominees were returned until the Reform Act of 1832. The franchise was then extended to about 2,000 householders, and finally in 1842 the corporation was abolished and replaced with an elected council in which many liberal merchants and manufacturers participated. O'Connell's attempt to carry his campaign into the heart of Ulster was defeated by huge counter-demonstrations that paralleled the popular appeal of the monster meetings. Ironically the 1868 Reform Act, hailed by liberals elsewhere, was a repulse for them in Belfast. The more prosperous voters, who had occasionally supported the liberals, were outnumbered by the newly enfranchised protestant working classes. These protestant workers swelled the ranks of the Orangemen.

Progress of orangeism

Increasingly the Orangemen in the province came to see their function as twofold — the defence of protestantism against impending 'papish' tyranny, and the maintenance of the union with Britain against the threat of Irish nationalism. In the early 1820s orangeism revived under the twin attacks of O'Connell's emancipation drive and Lord

Lieutenant Wellesley's attempts to ban Orange demonstrations. Peel, as home secretary in 1825, suppressed the Orange lodges at the same time as he suppressed the Catholic Association. This law lapsed in 1828 just at the time when O'Connell sent his agent, John Lawless, on a march through Ulster to show that orangeism was dead. The event merely provoked all of the militancy of the protestant peasantry, and O'Connell had to withdraw his agent when the police and military were unable to protect him. Catholic emancipation in 1829 stimulated a new phase of Orange demonstrations and clashes with Ribbonmen in the early 1830s. In 1835 an Orange spokesman claimed that the Order had about 200,000 members. This, if not a wild exaggeration, meant that more than half of the adult male protestants in Ireland belonged to the order. The involvement of the king's brother, the duke of Cumberland, as titular head of the Orange Order, and the link between a section of the tory party and the Orangemen enabled O'Connell and the British radicals and Under-Secretary Drummond to secure a second dissolution of the lodges in 1836. But the spirit of orangeism was strong enough to repulse O'Connell's attempt in 1841 to march through Ulster with his followers, and to bring about another revival of the order during the repeal agitation of the 1840s. In the eyes of the Orangemen, although the government's treatment of them left much to be desired, catholic domination and ascendancy were far worse to contemplate. The working class immigrants brought their orangeism with them from the countryside into Belfast. Although there was a relatively slow growth of the Orange Order among the bulk of the Belfast workers, their political conservatism coincided with that of the Orangemen.

The strength of the Orangemen was shown in the parade of up to 100,000 on 12 July 1848, and the rout of Ribbonmen at Dolly's Brae near Castlewellan, Co. Down in 1849, when a number of catholics were killed and many others injured. The event was one of the most notorious of the nineteenth-century sectarian encounters. It was afterwards celebrated in a song of victory adding to the number of offensive party tunes which played an important role in sectarian provocation:

> 'Twas on the 12th day of July, in the year of '49
> Ten hundreds of our Orangemen together did combine,
> In the memory of King William, on that bright and glorious day,
> To walk all round Lord Roden's park, and right over Dolly's Brae.

> And when we came to Dolly's Brae they were lined on every side,
> Praying for the Virgin Mary to be their holy guide;

> We loosened our guns upon them and we gave them no time to pray,
> And the tune we played was 'The Protestant boys' right over Dolly's Brae.[6]

Together with 'Croppies Lie Down', 'The Protestant Boys' and 'Boyne Water', 'Dolly's Brae' became one of the best known songs of Orange counter-rebellion.

In the 1860s Orangemen reacted to the fenian threat as earlier they had reacted to ribbonism. Presbyterian clergymen had earlier shied away from orangeism because of the episcopalian and aristocratic tone of the grand lodge, but with the disestablishment of the church of Ireland and the end of the subsidy paid to the presbyterian clergy, a substantial number of them began to join the lodges. Orangemen were an embarrassment to the government in ordinary times but reliable allies in emergencies, and for this aid they exacted a high price. Essentially the Orange Order was a counter-revolutionary movement which eventually came to combine protestant landowners and tenants, mill-owners and workers, and episcopalian and presbyterian clergymen for the defence of protestant dominance. Whereas many of the agrarian societies among the catholics had been touched by the broadening experience and the liberal politics of O'Connell, or by the patriotic nationalism of Young Ireland, or by the socialist leanings of the national agrarian movement, orangeism, in contrast, became entrenched, defensive and conservative, protecting the protestant ascendancy and the *status quo* of the union.

Despite its reactionary nature orangeism was also open to aspects of the democracy of the day. The Orangemen's conditional loyalty to the crown was based upon the principle of a contractual relationship which existed between the protestant community and the constituted authority. This was in the tradition of the glorious revolution and of British liberal thought. Another aspect of democracy penetrating the Orange Order was seen in the rule which said that each member of the elite grand lodge had also to be a member of a local lodge. This bound together the social classes in which all were in some sense equal in their common protestantism, and their common desire for security was strengthened by the shared secrecy of the order. In its own distorted way the right to party processions, however provocative to the other community, was an assertion of the democratic right to free assembly, free speech and freedom of movement. The right to parade was also, however, an assertion of dominance over the community through whose neighbourhood the procession passed.

Advancing democracy developed in opposite directions in the north and south. In Ulster it led on to unionism, whereas in the south it led on to nationalism. Individuals in the liberal tradition, both north and south, became apprehensive of these extreme dimensions at which democracy had arrived. The democratising tendencies transferred control in the south from the protestant ascendancy to catholic hands, but in the north-east protestant control was left unimpaired and even strengthened.

The democratisation of the Church of Ireland
Gladstone's Irish Church Act of 1869 marked the end of the age of aristocracy in the church of Ireland and introduced a new age of democratic government into that church. The act provided that the union between the churches of England and Ireland should be dissolved; that the church of Ireland should cease to be an established church; that its property, after equitable compensation was made, should be appropriated for the advantage of the Irish people. Disestablishment, by thus breaking the link which had existed between church and state, left the church free of parliament to determine its own dogma, discipline, appointments and financial arrangements. Following disestablishment a general synod of the church of Ireland was constituted as the highest deliberative body and given the powers to legislate on doctrine, discipline and diocesan organisation. This general synod was composed of an upper house and a lower house of representatives. The bishops sat in the upper house. The house of representatives consisted of one hundred representatives of the lower clergy and one hundred and fifty laymen elected from the dioceses. The two houses deliberated together but following the example of parliament they voted separately, which in effect gave a veto to the bishops.

To administer the finances of the disestablished church a representative church body was constituted. This body included the twelve bishops, two elected representatives from each of the twelve united dioceses — one lay and one clerical — and twelve other members to be co-opted. Before disestablishment land rental and tithe charges had been the major sources of revenue. Tithes now ceased altogether to be paid and most of the church lands were alienated. After 1869 the major sources of revenue were returns on investments and voluntary contributions.

The dramatic fall in episcopal incomes registered the decline in the church of Ireland's status. In 1830 the net income of the archbishop of Armagh was £14,000; as a result of the reforms of the 1830s it had fallen to less than £9,000 by 1867; after disestablishment it fell further to

£2,500 by 1919. The age of the ecclesiastical princes was over. Because of the structures provided for under the 1869 act only Irishmen were in practice selected thenceforward as bishops. In summary, perhaps the most revolutionary aspect of disestablishment was the role that had been assigned to the laity at all levels of church government. Committees on which laymen served with the clergy now selected local incumbents and maintained critical scrutiny of their professional performance. The clergy in fact became responsible to their parishioners who were now in control of about half of the clergyman's salary.

Like other bodies and institutions in the state the church of Ireland, for long a citadel of the aristocracy, had to respond to the changes forced upon it by an age of increasing democracy. Developments between 1800 and 1870 which affected Irish society as a whole also revolutionised the church of Ireland. This revolution in the position, status and structures of the now disestablished church accurately reflected the transformations that had occurred in Irish society.

Catholicism and Politics

An organised and visible institution that was so pervasive as the catholic church was bound to have both direct and indirect political influence. A parliamentary ally of Peel once described the Irish priesthood as 'the most formidable engine of political power ... ever wielded in any country'.[7] The direct influence was obvious enough: in the days of O'Connell the priests could act as his lieutenants and allies; in the 1850s the bishops could split the Independent Irish Party, and order the priests out of politics; in the 1860s they could launch the National Association, counter the Fenians and condemn secret societies. The indirect influence stemmed in the first instance from the fact that inside the status-symbol big churches, which had replaced the chapels of penal times, the massive captive audiences were easily turned into mobilised congregations. Outside the church doors these congregations acted as agents for the priesthood. Cardinal Cullen's hierarchical and centralised church made it easier for the mobilised catholics to think in terms of national as distinct from diocesan or local boundaries. This in itself made its own important contribution to the political notion of nationalism. The doctrine, preached by the bishops, of the separation of church and state with distinct roles for each, encouraged the Irish catholic people to think of themselves as politically separate from the English protestant government. The dogma of 'the one true church', which was central to catholicism, enabled catholics to turn a blind eye to non-catholic Ulster or regard it as an error with which there could be no compromise. The devotional fervour cultivated by the church among its people could, and did, spill over into politics; and this transfer of devotionalism produced persons who held their nationalism with all of the enthusiasm of missionaries and martyrs. Politics, thus inflamed, could become a substitute for religion — indeed another kind of religious conviction — for some among the Fenians. The devotional revolution, therefore, helped to pave the way for an Irish nationalism that could hardly be disentangled from religion thereafter.

The past repossessed
Nationalism, in both its democratic and elitist aspects, found a fertile soil in Irish catholic culture. The rapid growth of nationalism in nineteenth-century Ireland was also fed by a preoccupation with the past. The past which was being recovered by the scholars was also being repossessed by the people. A great boost to the recovery of Ireland's past was given by Macpherson's publication in the early 1760s of what he claimed to be the epic poetry of Ossian. The romantic interest that was thus aroused among European scholars soon spread from the early literature and literary remains to the language, history and archaeology of ancient Ireland. In Ireland Sylvester O'Halloran, followed by a whole generation of scholars, glorified ancient Ireland. The *Transactions* of the Gaelic Society, of the Iberno-Celtic Society of the Royal Irish Academy and of the archaeological societies fostered the cult of the history and antiquities of Ireland.

The Ordnance Survey of Ireland during the 1830s and 1840s brought together a number of experts who did pioneering work for the preservation of Ireland's past — John O'Donovan on Irish grammar, the annals and historical topography; Eugene O'Curry on the surviving manuscript materials in Irish, and early Irish history; and George Petrie on the round towers, inscriptions and Tara. The work of these scholars was popularised in the *Dublin Penny Journal* and elsewhere. Edward Bunting in the late eighteenth and early nineteenth centuries devoted his life to the collection and publication of the ancient music of Ireland. Petrie, who had collected much music over the years during his travels throughout the country, added to Bunting's collection.

'Native' writers at the turn of the century propagated the idea of an Ireland that had possessed an ancient splendour and greatness when the rest of the world was engulfed in a primordial mist of ignorance. One of these authors may have felt at times that he had 'nothing to inherit but the religion and misfortune of his ancestors', yet, on many other occasions he was given to dreams about 'the splendours of the court of Emania'.[8] O'Halloran liked to remind his readers that the present state of Ireland no more dimmed the former brightness than did nineteenth-century Greece darken the importance of ancient Athens.[9]

This golden portrait was in striking contrast with what they called the enslaved Ireland of the early nineteenth century. A people dissatisfied with the present was prepared to grasp at any vision of the past. During the first decade of the nineteenth century the native historical writers never went far beyond a romantic nostalgia for the days of ancient splendour. As the theme of native greatness became more extensive in the writings of the antiquarians, it also began to permeate other sections of the community, and as it did the nostalgia tended to develop into more active politics. Although the romantic scholars were not in themselves a threat to the government, the situation grew more alarming when their dreams were absorbed by a people organised to achieve definite political reforms. The one who popularised the 'ancient splendour-present misery' theme and facilitating its harnessing to contemporary politics, perhaps more than any other writer, was Thomas Moore, especially in his *Irish melodies* (1807–34).

Because the ballad singers of Ireland had got hold of Moore's melodies, argued Rev John Graham, chaplain to the Grand Orange Lodge, Moore was filling the peasants' heads with dreams about 'the full moon of freedom' which would replace 'the long night of bondage' and 'slavery's cloud'. Graham objected strongly to the effect lines like the following would have on a democracy organised by O'Connell:

> Weep on, weep on — your hour is past,
> Your dreams of pride are o'er
> The fatal chain is round you cast,
> As you are men, no more.

And Graham could see no less than incitement to treason in lines like:

> Thus, freedom now so seldom wakes,
> The only throb she gives
> Is when some heart indignant breaks,
> To show that still she lives.

'Ireland', argued Graham, 'possesses a freedom under the British government, unknown to her in the days of her petty feudal kings. So this mischievous rant appears calculated to rouse the angry passions of the ignorant servant, who may hear these melodies sung in drawing-rooms, at a time perhaps, when he may be strongly solicited to join in the Ribbon conspiracy.'[10] To counter the effects of songs and ballads of catholic nationalism, Graham himself wrote and edited a number of Orange ballads.

O'Connell, too, whose speeches were constantly adorned with the most enthusiastic lines from Moore, gave as his opinion that these melodies raised and encouraged the spirit of the catholics. Other reviews believed that the *Melodies* inflamed the vindictive passions of an ignorant and ferocious people. Moore may have been unaware of the part he played in the development of Irish nationalism, but it was part of the logic of the movement in which he was involved, that, after lingering over ancient greatness, he should turn to contemporary politics and insist, among other notes of patriotism, that Emmet's rising was to be kept green in Irish memory.

Moore was only the most popular representative of a group of writers who were linking up romantic nostalgia with impassioned contemporary politics. Survivors of '98 were now emboldened to popularise the principles of the United Irishmen. The hero-worship with which these writers looked back to their dead friends of '98 was a sign that national feeling was growing more intense. The lesson drawn by the political leaders from the historical writers was that 700 years of misery resulted from English dominion. As O'Connell said:

> Accursed be that day in the memory of all future generations of Irishmen when the invaders first touched our shores. They came to a nation famous for its love of learning, its piety, its heroism ... and foreign invaders doomed Ireland to seven centuries of oppression.

The conscious employment of the past for current political purposes reached its zenith in Young Ireland. The duty of history, according to Davis, was to inspire the virtue of patriotism. Taking his cue from a romantic French historian, Davis wrote: 'We must extract from our ancient chronicles a history capable of stirring the heart of the people.' This summed up the whole thrust of Young Ireland's objectives as propounded in the *Nation*, in the 'Library of Ireland', which provided cheap and popular volumes of history, and in the ballads. O'Connell had used history as a lawyer — producing the hostile witnesses of English sources in evidence of English misrule in Ireland, or pointing to the 'broken' treaty of Limerick, or the unconstitutionality of the Act of Union. In contrast the Young Irelanders treated historical events not as separate, selective, legalistic precedents but in the romantic light of an organic whole.

The most potent legacy of Davis and his friends was the myth of a continuous link of generations of Irish over hundreds of years attempting to repel the foreign invader. Not only did the Young Irelanders write the drama of the long tradition of asserting the right to independence by force of arms, but by participating in the 1848 insurrection they played a central role in that drama which they themselves had fashioned.

To be effective history had to be popular. Davis felt that the highest duties of history were best taught by a ballad history. Duffy described Moore's *Melodies* as 'the wail of a lost cause'. By contrast the *Spirit of the Nation* (1843), a collection of the historical ballads which had appeared in the *Nation* expressed, according to Duffy, 'the virile and passionate hopes of a new generation'. The Young Ireland ballads did not deal with the failures and tragedies of Irish history. They celebrated, instead, the glories of Ireland's past; the victories over the Danes and the Saxons; the feats of the Wild Geese and the Irish Brigade; and the bloodless triumph of Grattan's Volunteers. Tone and Emmet were openly hailed as heroes, and given the place of honour in Ireland's past. 'Step together', 'O'Donnell Abu', 'Who fears to speak of '98?', 'The croppy boy', 'A nation once again', 'The west's awake', 'Fontenoy', were only among the best known of those Young Ireland ballads fostering a martial spirit.

For Davis the ballad was the highest form of political journalism. It allowed him freedom from the constraints of prose to express his passionate convictions on the past and his reveries about the future in a mode which would not be considered extravagant or fantastic. The true history of Ireland, according to Davis, 'would people our streets, and glens, and castles, and abbeys, and coasts with a hundred generations besides our own'. This was the invention of a living past in which the noble peasant of Davis's time marched in step with the heroes of his race.

The historical ballads of Young Ireland struck a chord with a people who had their own strong tradition of folk songs. In the 1840s Crofton Croker published selections of the popular songs dealing with the Williamite wars and the French invasions. The folk songs reached out to the illiterate and semi-literate. They dealt with two main themes: one social, and the other political. Those in the social category dealt with the struggle against landlords, land agents, rents and tithes. They celebrated rough justice, secret societies, highwaymen, fugitives, faction fights, prophecies and dreams of liberation. The more specifically political songs condemned the union, and celebrated Grattan's Volunteers, the United Irishmen, '98, Tone, Emmet, O'Connell, emancipation, repeal, '48 and the Fenians. They were the compositions of anonymous broad-side makers, or of literary persons writing for the popular press and the cheap journals, and consciously trying to arouse political feeling and action. They were performed publicly before receptive audiences on market or fair-days. The notes of rebellion which they sounded were an indication that the people were ripe for enrolment into the nationalist movement, and responsive to the lessons of Young Ireland.

Republicanism
Nationalism, which had been fostered by O'Connell, grew more extreme in the post-famine decades, and became more specific and republican. Republicanism had been imported from revolutionary France in the days of Tone and the United Irishmen. With the suppression of the 1798 rebellion it had been eradicated — or so it seemed. Emmet's rebellion in 1803 had hardly touched beyond a section of the Dublin rabble, after which republicanism had lain dormant until the 1840s. The Young Irelanders were republicans implicitly before they knew it themselves, or before they had declared themselves as such. The hero-worship of Tone and Emmet and the literary cult of physical force prepared the ground for the growth of separatist ideals. The failure and frustration of O'Connell's parliamentarianism and constitutional nationalism; the politics of poverty which the famine occasioned; the declaration of the French republic in 1848, and the subsequent outbreak of revolution in the rest of Europe revived republicanism in Ireland. Influenced by these events, Mitchel, in his appropriately named newspaper, the *United Irishman*, Fintan Lalor and others preached rebellion in 1848 and 1849 and the establishment of an Irish republic. The young men who joined in the attempted coup of 1848-9 were the founders and organisers of the Fenians ten years later.

The characteristics of the republicanism which had emerged included the doctrine of physical force as the method whereby independence was to be won. It also preached — especially in the burning words of Mitchel — a holy hatred of English rule in Ireland as the chief virtue of Irish nationalism. The republicanism which Lalor represented with his agrarian gospel of 'the land of Ireland for the people of Ireland' had socialist leanings. Although the leadership was in some respects elitist, and even anti-democratic, believing that the people had no right to do wrong, the well-springs of Irish republicanism were populist. It was non-sectarian, even showed traces of anti-clericalism, and supported the principle of the separation of church and state. It was also anti-parliamentarian, and came to believe that an oath to the republic was more sacred than any even in religion. From the United Irishmen to the days of Young Ireland republicanism had been the privilege of middle-class, protestant intellectuals. With the Fenians republicanism was embraced for the first time by the catholic masses. The mass of the people had previously been regarded as political fodder, not as leader-producing material. The *Nation* of Young Ireland was essentially a middle-class concept. The *Irish People* of the Fenians was the more democratic concept. While the original fenian leaders were from comfortable middle-class backgrounds their lieutenants, and therefore the next generation of fenian and land league leaders, had sprung from the working class. This was true of Michael Davitt, the founder of the land league, whose family had been evicted from their peasant holding of a few acres in 1850. It was true of Patrick Egan, the treasurer of the land league, and of Thomas Brennan, the secretary, both of whom had begun life as junior commercial clerks in Dublin. It was true of Thomas Sexton, one of the head organisers of the league, who was the son of a policeman, and who had started out as a railway clerk. It was true of John Barry, son of a Wexford coastguard, who organised support for the league in Britain. It was true of John Devoy, their man in America, whose father was a labouring man. And it was true of at least two of the land league's strongest parliamentary supporters, Joseph Biggar and John O'Connor-Power. And adding to the threat which these sons of the people now posed for landlordism in Ireland was the fact that all of them were not only land leaguers but also leading fenian activists.

The face of this new Irish democracy was far from handsome to behold, for it was pock-marked as in the case of O'Connor-Power who, despite his double-barrelled name, was probably the illegitimate son of an RIC man, and had been brought up in Ballinasloe workhouse. And it was hunch-backed as in the case of Joseph Biggar, the grocer from Belfast. And it was one-armed as in the case of Davitt himself, who had lost a limb in the Lancashire cotton mill where he worked as a boy. And the tone of its language was also ugly, as might indeed be expected of Fenians come into the open, but still preaching revolution.

Democracy in its first tentative stages was liberal, demanding civil rights for the catholics; then progressively it became nationalist, vaguely aiming at independence for the nation; finally it became tinctured with republicanism, specifically demanding political separation from England, and the dismantling of the old landlordism. The forces which had been at work through catholic culture, through the developments taking place in nationalist politics, and through the conscious evocation of a romantic past all tended in the direction of separation, and had the effect generally of making democracy in Ireland republican. By 1870 a complex of liberal, catholic, nationalist, historical, republican, middle-class and peasant attitudes constituted the predominant democracy that had dawned in Ireland.

Notes

Chapter 1
1. Seamus Heaney, 'Act of Union', in *North* (London, 1975), p. 49.
2. W E H Lecky, *History of Ireland in the eighteenth century* (London, 1892), v, 416.
3. Lecky, *Ire.*, v, 171.
4. J H Rose, *William Pitt and national revival* (London, 1911), p. 429.
5. James Winder Good, *Irish unionism* (Dublin, 1920), p. 3. Good asserted that every Irish child knew these verses.
6. W E H Lecky, *Leaders of public opinion in Ireland* (London, 1871), p. 194.
7. Oliver MacDonagh, *Ireland: the union and its aftermath* (London, 1975), preface.
8. *Collected works of P H Pearse: political writings and speeches* (Dublin [1917]), 'Ghosts', pp 231-2.
9. W E H Lecky, *Leaders of public opinion in Ireland* (3rd ed. London, 1903), i, 270.
10. D O Madden, ed., *Select speeches of the Rt Hon Henry Grattan* (Dublin, 1845), p. 82; *Memoirs of the life and times of the Rt Hon Henry Grattan*, by his son (new ed., London, 1849), ii, 236; S Gwynn, *Henry Grattan and his times*, (Dublin, 1939), (16 Apr. 1782), p. 125. Gwynn has 'paternal' where the others have 'eternal'.
11. Madden, op. cit., p. 293; *Memoirs*... v, 176; Grattan's *Speeches* (ed. by his son) iv, 1-23; Lecky, *Ireland*, v. 412-3, Gwynn, op. cit., p. 360 (26 May 1800). Gwynn has '*my* country', not '*the* country'.
12. J A Froude, *The English in Ireland in the eighteenth century* (London, 1874), iii, 497-8.
13. James Connolly, *Labour in Irish history* (Dublin, 1910), pp 64-5 quoting Tone's pamphlet, *An argument on behalf of the catholics of Ireland* (Sept. 1791); also Lecky, *Ireland*, iii, 10; also F MacDermott, *Theobald Wolfe Tone* (Tralee, 1968), pp 67-8.
14. *Life of Theobald Wolfe Tone*, edited by his son (London), p. 48.
15. [Christopher Manus O'Keefe], *Life and times of Daniel O'Connell* (John Mullany, Dublin, 1870) i, 83.

Chapter 2
1. D Bowen, *The protestant crusade in Ireland 1800-1870* (Dublin, 1978), p. 41.
2. D H Akenson, *The Irish educational experiment* (London, 1970), p. 92.
3. Hereward Senior, *Orangeism in Ireland and Britain 1795-1836* (London, 1966), p. 180.
4. E Larkin, 'The devotional revolution in Ireland 1850-75', in *American Historical Review* (1972), lxxvii, 3, 625-52.
5. Francis Plowden, *An historical review of the state of Ireland* (London, 1803), i, 1-5.
6. James Bentley Gordon, *History of the rebellion in Ireland in the year 1798* (2nd edition, Dublin, 1803).
7. M R O'Connell (ed)., *Correspondence of Daniel O'Connell*, (Shannon, 1972) i, 158.
8. [O'Keefe], *Life and times of Daniel O'Connell* (Dublin, 1870), i, 89.

9. William Parnell, *An enquiry into the causes of popular discontents* (Dublin, 1804), pp 65–6.
10. O'Connell to his wife, 12 Aug. 1810 (M R O'Connell ed., *Correspondence of Daniel O'Connell*, i, no. 291).
11. *Irish Magazine*, July 1808, p. 357.
12. Ibid., Sept. 1808, pp 432–3.
13. *Parliamentary debates*, 23 May 1808.
14. J Curry, *An historical and critical review of the civil wars in Ireland* (Dublin, 1810), see dedication.
15. D Taaffe, *History of Ireland* (Dublin, 1809–11), iii, 279.
16. Eneas Mac Donnell to O'Connell, 30 Jan. 1811 (M R O'Connell, ed., *Correspondence of Daniel O'Connell*, i, no. 320).
17. Lecky, *Historical and political essays* (London, 1908), p.165; *Life and times of Daniel O'Connell*, i, 151–2.
18. M MacDonagh, *Daniel O'Connell and the story of catholic emancipation* (Dublin, 1929), p. 63.
19. [O'Keefe], *Life and times of Daniel O'Connell* (Dublin, 1870), i, 232.
20. Mac Donagh, *O'Connell and the story of catholic emancipation*, p. 91.
21. Ibid., p. 93.
22. Ibid., pp 95–6.
23. W E H Lecky, *Leaders of public opinion in Ireland* (new edition, New York, 1912), ii, 25.

Chapter 3
1. T B Howell, *State trials*, xxx, (8 Dec. 1806), pp 82–96.
2. *Speeches of W C Lord Plunket*, ed. J C Hoey (Dublin, 1865), pp 96–106.
3. Plowden, *History of Ireland 1801–1810* (Dublin, 1811), iii, 612–13. See T B Howell, *State Trials* (London, 1822), xxxi, 423 for a slightly different wording of this speech.
4. Another version of the origin of the nickname was given at the trials before the Special Commission in 1811, when it was said that at the execution of Hanly, his enemy, Pawdeen Gar, punned that he would not leave the place until he saw the 'caravat' (ie rope) about the fellow's neck.
5. Tom Garvin, *The evolution of Irish nationalist politics* (Dublin, 1981), pp 36–7; Sailbheastar Ó Muireadhaigh, 'Na Carabhait agus na Sean-Bheisteanna', in *Galvia*, viii (1961), p. 11.
6. Paul E W Roberts, 'Caravats and Shanavests: Whiteboyism and faction fighting in east Munster, 1802–11', in Clarke and Donnelly (ed), *Irish peasants: violence and political unrest 1780–1914* (Manchester, 1983), pp 66-7.
7. This claim is made by Roberts, op. cit., p.67.
8. Bushe's speech is reported in T B Howell, *State Trials*, xxxi, 418ff.
9. James S Donnelly, Jr., 'The social composition of agrarian rebellions in early nineteenth-century Ireland: the case of the Carders and Caravats, 1813–16', in P J Corish (ed), *Radicals, rebels and establishments* (Belfast, 1985), pp 161–4.
10. Michael Beames, *Peasants and power* (Brighton, 1983), p. 175.
11. O'Connell in evidence given in *Report from the select committee on the state of Ireland*, H.C. 1825 (129), p. 71.
12. A M Sullivan, *New Ireland*, i, 33–45.
13. *Report from select committee on the state of Ireland*, H.C. 1825 (129), p. 136. Evidence of Mr John Astle.

14. For the organisational structure of Ribbonism apart from Garvin and Beames see the evidence of Major Warburton in *Minutes of evidence taken before the select committee of the House of Lords 1824,* H.C. 1825 (200), pp 81–5 and *Report of the trial of Michael Keenan* (1822), pp 42–5. For an account of an induction ceremony around 1813 and the oath that was administered see Wm Carleton, *Autobiography* (London, 1968), pp 76–84, and the same author's novel, *Rody the Rover, or the Ribbonman* (Dublin, 1845), p. 66.
15. Sailbheastar Ó Muireadhaigh, 'Na Fir Ribín', in *Galvia*, x, (1964–5), p. 25.
16. Beames, 'The ribbon societies: lower class nationalism in pre-famine Ireland', in *Past and present*, no. 97 (1982), p. 141.
17. Ibid., p. 143.
18. W Steuart Trench, *Realities of Irish life* (2nd ed., London, 1869), pp 47–9.
19. Joseph Lee, 'The Ribbonmen', in T D Williams (ed.), *Secret societies in Ireland* (Dublin and New York, 1973), pp 26–35.
20. Tom Garvin, 'Defenders, Ribbonmen and others: underground political networks in pre-famine Ireland', in *Past and present*, no. 90 (Aug. 1982), p. 134.
21. Barrington's evidence in *Report from the select committee on the state of Ireland*, H.C. 1825 (129), p. 573. Dillane's evidence is reported in *Dublin Evening Post*, 6 August 1822.
22. *Dublin Evening Post*, 28, 29 September 1821.
23. Barrington's evidence in *Report from the select committee on the state of Ireland*, H.C. 1825 (129), p. 573.
24. *Dublin Evening Post*, 3 May 1823.
25. *Dublin Evening Post*, 7 August 1823.
26. Evidence of George Bennett, *Minutes of evidence taken before the select committee of the House of Lords 1824*, H.C. 1825 (200), p. 26.
27. Ibid., pp 24–36.
28. *Dublin Evening Post*, 13, 16, 23, 27 Sept. 1823; 15 April, 28 Aug. 1824; 20 Aug. 1825. An account of the Franks affair is also given in J. Roderick O'Flanagan, *The bar life of O'Connell* (Dublin, 1875), pp 134–8.
29. *Report of the select committee on the state of Ireland*, H.C. 1825 (129), pp 584–6.
30. *Dublin Evening Post*, 16 April 1822.
31. *Minutes of evidence taken before the select committee of the House of Lords 1824*, H.C. 1825 (200), p. 85.
32. Ibid., p. 92.
33. *Dublin Evening Post*, 22 December 1821.
34. *Report of the select committee on the state of Ireland*, H.C. 1825 (129), pp 584–6.
35. See the evidence of Bennett, Blackburn, Willcocks and others in *Minutes of evidence taken before the select committee of the House of Lords 1824*, H.C. 1825 (200), pp 7, 51, 109.
36. Mortimer O'Sullivan, *Captain Rock detected* (1824), pp 282–3.
37. *Minutes of evidence taken before a select committee of the House of Lords 1824*, H.C. 1825 (200), p. 198.
38. Blackburn's evidence in *Minutes of evidence taken before a select committee of the House of Lords 1824*, H.C. 1825 (200), pp 7ff.
39. *Report of the select committee on the state of Ireland*, H.C. 1825 (129), p. 197.
40. O'Connell to the Knight of Kerry, 8 April 1821.
41. O'Connell to Attorney General Plunket, 1 July 1822.
42. O'Connell to Wellesley, 11 July 1822.
43. O'Connell to his wife, 12 October 1821.

44. Ibid.
45. O'Connell to Wellesley, 11 July 1822.
46. O'Connell to his wife, 12 March 1822.
47. Ibid.
48. Fitzpatrick, *Correspondence of O'Connell* (London, 1888), i, 90.
49. [Thomas Moore], *Memoirs of Captain Rock* (London, 1824), p. 187.
50. Ibid., p. xiii.
51. Ibid., p. 23.
52. Ibid., pp 50–51.
53. Ibid., p. 371.
54. Ibid., p. 131.
55. Ibid., p. 152.
56. Thomas Moore, *Memoirs, journal and correspondence* (London, 1853), iv, 224.
57. Terence de Vere White, *Tom Moore: the Irish Poet* (London, 1977), p. 184.
58. Michael J Whitty, *Captain Rock in London or the Chieftain's Gazette* (London, 1825–7), p. 2.
59. Ibid., p 1.
60. Whitty, *Captain Rock in London*, Dedication to the people of Ireland, p iii.
61. Ibid., Address to the king, p. i.
62. Ibid., p. i.
63. Ibid.
64. Ibid., Dedication, p. ii.
65. *Letters to his majesty King George IV by Captain Rock* (London, 1828), p. 363.
66. *Quarterly Review*, xxxviii, p. 544.

Chapter 4

1. [O'Keefe] *Life and times of Daniel O'Connell* (Dublin, 1870), ii, 315–6.
2. Quoted in J A Reynolds, *The catholic emancipation crisis in Ireland 1823–1828* (Yale, 1954), p. 46.
3. W E H Lecky, *Leaders of public opinion in Ireland* (New York, 1912), ii, 59.
4. Edward Wakefield, *An Account of Ireland, statistical and political* (London, 1812), ii, 384.
5. *Freeman's Journal*, 26 June 1826.
6. *Dublin Evening Mail*, 26 June 1826.
7. Ibid., 28 June 1826.
8. K Theodore Hoppen, *Elections, politics and society in Ireland 1832–85* (Oxford, 1984), p. 1.
9. *The letters of Rev James Maher, DD,* ed. P F Moran (Dublin, 1877), pp xliii–xlv.
10. M F Cusack (ed.), *Speeches and public letters of the Liberator* (Dublin, 1875), i. 127 (22 June 1831).
11. Ibid., i, 135 (12 July 1831).
12. M F Cusack (ed.), *Speeches and public letters of the Liberator*, i, 134–5 (12 July 1831).
13. Ibid., i, 238–240 (13 July 1832) i, 283 (5 July 1833).
14. For the evidence of Fr O'Connor and Matthew Barrington see *Report from the select committee on the state of Ireland*, H.C. 1832 (677) pp 179ff.
15. Ibid., p. 181.
16. Ibid.
17. John O'Hanlon, *History of the Queen's County* (Dublin, 1914), ii, 651.

18. Cusack, op. cit., i, 208 (31 May 1832).
19. Major General Robert Crawford's evidence in *Report from the select committee on the state of Ireland*, H.C. 1832 (677), pp 124–5.
20. *Report from the select committee on the state of Ireland*, H.C. 1832 (677), pp 5–6; appendix IX; *minutes of evidence*, pp 271–2.
21. O'Hanlon, *History of the Queen's County* (Dublin, 1914) ii, 645.
22. *Report from the select committee on the state of Ireland*, H.C. 1832 (677, appendix pp 69–77.
23. *Report from the select committee on the state of Ireland*, H.C. 1832 (677), p. 134.
24. Drummond to Lord Donoughmore, 22 May 1838, quoted in J. F. McLennan, *Memoir of Thomas Drummond* (Edinburgh, 1867), p. 322.
25. Doyle to Parnell, 20 Dec. 1832, in O'Hanlon, *History of Queen's County*, ii, 685–6.

Chapter 5
1. Lecky, *Leaders of public opinion in Ireland* (New York, 1912), ii, 245–6.
2. John Mitchel, *Jail journal* (Dublin, 1913), p. 141.
3. L M Cullen, 'Irish history without the potato', in *Past and Present*, no. 40 (1968), has argued that the dissemination of the potato came after population expansion was already in progress.
4. The 1841 census indicates a mean age of marriage similar to that in western Europe generally. The birth-rate, however, was much higher in Ireland than in Europe.
5. James S Donnelly Jr., *Landlord and tenant in nineteenth-century Ireland* (Dublin, 1973), p. 45; Barbara L Solow, *The land question and the Irish economy 1870–1903* (Cambridge, Mass., 1971), p. 55.
6. K Theodore Hoppen, *Elections, politics, and society in Ireland 1832–1885*, pp 17–18, 32–3.
7. R V Comerford, *The fenians in context* (Dublin, 1985), p. 124.
8. J C Beckett, *The making of modern Ireland 1603–1923* (London, 1969), p. 361.

Chapter 6
1. John Coolahan, *Irish Education: its history and structure* (Dublin, 1981), p. 19.
2. Maurice Earls, 'The Dublin press 1815—1850' (unpublished Ph.D. thesis, U.C.D., 1984).
3. E R R Green in *Ulster since 1800*, ed. T W Moody and J C Beckett, (London, 1954), p. 28.
4. M Daly, *Dublin: the deposed capital* (Cork, 1984), pp 2–3.
5. Fergus O'Ferrall, *Daniel O'Connell* (Dublin, 1981), p. 86.
6. G D Zimmermann, *Songs of Irish rebellion* (Dublin, 1967), pp 311–12.
7. Lord Lyndhurst quoted in Kerr, *Peel, priests and politics* (Oxford, 1982), p. 69.
8. Rev Charles O'Conor, *Memoirs of the life and writings of the late Charles O'Conor of Belanagare* (Dublin, 1796), i, 168, 165.
9. O'Halloran, *An Introduction to an History of Ireland* (Dublin, 1803), i (see advertisement).
10. Rev John Graham, *An historical poem on the state of Ireland* (Dublin, 1820), pp 25ff.

Bibliographical note

General surveys:
Recommended general surveys dealing with this period include J C Beckett, *The making of modern Ireland 1603-1923* (London, paperback edition, 1969); G Ó Tuathaigh, *Ireland before the famine 1798-1848* (Dublin, 1972); Joseph Lee, *The modernisation of Irish society 1848-1918* (Dublin, 1973); F S L Lyons, *Ireland since the famine* (London, 1971); P J O'Farrell, *Ireland's English question: Anglo-Irish relations 1534-1970* (London, 1970); R Kee, *The green flag: a history of Irish nationalism* (London, 1972); Tom Garvin, *The evolution of Irish nationalist politics* (Dublin, 1981); R B McDowell, *Public opinion and government policy in Ireland 1807-1846* (London, 1952); L M Cullen, *An economic history of Ireland since 1660* (London, 1972); Mary E Daly, *Social and economic history of Ireland since 1800* (Dublin, 1981).

The union
G C Bolton, *The passing of the Irish act of union* (Oxford, 1966) is an objective revision of earlier and more political accounts; O MacDonagh, *Ireland: the union and its aftermath* (London, revised edition, 1977), is a well-written perceptive analysis; Volume v of Lecky's *Ireland* (London, 1892) is an older, detailed and still valuable account of the period from 1798 to 1800. For details of the Act of Union see Edmund Curtis and R B McDowell (ed.), *Irish historical documents 1172-1922* (London, 1943).

O'Connell, emancipation and reform
An essential source for O'Connell's career is Maurice R O'Connell (ed.), *The correspondence of Daniel O'Connell*, 8 vols. (vols i–ii Shannon, vols iii–viii Dublin 1972-80). There are several biographies of O'Connell, of the older ones the most useful are: W E H Lecky, *Leaders of public opinion in Ireland* (3rd ed. London, 1903); M MacDonagh, *Daniel O'Connell and the story of catholic emancipation* (Dublin, 1929); S Ó Faoláin, *King of the beggars* (London, 1938; 2nd ed. Dublin, 1970). Also useful are D Gwynn, *The struggle for catholic emancipation, 1750-1829* (London, 1928); R Dudley Edwards, *Daniel O'Connell and his world* (London, 1975). A good recent biography is F

O'Ferrall, *Daniel O'Connell* (Dublin, 1981). O'Connell's impact outside of Ireland is dealt with in D McCartney (ed.), *The world of Daniel O'Connell* (Dublin, 1980). Essays on various aspects of O'Connell's career are to be found in M Tierney (ed.), *Daniel O'Connell: nine centenary essays* (Dublin, 1948), and K B Nowlan and M R O'Connell (ed), *Daniel O'Connell: portrait of a radical* (Belfast, 1984). For the Catholic emancipation struggle see also J A Reynolds, *The catholic emancipation crisis in Ireland, 1828-9* (New Haven, 1954); G I T Machin, *The Catholic question in English politics, 1820-30* (Oxford, 1964); A Macintyre, *The liberator: Daniel O'Connell and the Irish party, 1830-47* (London, 1965); G Ó Tuathaigh, *Thomas Drummond and the government of Ireland, 1835-41* (Dublin, 1978).

Secret societies
Agrarianism, peasant unrest and secret societies have recently been receiving a good deal of attention from historians. Some of the results of this research have been brought together in, for example, Samuel Clarke and James S Donnelly Jr (ed.), *Irish peasants: violence and political unrest 1780-1914* (Manchester, 1983); Michael Beames, *Peasants and power: the Whiteboy movement and their control in pre-famine Ireland* (Sussex and New York, 1983); and T D Williams (ed.), *Secret societies in Ireland* (Dublin, 1973).

The classic contemporary survey of agrarian disturbances is G C Lewis, *On local disturbances in Ireland* (London, 1838). The attempt by the authorities to enforce law and order is considered in G Broeker, *Rural disorder and police reform in Ireland 1812-36* (London, 1970).

Repeal, electoral politics, the famine and the land questions
For repeal see K B Nowlan, *The politics of repeal* (London, 1965); and D Kerr, *Peel, priests and politics 1841-46* (Oxford, 1980). Essential for electoral politics are B M Walker (ed.), *Parliamentary election results in Ireland, 1801-1922* (Dublin, 1978), and K T Hoppen, *Elections, politics and society in Ireland 1832-1885* (Oxford, 1984). On the famine see M E Daly, *The famine in Ireland* (Dublin Historical Association, 1986), and the standard works: R Dudley Edwards and T Desmond Williams (eds), *The great famine* (Dublin, 1956), and Cecil Woodham-Smith, *The great hunger, Ireland 1845-9* (London, 1962). Joel Mokyr, *Why Ireland starved* (London, 1983) is an analysis of pre-famine Irish society.

Important recent works on the land question in the nineteenth century include: E D Steele, *Irish land and British politics* (Cambridge, 1974); Samuel Clarke, *Social origins of the Irish land war* (Princeton,

1979); Barbara Solow, *The land question and the Irish economy 1870-1903* (Harvard, 1971); James S Donnelly Jr, *The land and the people of nineteenth-century Cork* (London, 1975); W E Vaughan, *Landlords and tenants in Ireland 1848-1904* (Dublin, 1984).

Constitutional politics and fenianism
Constitutional politics of the 1850s and 60s are dealt with in: J H Whyte, *The independent Irish party, 1850-9* (Oxford, 1958); P J Corish (ed), *A history of Irish catholicism* vol v; 2-3, (Dublin, 1967) and E R Norman, *The catholic church in Ireland in the age of rebellion 1859-1873* (London, 1965). For the Fenians see T W Moody (ed), *The fenian movement* (Cork, 1968); R V Comerford, *The fenians in context* (Dublin, 1985); L O Broin, *Fenian fever: an Anglo-American dilemma* (London, 1971).

Education
For education see D H Akenson, *The Irish educational experiment: the national system of education in the nineteenth century* (London, 1970); Norman Atkinson, *Irish education: a history of educational institutions* (Dublin, 1969); P J Corish (ed), *A history of Irish catholicism* vol. v, 6, (Dublin, 1971); John Coolahan, *Irish education: its history and structure* (Dublin, 1981).

Ulster, presbyterianism, orangeism
On Ulster and the presbyterians see T W Moody, *The Ulster question 1603-1973* (Cork, 1974); T W Moody and J C Beckett (ed.), *Ulster since 1800: a political and economic survey* (London, 1954); D W Miller, *Queen's rebels: Ulster loyalism in historical perspective* (Dublin, 1978); A T Q Stewart, *The narrow ground: aspects of Ulster 1609-1969* (London, 1977); Peter Gibbon, *The origins of Ulster unionism* (Manchester, 1975); I Budge and C O'Leary, *Belfast, approach to crisis: a study of Belfast politics, 1603-1970* (London, 1973). A non-partisan account of early orangeism is Hereward Senior, *Orangeism in Ireland and Britain, 1795-1836* (London, 1966).

Catholic Church
For the role of the catholic church consult, besides Corish mentioned above, Emmet Larkin, *The making of the Roman Catholic Church in Ireland, 1850-1860* (North Carolina Press, 1980); S J Connolly, *Priests and people in pre-famine Ireland 1780-1845* (Dublin, 1982); D J Keenan, *The catholic church in nineteenth-century Ireland* (Dublin, 1983).

Church of Ireland
D H Akenson, *The Church of Ireland ecclesiastical reform and revolution, 1800–1885* (London, 1971); R B McDowell, *The Church of Ireland 1869–1969* (London, 1975); Desmond Bowen, *The protestant crusade in Ireland, 1800–1870* (Dublin, 1978).

Index

Abbeyfeale, Co. Limerick, 90
Abbeyleix, Queen's County, 137, 147
Aberdeen, Lord, prime minister, 181
Act of Union, 2, 121, 149, 210
— articles of, 3–5
— attitudes towards, 5–12
— carried, 12–15
— effects of, 15–19, 26
— repeal of, 119
Adare, Co. Limerick, 97
Addington, Henry, prime minister, 40
Anglo-Normans, 2, 26, 134
An historical apology for the Irish catholics, 43
Annals of the Irish rogues and rapparees, 107
Antrim, Co., 11, 31, 94, 200
Armagh, Co., 11, 31, 34, 82, 84, 94, 200

Ballagh, Co. Tipperary, 81
Ballina, Co. Mayo, 65
Ballingarry, Co. Tipperary, 75
Ballybricken butchers, 115
Bandon, Co. Cork, 82, 96
Barrington, Matthew, 90, 138
Barron, Philip, 178
Barry, John, 213
Beaumont, Gustave de, 38, 160
Belfast Academical Institution, 31, 196
Belfast, city of, 18, 82, 122, 157, 158, 204
— industrial revolution in, 200–203
Belfast News-Letter, 203
Bellew, Sir Edward, 41
Bennett, George, 98
Beresford, George de la Poer, bishop of Clonfert, later of Kilmore, 28
Beresford, Lord George, 114, 115, 116, 117, 132
Beresford, Lord John George, bishop of Cork, later archbishop of Armagh, 27, 28
Beresford, J. C., inspector-general of imports and exports, 10
Beresford, John, 113
Beresford, William, archbishop of Tuam, 28
Bessborough, Lord, 76
Biggar, Joseph, 213
Blackburn, Francis, 98, 100, 101
Blackfeet, 130, 136, 138, 139, 140
Blood, William, 133
Board of Érin, 84
Bompart, Admiral, 5
Bonaparte, Letitia, 115
Bonaparte, Napoleon, 40, 45, 46, 47, 59, 86, 115, 165, 183
Bray, Thomas, archbishop of Cashel, 8
Brennan, Thomas, 213
Brotherhood of St Patrick, 186
Bruen, Henry, 125–130
Bunting, Edward, 208
Burke, Edmund, 140
Bushe, Charles Kendal, solicitor-general, 68, 72, 75, 77–8

Butt, Isaac, 147
Buttevant, Co. Cork, 94

Callan, Co. Kilkenny, 179
Captain Rock detected, 106, 109
Captain Rock in London or the chieftain's gazette for 1825, 106, 107
Caravats, 72–79, 79–82, 89, 138
Carders, 63, 79
Carlow corporation, 147–8
Carlow Co., 11, 93, 100, 137
Carlow elections, 121, 123, 125–130
Carmelites, 38, 196
Carnygallan, Co. Leitrim, 67
Carrick-on-Shannon, Co. Leitrim, 68
Carrick-on-Suir, Co. Tipperary, 94
Carrickshock, Co. Kilkenny, 136
Cassels, Richard, 17
Carton Watt, Co. Sligo, 64
Cashel, Co. Tipperary, 72, 73, 81, 121
Castlebar, Co. Mayo, 65, 67, 68, 72
Castlecomer, Co. Kilkenny, 137
Castlereagh, Lord, chief secretary, 7, 8, 11, 12, 23, 51
Catholic Association, 98, 104, 108, 110–119, 131, 132, 151, 204
Catholic Board, 53, 57, 59, 61, 110
Catholic Board of England, 59
Catholic Church, 35–39, 207–8
Catholic Committee, 41, 43, 44, 49, 50, 51, 52, 53, 67, 106
Catholic Defence Association, 180–2
Catholic Directory, 36, 195
Catholic Relief Act (1829), 86, 202
— (1793), 196
Catholic question 1800–1823, 39–62
Catholic University, 36, 197–8
Caulfield, James, bishop of Ferns, 8
Cavan, Co., 11, 63, 67, 68, 86
Cavour, Count Camillo, 161
Charitable Bequests Act (1844), 157–8, 159
Charleville, Earl of, 123, 148
Church Education Society, 194
Church of Ireland, 26–31, 206–7
Church Temporalities Act (1833), 29
Churchtown, Co. Cork, 95, 103
Clare, Co., 79, 80, 82, 85, 98, 99, 130–134, 168
Clare election (1828), 86, 111, 116–118, 124, 130, 132, 160, 175
Clare Journal, 131
Clare, Lord, lord chancellor, 6, 7, 11, 12, 21, 22, 24
Claremorris, Co. Mayo, 63
Clinch, barrister, 41
Clogheen, Co. Tipperary, 75
Clonee, Co. Leitrim, 67
Clonmel, Co. Tipperary, 72, 73, 77
Cloughjordan, Co. Tipperary, 82
Columbanus ad Hibernos, 48
Connaught, 11, 27, 59, 72, 82, 83, 85, 86, 89, 99, 108, 134, 175

224

Connemara, 30
Constabulary Act (1822), 144
Convention Act (1793), 51, 52, 53
Cooke, Dr Henry, 33, 203
'Cooping', 122, 126, 128
Cork, city of, 11, 157, 177
Cork, Co., 75, 76, 93, 94, 95, 96, 97, 100
Corofin, Co. Clare, 131, 132
Cornwallis, Lord, lord lieutenant, 7, 11, 39, 45
Courtenay, estate, 90, 97
Cox, Watty, 44, 45
Crawford, Sharman, 159, 179
Croke, T. W., archbishop of Cashel, 198
Croker, Crofton, 211
Croker, John Wilson, 54
Crossmolina, Co. Mayo, 66
Cullen, Paul, archbishop of Dublin, 30, 36, 164, 181, 185, 186-7, 198, 207
Curragh, Co. Kildare, 87
Curraghmore estate, 115
Curry, John, 49

D'Alton, Richard, 178
Davis, Thomas, 21, 151, 154, 158-9, 164, 178, 210-11
Davitt, Michael, 89, 213
Decies, Co. Waterford, 73, 93
Defenders, 34, 82, 84, 89, 156
Delany, Daniel, bishop of Kildare and Leighlin, 8
Derry, city of, 82
Derry, Co., 11
Derrynane, Co. Kerry, 24
Devoy, John, 184, 190, 213
Dillane, Patrick, 90
Dillon, Edward, archbishop of Tuam, 8
Dillon, John Blake, 151, 156, 186
Disfranchisement Act (1829), 122
Dolly's Brae, Co. Down, 204-5
Dominicans, 38, 193, 196
Donegal, Co., 177
Donegall family, 203
Doneraile, Co. Cork, 96, 97
Down, Co., 31, 94, 200
Downes, Chief Justice, 67
Doyle, James Warren, bishop of Kildare and Leighlin, 30, 54, 87, 94, 101-2, 109, 112, 124, 125, 130, 134, 135, 137, 139, 140, 142, 146, 194
Drogheda, 107
Dromgoole, Doctor, 42
Drummond, Thomas, 144-5, 204
Dublin castle, 9, 14, 24, 25, 39, 57, 81, 144, 145
Dublin, city of, anti-unionism in, 10, 18
— effects of union on, 16-18
— 35, 38, 53, 55, 59, 82, 100, 110, 111, 113, 144, 147, 148, 161, 188, 201, 212
Dublin, Co., 10-11, 27, 47, 82, 84
Dublin Evening Mail, 115, 131
Dublin Evening Post, 92, 93, 94
Dublin Penny Journal, 199, 208
Dublin University Magazine, 158
Duffy, Charles Gavan, 151, 159, 163, 164-5, 179, 181, 211
Duhallow Hunt, 94
Duigenan, Patrick, 39, 42

Dungarvan, Co. Waterford, 125

Ecclesiastical Titles Bill, 180, 182
Edinburgh Review, 40
Education, primary, 192-5
— secondary, 195-6
— university, 196-8
Egan, Patrick, 213
Emancipation bill (1813), 57
— (1819), 61
— (1821), 61
Emmet, Robert, 24, 150, 156, 210, 211, 212
Encumbered Estates Act (1849), 173, 179
Ennis, Co. Clare, 52, 101
Evangelicalism, 29-31, 177

Famine (1845-9), 166-174
— (1817, 1821), 90, 99
Fenians, 19, 88, 89, 106, 155, 164, 178, 207, 208, 212, 213
— origins and spread of, 182-4
— and the church, 185-8
— Rising and its aftermath, 188-191
Fenian Amnesty Association, 106, 188, 190
Fermanagh, Co., 11, 31, 86, 196
Ffrench, Lord, 42, 43
Fingall, Earl of, 8, 41, 42, 43, 45, 47, 50, 53, 86, 106, 142
Finnerty, Peter, 51
Fitzgerald, Vesey, 117
Fitzpatrick, Hugh, 49, 61
Foras Feasa ar Éirinn, 178
Forty-shilling freehold vote, 10, 115, 116, 117, 119, 122, 125, 175
Foster, John, speaker of the Irish house of commons, 10, 22, 23
Fox, Charles James, 41
France, 1, 3, 5, 6, 12, 15, 22, 23, 24, 69, 99, 212
Franchise Act (1850), 180
Franciscans, 38, 193
Franks family, 95-6, 103
Freeman's Journal, 115, 179

Gaelic societies, 177-8, 208
Gallan, barony of, 63
Galway, city of, 11, 102, 122, 157
Galway, Co., 82, 85, 108, 134, 194
General history of the christian church . . ., 99, 101
George III, king, 6, 39, 43, 55
George IV, king, 109
George, Baron, 67
Gladstone, W. E., prime minister, 190-1, 206
Glasgow, 82
Glensheen, near Kilmallock, Co. Limerick, 97
Goderich, Lord, prime minister, 121
Going, Major, 92, 102
Golden, Co. Tipperary, 77
Goold, Honora, 90
Gordon, Rev. James Bentley, 39
Government of Ireland Act (1920), 118
Graham, Rev. John, 209-210
Graiguenamanagh, Co. Kilkenny, 135
Grattan, Henry, MP, 10, 14, 19, 20, 21, 22, 23, 24, 41, 43, 45, 47, 49, 52, 57, 61

Granard, Co. Longford, 66
Granard, Lord, 66
Gray, John, 179
Grenville, Lord, prime minister, 41, 42, 43, 47, 48, 56
Grey, Charles, 47
Griffith, Arthur, 165
Gwynn, Denis, 120

Harland, Edward, 201
Hay, Edward, 40, 51
Hayes, Richard, 60
Henry VIII, 2, 3
Higgins, William, bishop of Ardagh, 153, 157
Hillsborough, Co. Down, 33
History of Ireland, 164
Hoche, General, 5
Hohenloe, prince, 101, 107
Hoskins, 90, 92, 102
Humbert, General, 5
Hussey, Thomas Bodkin, 41

Illustrated London News, 170
Independent Club, 125
Industrial revolution, 167, 199-203
Inchyrourke, near Askeaton, Co. Limerick, 92
Independent Irish Party, 180-2, 207
Insurrection Act (1814), 81, 94, 98, 99, 101
Irish Church Act (1869), 191, 206
Irish Church Missions, 30, 194
Irish Confederation, 159
Irish language, 38, 150, 174-179
Irish Magazine, 44
Irish melodies, 209-211
Irish parliament, 2, 3, 6, 8, 11, 16, 18, 22, 23, 24, 150
Irish People, 183-4, 185, 187, 188, 189, 213
Irish Republican Brotherhood, 183
Irish Sons of Freedom, 84

Jackson, Charles, 39
James II, king, 3
Jebb, Dr John, bishop of Limerick, 119
Jesuits, 17, 36, 38, 119, 196, 197
Johnson, Francis, 17
Jones, Richard, 84, 86, 87

Kanturk, Co. Cork, 96
Kavanagh, Thomas, 125-127
Kearney, Wm., 64
Keating, Geoffrey, 178
Keeffe, Fr Matthew, 179
Keenan, Sir Patrick, 176
Keenan, Michael, 84, 86, 87
Kelly, Oliver, archbishop of Tuam, 85
Kelly, Patrick, bishop of Waterford, 115
Kenmare, Lord, 8, 11, 41, 142
Kennedy, Captain Arthur, 169-170
Keogh, John, 47
Keogh, William, 164-5, 180, 181
Kerry, Co., 9, 11, 46, 73, 76, 78, 93, 96
Kickham, Charles, 184, 187
Kildare, Co., 11, 82, 87, 94, 95
Kildare Place Society, 137, 193, 199
Kildorrery, Co. Cork, 95

Killarney, Co. Kerry, 51
Kilkee, Co. Clare, 168
Kilkenny, city of, 46, 128
Kilkenny, Co., 46, 72, 75, 76, 77, 78, 79, 93, 94, 97, 128, 134, 135, 136, 137, 138
Kilkenny, statute of, 3
Killeen, Lord, 142
Kilrush union, 168-172
King's County (Offaly), 79, 81, 82, 93, 94, 95, 99
Kingston estate, 95
Kirwin, Thomas, 53
Knights of St Patrick, 87
Knocknagow, 184

Lagan Valley, 167
Lalor, James Fintan, 135, 169, 212
Lalor, Patrick, 135-6, 142, 146, 147
Lamartine, Alphonse de, 161
Land Act (1870), 191
Lanigan, James, bishop of Ossory, 8
Last conquest of Ireland (perhaps), 164
Lawless, Jack, 49, 204
Laurence, Richard, archbishop of Cashel, 27
Lavelle, Fr Patrick, 186-8
Lavin, Thady, 65, 66, 71
Lecky, W. E. H., historian, 10, 14, 113, 153
Leinster, 27, 79, 80, 82, 83, 86, 93, 95, 98, 108, 134, 137
Leitrim, Co., 63, 67, 196
Letters to his majesty King George IV by Captain Rock, 106, 108
Liberal clubs, 116, 126, 140
Liberty Rangers, 74, 75
Lichfield House Compact, 144
Limerick, city of, 11, 82, 84, 122
— treaty of, 54, 210
Limerick Co., 74, 75, 78, 79, 80, 81, 90, 92, 93, 104, 110, 169
Lita, Cardinal, 60
Liverpool, 82
Liverpool, Lord, prime minister, 55
Lloyd, John, 99
London Hibernian Society, 131
Longford, Co., 63, 66, 68, 79
Louth, Co., 11, 125
Louth election (1826), 116
Loyal National Repeal Association, 151, 157, 159, 161
Luby, Thomas Clarke, 183, 184
Lucas, Frederick, 179, 181
Lugnadiva, Co. Sligo, 65

MacDonnell, Thomas, 41
McDonagh, John, 64
MacHale, John, archbishop of Tuam, 152, 158, 159, 178, 186-8, 194
McKnight, James, 179
MacManus, Terence Bellew, 183, 186
Magee, Thomas D'Arcy, 162
Maher, Fr James, 126, 129
Mallow, Co. Cork, 93
Manchester, 82
Manchester Martyrs, 188-190
Morning Register, 111
Marum, bishop of Ossory, 97

Maryborough (Portlaois), 136, 137, 140
Mathew, Fr Theobald, 153
Mayo, Co., 50, 63, 65, 66, 85, 93
Maynooth, 15, 35, 46, 49, 112, 135, 157, 158, 191
Mazzini, Guiseppe, 161
Meath, Co., 11, 84
Mechanics Institute (Dublin), 178
Melbourne, Lord, prime minister, 144
Memoirs of Captain Rock, 106, 107, 109
Memoirs of Jack the batchelor, 107
Memoirs of the different rebellions in Ireland, 39
Metternich, Prince, 119, 160
Millenialism, 99–102
Milner, John, bishop, 45, 47, 48, 49
Minola, Co. Mayo, 65
Mitchel, John, 6, 159, 163, 164, 165, 173, 174, 186, 212
Moira, Lord, 41
Moll Doyles, 78, 92, 93
Molly Maguires, 83
Monaghan, Co., 11, 82, 84
Monaghan election (1826), 116
Monster meetings, 152–8
Montalembert, Charles, Comte de, 161
Montgomery, Rev. Henry, 33, 203
Moore, George H., M.P., 180, 181
Moore, Sergeant, 67, 68
Moore, Thomas, 55, 106, 107, 109, 124, 150, 209, 210
Moriarty, David, bishop of Kerry, 185
Moylan, Francis, bishop of Cork, 8
Mountmellick, Queen's County, 82, 137, 147
Mountrath, Queen's County, 82, 137
Moyle Rangers, 73, 74
Municipal Corporations Act (1840), 147
Munster, 25, 59, 79, 80, 83, 85, 86, 90, 92, 93, 94, 95, 96, 97, 98, 102, 108, 110, 134, 138
Murray, Daniel, archbishop of Dublin, 36, 59, 60, 101
Musgrave, Richard, 39, 44, 45

Nation, 151, 158, 159, 164, 178, 179, 183, 190, 210, 211, 213
National Association, 191, 207
Newcastle West, Co. Limerick, 90
Newman, John Henry, 197, 198
Newspapers, 198–9
Newtown, Co. Kilkenny, 137
Newtownbarry, Co. Wexford, 136
Norbury, Lord, chief justice, 77
Northern Union, 84, 87
Northern Whig, 202–3

O'Brien, Wm Smith, M.P., 169, 186
O'Connell, Daniel, 10, 38, 98, 101, 108, 132, 150, 173, 175, 185, 186, 188, 196, 204, 205, 207, 209, 210, 212
— and the union, 8–9
— and Emmet's rising, 24
— and the Catholic Committee, 40–4, 50–6
— and the veto, 46–9, 57–62
— and secret societies, 83, 85–7, 90, 102–9, 134
— and the Catholic Association, 110–119
— and reform of parliament, 120–3
— and his party, 124–30, 143, 149, 151, 180, 182
— and the Terry Alts, 130–134
— and the Tithe war, 134–143
— and the Whigs, 143–8
— and repeal, 151–8, 203
— and Young Ireland, 158–9
— and his impact abroad, 159–163
— and the changing image of, 163–6
— and the Irish language, 178
O'Connell, Daniel (son), 129
O'Connell, John (son), 165
O'Connell, Maurice (son), 129
O'Connell Tribute, 151
O'Connor, Matthew, 54
O'Connor, Fr Nicholas, 138
O'Connor, Roger, 106, 108, 109
O'Connor-Power, John, 213
O'Conor, Rev. Charles, 48, 49
O'Conor, Charles of Belanagare, 48
O'Curry, Eugene, 198, 208
O'Donovan, John, 208
O'Donovan Rossa, Jeremiah, 178, 183, 184, 190
Ó Faoláin, Seán, 120
O'Grady, Standish, chief baron, 77
O'Hagan, John, 13
O'Halloran, Sylvester, 208–9
O'Hegarty, P. S., 120
O'Leary, Fr Arthur, 39
O'Leary, John, 184
O'Mahony, John, 178, 182
Orangemen, 10, 26, 29, 33, 34–5, 54, 82, 83, 84, 86, 92, 96, 98, 100, 101, 103, 114, 128, 131, 138, 143, 145, 203–6, 209–10
Order of Liberators, 132
Ordnance Survey of Ireland, 208
O'Reilly, archbishop of Armagh, 8
O'Shea, Fr Tom, 179
Ossian, 208
O'Sullivan, Rev. Mortimer, 106, 109

Palatines, 96–7, 100
Parnell, Charles Stewart, 19, 106, 155, 181, 185
Parnell, Henry, 54, 137, 143, 146
Parnell, Sir John, chancellor of the exchequer, 10, 12, 22
Parnell, Wm., 43, 44
Passionists, 36, 38
Pastorini, 85, 99–12, 107, 139, 157; see Walmesley
Patrick's Well, Co. Limerick, 93
Peace Resolutions (July, 1846), 159, 161
Peace Preservation Act (1814), 81, 144
Pearse, P. H., 20, 190
Peel, Sir Robert, 29, 35, 55, 56, 81, 117–8, 151, 155, 156, 157, 158, 172, 196, 204, 207
Penny journals, 199
Perceval, Spencer, prime minister, 47, 54, 55
Petrie, George, 208
Phoenix Society, 183
Pidal, Menendez, 1
Pilot, 159
Pitt, William, prime minister, 6, 8, 12, 23, 39, 40, 41, 56
Pius VII, 60
Pius IX, 185
Plowden, Francis, 40, 43, 44, 48
Plunket, Baron Thomas, archbishop of Tuam, 28
Plunket, W.C., M.P., 10, 12, 23, 61, 68–70, 86

'Pocket-boroughs', 121
Pole, William Wellesley, chief secretary, 52
Ponsonby, George, M.P., 10, 23, 41, 45, 52, 57
Ponsonby, William, M.P., 10
Poor Law Act (1838), 143, 146–7, 168, 169
Pope's Brass Band, 180
Portland, Duke of, 43, 45, 47
Portlaw, Co. Waterford, 115
Powis Commission (1868), 193
Precursor Society, 151
Presbyterianism, 31–34

Quarantotti, Monsignor Giovanni Baptista, 59
Queen's Colleges, 157–8, 159, 196–7
Queen's County (Laois), 79, 86, 130, 132, 134–143, 146, 147

Raphael, Alexander, 128–9
Rathvilly, Co. Carlow, 93
Rebellion (1798), 6, 8, 12, 22, 24, 32, 39, 40, 46, 82, 132, 156, 190
— (1803), 16, 24, 190, 210, 212
— (1848), 16, 182, 190, 210, 212
— (1867), 16, 188–190
— (1916), 16, 190
— (1919–21), 16
Redemptorists, 38
Realities of Irish life, 88
Reform Bill (1832), 121, 122–4, 147, 203
— (1868), 203
Regency crisis, 6
Republicanism, 212–3
Review of the civil wars in Ireland, 49
Ribbonmen, 34, 82–89, 92, 99, 100, 101, 102, 132, 136, 137, 204, 210
Richmond, Duke of, lord lieutenant, 56
Rifle Brigade, 95, 103
Rightboys, 63, 92
Rockism, impact of, 103–109
Rockites, 85, 89–103, 132, 136
Rome, 35, 39, 45, 59, 60, 61, 62, 119, 160, 181, 185, 187, 188, 197
Roscommon, Co., 79, 82, 85
Rowan, Hamilton, 11
Royal Irish Academy, 177, 208
Russell, Lord John, 15, 172
Ryan, James, 41, 42

Shanagolden, Co. Limerick, 93
Sadleir, John, 164–5, 180, 181
Sally Cavanagh, 184
Saurin, Wm., attorney-general, 35, 61
Scrope, Paulett, M.P., 169
Scully, Denys, 40, 41, 48, 49, 54
Seminaries, 177
Sermons (Gallagher), 177
Sexton, Thomas, 213
Shanavests, 72–79, 89, 138
Shakers, 63, 64
Sheil, Richard Lalor, 37, 61, 124, 125
Sheehan, Fr John, 115, 125
Sligo, Co., 63, 64, 65, 66, 68, 82

Smith, Baron Sir William, 140–1, 146
Sons of the Shamrock, 87
Southey, Robert, 109
Spirit of the Nation, 158, 211
Stephens, James, 182–3
Stradbally, Queen's County, 137
Stuart, H. Villiers, 114, 115, 116
Stuart, William, archbishop of Armagh, 28
Sullivan, A. M., 83
Sullivan, T. D., 189–190
Syllabus of Errors (1864), 185
Synge, Edward, 131–3

Taaffe, Denis, 40, 49
Tablet, 179
Tarbert, Co. Kerry, 82, 100
Taylor, George, 39
Tenant League, 179–182
Terry Alts, 130–134
Threshers, 63–72, 79, 89
Thurles, national synod of, 197
Ticket-voting, 126
Tierney, Michael, 120
Tipperary, Co., 40, 46, 72, 74, 75, 77, 78, 79, 80, 81, 82, 88, 93, 94, 96, 124, 138, 178
Tithes, 28, 94, 107, 124–5, 133, 134, 139, 140–45
Tithe Composition Acts (1832, 1834), 135
Tithe Rent-charge Act (1838), 29, 145–6
Tithe-war, 134–143, 145–6
Tommaseo, 161
Tone, Theobald Wolfe, 22, 24, 156, 211, 212
Tralee, Co. Kerry, 51
Trench, Power le Poer, archbishop of Tuam, 28
Trench, Richard Chenevix, archbishop of Dublin, 27
Trench, W. Steuart, 88
Trent, council of, 35
Trimleston, lord, 41, 42
Trinity College, Dublin (Dublin University), 25, 27, 122, 196, 197
Troy, John Thomas, archbishop of Dublin, 8, 11
Tubbercurry, Co. Sligo, 65
Tuohy, Charles, bishop of Limerick, 101
Turneen, Co. Mayo, 66
Tyrawley, Co. Mayo, 63
Tyrone, Co., 11, 196

Ulster, 11, 28, 32, 35, 82, 83, 84, 89, 108
— industrial revolution in, 14, 199–203
— religious affiliation in, 27, 31
Ulster-custom, 179, 191
Ulster Tenant Right Association, 179
United Irishman, 212
United Irishmen, 5, 6, 32, 44, 68, 74, 82, 84, 85, 88, 89, 99, 102, 108, 150, 156, 202, 212, 213

Vincentians, 38, 196
Veto, 9, 45–50, 57–62, 119
Veuillot, Louis, 160

Wakefield, Edward, 113
Wales, Prince of, 41, 51, 53, 54, 55, 56
Walmesley, Charles ('Pastorini'), 99–102, see Pastorini

Warburton, Major George, 85, 99
Waterford, city of, 11, 46, 122
Waterford, Co., 11, 72, 75, 77, 78, 79, 80, 122, 125, 130, 178
Waterford election (1826), 111, 113–116, 122, 124, 132, 175
Wellesley, Lord Richard Colley, lord lieutenant, 61, 113, 203–4
Wellington, Duke of, 75, 117, 118, 155, 156
Westmeath, Co., 79, 81, 82, 136, 175
Westmeath election (1826), 116
Westminster, UK parliament at, 2, 4, 5, 7, 8, 9, 15, 19, 22, 23, 24, 41, 121, 122, 123, 149
Wexford, Co., 11, 32, 40, 46, 87, 135
Whately, Richard, archbishop of Dublin, 27
Whiteboys, 72, 73, 74, 85, 88, 89, 92, 95, 100, 102, 105, 106, 132, 134, 137, 138
Whiteboy Acts (1766, 1777), 70, 71
Whitechurch, Co. Waterford, 74
Whitefeet, 78, 89, 130, 132, 134, 136, 137, 138, 139, 140, 143
Whitelegs, 137
Whitty, M. J., 106
Wicklow, Co., 11, 27, 86, 196
Willcocks, Major Richard, 98
William of Orange, 3
Windy Gap, Co. Sligo, 64
Wyse, Thomas, 114, 115, 124, 125, 143, 194

Yeats, W. B., 174, 184